Alfredo Barili
and
the Rise of Classical Music in Atlanta

Alfredo Barili
and
the Rise of Classical Music in Atlanta

N. Lee Orr
Georgia State University

Scholars Press
Atlanta, Georgia

Alfredo Barili
and
the Rise of Classical Music in Atlanta

N. Lee Orr

©1996
Cherry Logan Emerson

Library of Congress Cataloging-in-Publication Data
Orr, N. Lee, 1949–
    Alfredo Barili and the rise of classical music in Atlanta / by N. Lee Orr.
      p. cm.
    Includes bibliographical references (p.   ) and index.
    ISBN 0-7885-0137-2 (alk. paper)
    1. Music—Georgia—Atlanta—History and criticism. 2. Atlanta
(Georgia)—History. 3. Barili, Alfredo. 4. Musicians—Georgia—
Bibliography.   I. Title.
ML200.8.A   0
780'.9758'2310904—dc20   95-30174
                                                 CIP
                                                          MN

Printed in the United States of America
on acid-free paper

For Cherry, Elaine, and Victor

TABLE OF CONTENTS

PHOTOGRAPHS

Alfredo Barili at his
Steinway, about 1920

INTRODUCTION

This book has been needed for a long time. For decades Atlanta has enjoyed a steady stream of studies examining nearly every aspect of her life as a struggling city, strategic military hub, state capitol, and today, "the center of the New South," as Henry Grady affectionately christened it. I brought together many of these studies, along with numerous other sources, in my two-volume *Atlanta and Environs* (1954). Since then, many other scholars in widely - varying fields have built upon my work in celebrating this remarkable city. But no one has seriously investigated the life of classical music in the city. Now, as Atlanta hosts the Olympics in 1996, which appropriately marks the centennial of Atlanta's *first* major International Exhibition—the Cotton States Exposition of 1895—someone has finally told the story of the city's first professional musician and the history of Atlanta's artistic musical heritage.

From her earliest days as a railroad junction, Atlanta's citizens enjoyed all types of music. Even though she was founded as a commercial center, she soon had a thriving concert life which drew some of the most celebrated touring musicians of the day. The dark years of the Civil War interrupted only momentarily her passion for operas, pianists, singers, instrumentalists, ensembles, and choral concerts. After the war, even before all the rubble was cleared, concert life reappeared, more vibrant than ever. As Atlanta grew in importance as a commercial and railroad center, her musical life prospered accordingly. By the beginning of this century she had an impressive number of theaters—most importantly the majestic Degive's Grand Opera House—and she enjoyed perhaps the richest musical fare of any southern city.

Alfredo Barili moved into town in 1880 and Atlanta acquired one of the finest pianists, teachers, and musicians of the period. While it took the citizens a while to recognize this, by the 1890's he was being touted as the most important musician in the South. It almost seems fitting that the growing capitol of the South would attract someone of his stature. He played, taught, conducted, and perhaps most importantly, he inspired. Accounts of his teaching for almost fifty years laud his ability to evoke the finest from his students and choral groups. Even those Atlantans who rarely attended a concert or enjoyed music of any kind had heard of Alfredo Barili and how much he had done for the cultural life of the city. This work presents his story, much of which is also Atlanta's musical story. It also brings us closer to completing the chronicle of the city's extraordinary history.

Franklin M. Garrett
Atlanta
April, 1995

FOREWORD

With Recollections of a Student

This book is a tribute to the life of Alfredo Barili and his family. Born in Florence in 1854, he came to Atlanta by a circuitous route establishing himself here with his family in 1880, this being only fifteen years after the Federal army departed from the Confederate city.

Atlanta was rebuilding fast, but if one thing was needed to rekindle its spirit that thing was music. Music was what Alfredo Barili brought with him. Soon there was a choral society, a Barili school of music, a Polymnia Club, instrumental and voice training and then in 1883 an Atlanta Music Festival. Alfredo Barili formed and trained the chorus, the orchestra of Theodore Thomas came from Chicago and for a week Atlanta was full of music attended by thousands of its citizens. The cultural development of Atlanta was under way.

The true and significant story of Alfredo Barili begins long before this, however. Caterina Chiesa, a young Italian girl of much musical talent went singing her way one morning to a water fountain south of Rome. Hearing her, Francesco Barili, a musician became first her teacher and then her husband. Caterina gave birth to three Barili sons (among them Ettore) and one daughter. After Francesco died, Caterina married Salvatore Patti. Together they produced one son and three daughters, the last of whom was Adela, to be known to the world as Adelina Patti. Here you have the story of one Italian woman who produced the entire Barili/Patti clan: the only description is *How amazing*.

Ettore Barili was the father and Antoinetta Sampo of Barcelona the mother of Alfredo Barili; Ettore brought his family from Florence to New York, then Philadelphia, then Montgomery, Alabama, then Philadelphia again, from whence (after three years of study at the Cologne Conservatory) Alfredo Barili came to Atlanta and stayed.

The director of the Cologne Conservatory and mentor of Alfredo was Ferdinand Hiller who studied under Johann Hummel, a student and protege of Wolfgang Amadeus Mozart. Mozart's unique style of playing the pianoforte was perpetuated through his students and arrived in Atlanta in 1880 with Alfredo Barili! It was at Cologne that Alfredo met Emily Vezin from a French family of great talent - two brothers (Charles and Frederick) both members of the Royal Academy of Arts (London) and herself a fine musician, studying seriously at the Conservatory. Her family resided at this time in Philadelphia and it was there upon their return from Cologne that she and Alfredo were married in 1877. Their first child born there died. In 1880, in Atlanta, their daughter Louise become the first native Atlantan of the Barili/Patti clan.

Alfredo Barili (b.1854) was only 11 years the junior of his Aunt Adelina Patti (b.1843), and they maintained a very close relationship until her death in 1919. More than once, Adelina who was childless pursued the idea of adopting Louise, but to no avail. Other children of Alfredo and Emily were Viola (who moved to New York and married there) and Alfredo II who studied in New York and became a highly respected Atlanta architect.

In 1931, I met Alfredo Barili for the first time. At seventy-seven he seemed like a grandfather. I was a lad of fourteen with very slight pianistic abilities. Why he took me in as a student, I cannot say with any assurance except to point out that my maternal grandfather W. Woods White was his longtime friend and financial advisor. Although I knew nothing of significance about music, I loved it and it was thus that we began together, he to teach and I to learn everything that I could absorb.

One of my first projects with Professor Barili was to find a piano to replace the old upright in my home on Pelham Road. After a diligent search, I introduced him to a six foot Steinway grand, made in 1929 (Serial # 265625) at the Carter Piano Company. After a few arpeggios and scales, he pronounced, "This is the piano for you, Cherry." At this point I began a negotiation with Mr. Carter who at first offered the piano to me at $1100. Over the next few weeks he reduced his price by $100. Then I had a great idea; I appeared the next day at his emporium with my saving bank book showing $685.03.[1] I handed it to him with the statement (true enough) that it showed all of the money in the

---

[1] If you want to know where this $685.03 came from, I earned it over a three year period selling Coca-Cola to workmen who were constructing homes in rapidly developing Morningside. They were eager to pay 10 cents per bottle delivered on their scaffolds, ice cold. I paid 2 cents per bottle most mornings for 48 bottles and never failed to sell them. Thus Coca-Cola performed a double service.

world which belonged to me; I asked if he would sell that piano to me for that amount of money. Without a moments hesitation, he snatched the book from my hand, waved it high in the air and shouted to his salesmen: "Fellows come over here." They gathered quickly and he showed them the book. "Shall we sell the piano to this kid for this amount of money" was the question; the answer from all of them was "Yes!" So it came to pass that by handing to Mr. Carter a bank check for $685.03, one half hour later, I became the owner of Steinway 265625 which was delivered next morning to my home in Morningside. It has remained with me to this day and after many millions of notes, sounds as sonorous as a Steinway should.

Progress in my studies with Professor Barili was rapid. I developed, under his strict guidance, a substantial repertoire of piano solos and a tremendous improvement in piano technique. Then came the Beethoven bible and from it Opus 13; this lifted me to a completely new understanding of piano music and with it a desire to learn much more. The Mendelssohn Concerto in G minor, Opus 25 followed. Could I have become a professional musician? Even in the depth of the great depression I realized (and was so advised by Alfredo Barili) that I must make my living some other way.

One of my favorite pieces was the *Scotch Poem* by Edward MacDowell. This is a dramatic little piece of high intensity; I played it many times as it caught my fancy. Once after playing it under the studious oversight of Alfredo Barili, he said simply: "Cherry, Padarewski could not have done it better." This certainly marked the high point in my technical advancement at the piano and much more than that, shows so well how he gave inspiration to his students.

The Cradle Song, Opus 18 of Alfredo Barili was also in my repertoire. I would study and play it repeatedly but was never able to satisfy my mentor fully. Most often when I was not yet finished, he would gently replace me at the bench to show what was the perfect phrase at that point. Even when I completed the study with the feeling that "this time he cannot complain," he would add further insight to improve my presentation. My advice to all students of the piano is never to play a composition of your teacher while he is observing!

As the years went by (From age 14 to 18 for me), Professor Barili and I became good friends and would walk together occasionally around his neighborhood. We also took weekend drives into the north Georgia mountains where he seemed to be most at ease with the world. In all of these excursions, no time was ever wasted; they were meetings of the teacher and his student. It was during these discussions that I absorbed the lore of nineteenth century music - the music of Mendelssohn, Brahms, Schubert and, going back in time, Mozart and Beethoven, Handel, and Haydn - treasures in my memory.

As all good things must sometime end, so did this confluence of two lives. It was on November 17, 1935 that Alfredo Barili at nightfall stepped from the curb at Myrtle Street and Ponce de Leon Avenue, was struck by a city bus and died immediately. He left a legacy of hundreds of well trained students, all introduced thoroughly to classical music; he left to Atlanta a musical culture which had grown primarily by his efforts from almost nothing to a robust and burgeoning industry. Atlanta owes a tribute to his life which I hope that this book will bring.

The author of this book is Professor N. Lee Orr of Georgia State University. We have known one another since he published in 1984 in *American Music* a short sketch of the work of Alfredo Barili in Atlanta. Lee is scholarly, erudite and quite interested in the Barili/Patti clan. How could one have found a better colleague than Lee to write this book?! Who knows what will happen when this book is published: will Atlanta finally wake up to full appreciation of the man named Alfredo Barili?

Cherry Logan Emerson
April 1995

PRELUDE

One day in 1979, after recently assuming a teaching position at Georgia State University in Atlanta, I was talking to a friend from graduate school, Brent Holcomb. I cannot remember how we wandered around to discussing music in the South, but as we did Brent remembered a piece he had learned years earlier as a young piano student in South Carolina, the *Cradle Song*. It seems that his piano teacher at the time had studied the work years earlier with its composer, Alfredo Barili. "Barili was quite well known in those days, and I think he lived in Atlanta," Brent recalled. "Why don't you look into what you could find out about him? It might prove very interesting." Little did I know at the time, but this conversation would start me on a fifteen-year relationship with of one of the South's greatest musicians.

After some searching, I discovered that two of Barili's granddaughters still lived in Atlanta. Seeking them out, I found my interest in this nearly-forgotten musician raised, and, with their encouragement started my investigations. Much of the family collection had already been placed in the Georgia Department of Archives and History (GDAH). As I examined the scrapbooks, newspaper and journal articles, programs, letters, notices, comments, family histories, and other materials, I found myself face-to-face with a musician of the first rank. Even more, I discovered that Barili had not only been one of the South's leading musicians, but had also belonged to one of the most remarkable musical families in nineteenth-century America. Before I knew it I was hooked—Alfredo Barili had captivated me, as he did so many during his fifty-five years in Atlanta.

1

By the time I satisfied my curiosity about this extraordinary musician, I had collected a considerable amount of information. So, I dispatched an article on Alfredo Barili to *American Music*, which promptly published it in 1984.[1] While I was glad to complete this project, in the years following I could not rid myself of an uneasy feeling that there remained much to be done. Then I met Cherry Emerson.

Emerson had been a student of Barili from 1931 to 1935 while studying chemistry at Emory University. The two had developed a fast friendship, which Emerson has cherished ever since. After an extremely successful career as an engineer, Emerson returned to Atlanta, where I met him in 1994. He proposed that I write a full-length study of Barili, which delighted me. Now I could return to those loose threads and dangling questions left hanging ten years earlier. In the meantime, the family had given most of the remaining materials on their beloved grandfather to the Georgia Archives. I plunged into the project immediately, excited over the prospect of what I might find.

This begun, I sought information on the larger music scene in Atlanta in which Barili worked following his move here in 1880. I was shocked to discover that virtually no serious study existed of classical music in Atlanta during the nineteenth century. The considerable amount of scholarship dedicated to nearly every other aspect of Atlanta since its founding—military, economic, political, religious, sociological, popular entertainment, and more— remained silent concerning the rise of classical music in the city. As incredible as it may seem, the cultural life in the capitol of the South still awaited careful examination.

To judge the impact which Barili made on Atlanta's music, it became necessary for me to construct a history of classical music in the city, a daunting task that involved an exhaustive investigation of general nineteenth-century sources about Atlanta. Primary here was the *Atlanta Constitution*, nearly every issue of which from 1870 to 1920 was read (abbreviated to *AC* in the notes). In addition, virtually every other pertinent document concerning the city's concert life was investigated—periodicals, city directories, programs, church bulletins, city histories, sheet music, concert flyers, and numerous other items. Students and family who knew Barili also added much to the picture: Cherry Emerson, Evelyn Wall Robbins, Ned Hanley, Mary Barili Goldsmith, and Randy Barili Harris.

---

[1] N. Lee Orr, "Alfredo Barili: Atlanta Musician, 1880-1935," *American Music* 2, No. 1 (Spring 1984): 43-60.

The work thus has a dualistic structure: a biographical study on Alfredo Barili intertwined with discussions of contemporaneous classical-music activity in Atlanta. These respective sections alternate within each chapter, which covers roughly a decade each. Together, they work to complete the picture of Barili's career in Atlanta.

The resulting literary portrait of Alfredo Barili had to be drawn painstakingly, from the outside in. Barili rarely speaks for himself; virtually no personal letters or documents remain, aside from his music. He touched so many others, however, and they left such a rich record of their impressions, that it did not prove difficult to paint a fairly complete picture of the man and the artist. It did make for careful thought, though, in reconstructing this picture from external sources. I have tried to produce a convincing, compelling, and personal portrait, while not straying unduly beyond my material. Lytton Strachey well articulated my task when he described biography as "the most delicate and humane of all the branches of the art of writing."

* * * * * *

Like many books, this one too results from a collaboration of a number of people. First is Cherry Emerson, whose affection for Alfredo Barili and encouragement, insight, and support made my whole study possible. Next, are the two engaging family members who worked with me, Barili's granddaughter Mary Barili Goldsmith, and his great-granddaughter, Randy Barili Harris. If Alfredo possessed half their charm, then I see why many people loved him so.

Nor would the book have been completed without the help of Susan Stephens, Ron Payne, and John Van Sant. Their patient, fastidious, and encouraging assistance in plowing through the daunting amounts of primary material proved indispensable. Andy Phrydas at the Georgia Department of Archives and History also did everything he could to make my authorial life easier by his cheerful and unflagging cooperation. Vera Brodsky Lawrence helped fill in a number of places by graciously sending me a pre-publication copy of the second volume of her magisterial study on George Templeton Strong—*Strong on Music: The New York Music Scene in the Days of George Templeton Strong. Volume 2: Reverberations: 1850-1856* (Chicago: University of Chicago Press, 1995).

In pursuit of trying to bring some stylistic unity to an enormously varied amount of material, I have corrected spellings, especially the titles of works and composer's names. Problematic materials in quotation have been left unaltered but designated by [sic].

N. Lee Orr
Atlanta, 1995

1

MUSICAL AMERICA'S
FIRST FAMILY

Alfredo Barili belonged to that "phenomenal clan of Barilis and Pattis who so significantly inhabited the musical nineteenth century," as Vera Brodsky Lawrence deftly phrases it. "What a family!" the colorful pianist Louis Moreau Gottschalk exclaimed. "Do you know many others in art whose quarterings of nobility are better than those I have just enumerated?" No other family in American musical life produced such a dazzling array of talent. For most of the nineteenth century members of the Barili-Patti clan strode across the musical stages of the western world. They seemed to turn up everywhere, from Naples, Italy to Atlanta, Georgia; from San Francisco, California to Lima, Peru; from St. Petersburg, Russia to Philadelphia, Pennsylvania. Rare was the music-lover who attended an opera, heard a concert, or read a newspaper without encountering a Barili or Patti singing, playing, conducting, composing, producing, or teaching. Their talents were so prodigious, their passion so stirring, and their performances so striking that the name Barili-Patti became synonymous with music by the end of the century.[1]

That one family could produce so many musicians with so much talent is nothing short of astonishing—as Verdi put it, they were "A constellation of stars." The first generation of the family, born in southern Italy at the turn of the nineteenth century, came into their artistic maturity along with the first phase of Italian romantic opera. In the late 1820's and 1830's, as operatic music spread in popularity, especially in the works of Donizetti and Bellini, members of the Barili-Patti family assumed lead roles as well as important secondary parts, at times introducing new works. While these first Barili-Pattis were singing their way across Europe, they produced a new generation of even *more* talented children, who in turn took their places on the stage, in the orchestra pit, at the piano, or in the teaching studio. After their successes in Europe, and seeing that better opportunities awaited them in the new world, they followed the first wave of Italian opera as it migrated to America.

The musical climate in this country had ripened for Italian opera by the 1850's. Until that time, the American theater had depended on the culture and repertory of Great Britain for everything—the plays, actors, operas, singers, managers, even some of the costumes and sets. Everything was imported, except the buildings which housed the performances. By the 1840's, however, this situation began to change. As economic activity in the United States prospered and the population increased, the country developed a growing appetite for musical performances. Fueling this interest were the number of touring troupes that offered an enormous variety of operatic and musical productions in both English and Italian. From 1847 through 1860, between three and six Italian companies were touring the country in any one year, gradually moving further toward the interior. At the same time, English opera companies, which presented not only *English* operas but more often featured foreign-language operas in translation, took to the road as well.[2]

By the end of the 1840's, these traveling English, French, and Italian opera companies, with their expanded numbers and high-quality soloists, made dramatic music the most popular stage entertainment of the day. As American-music scholar Richard Crawford points out, "the most significant force to hit the American performing world in the first half of the nineteenth century was Italian opera . . . ." Opera proved just the vehicle to express the forceful, emotional, and volatile American character. The melodramatic stories, set to thrilling music, and sung passionately by larger-than-life characters, moved American audiences to rage, love, grief, and joy. In an era that circumscribed expressing personal feelings, the opera singers symbolically provided a much-needed emotional release for their listeners. "Their skill at capturing, distilling, protracting, and communicating the human passions with utter conviction was surely the ingredient that enabled opera to cut across social and class lines, attracting a wide range of nineteenth-century American listeners in performance."[3]

It is difficult to state the ubiquity of operatic music in the United States at the time; American audiences embraced it with an unbridled fervor. George Templeton Strong, a recent—and reluctant—convert to operatic pleasures, saw Bellini's *La sonnambula* at New York's Castle Garden in the summer of 1851. "Everybody goes, nob and snob, Fifth Avenue and Chatham Street, sit side by side fraternally on the hard benches," he noted in his journal. His upper-class sensibilities shuddered at the audience's *outre* reaction to the soprano in Bellini's

Norma: "The house was crowded and enthusiastic," he pooh-poohed; "the louder this lady screamed, the more uproariously they applauded, and her solitary windpipe was a fair match for the vociferous bravos of her 5,000 admirers . . . Norma hollered so . . . and so made the fur fly, that the exaltation of the audience knew no bounds." But operatic music also enjoyed wide popularity outside the opera house. Unlike today, Americans experienced opera as a part of their everyday lives. The popular songs adapted from these operas soon found their way into almost every heart and home. These songs formed a major part of the song repertory in America; operatic songs were sung in the parlor, parlor songs sung in operas; any and all could appear on a concert. Arrangements of music from *La sonnambula* for dancing in *Deux Quadrilles De Contredanses pour le Piano Forte* typified the countless instrumental arrangements which operatic music underwent. The widespread popularity of band music in nineteenth-century America brought opera an even wider audience. In 1861 part of the band music accompanying President Lincoln's inauguration came from *Rigoletto*. The touring European pianists in the 1840's and 1850's filled their concerts with glittering operatic transcriptions and fantasies on favorites such as *Lucia di Lammermoor, Norma, I Puritani, Lucrezia Borgia*, and others. Well into the last part of the century, opera "provided the American vernacular theater, and the musical scene in general, with a vitalizing force of great richness."[4]

It was into this rich musical situation that the Barili-Pattis stepped. More than any other single family, they played a central role in introducing and establishing Italian opera in the United States. First in New York, then throughout the Northeast, and finally with their wide-ranging tours, they sang, played, and managed operas and concerts across the country. Even more, they did much to bring new operas to life in America. Many of opera's first performances on these shores found at least one, if not more, Barili-Pattis on the stage or in the orchestra pit. They produced the first Verdi opera performed in the United States, *I Lombardi*, as well as the American premieres of Donizetti's *Linda di Chamounix* and Antonio Copolla's *Nina, la pazza per amore* (1847); they worked in two *more* debuts the next year—Mercadante's *Il giuramento* and Verdi's *Nabucco*; Salvatore Patti sang in the first performance of Donizetti's *Maria di Rohan* (1849); Ettore Barili premiered the role of *Rigoletto* in this country (1855); and Adelina Patti sang Dinorah in the American premiere of Meyerbeer's *Le Pardon de Ploermel* (1860). As opera gained in popularity in this country their careers blossomed. Members of the family with young Adelina Patti in tow gave more than two hundred concerts throughout the country by the end of the decade. After departing for Europe in 1861, Adelina became *the*

Queen of Song, reigning for more than thirty years. Her sisters Carlotta and Amalia were right behind her, garnering accolades and renown during their long singing careers.

The family added another to its list of firsts when Amalia married Maurice Strakosch, one of the country's first impresarios. His partnership with Bernard Ullman became a watershed in the history of American musical culture. Strakosch and Ullman's methods in managing opera companies established the basic operating format for arts' management in the United States. Finally, as one of the first generation of notable American pianists, Alfredo Barili captivated the New York musical world when he made his debut in 1865. He would go on to become the leading musician in Georgia, if not the entire South, by the end of the century. As the *Atlanta Constitution* reported in 1895, "It is not unreasonable to declare that Atlanta owes more to Alfredo Barili than to any other musician . . . ."[5] His story is their story, which begins in Italy.

* * * * * * *

Caterina Chiesa, Barili's paternal grandmother, was raised in southern Italy—land of song, passion, and splendidly handsome people. She bequeathed to her family looks, talent, and temperament. Born in Rome about 1810 to Giovanni Chiesa and Luisa Caselli, she was singing before she was in her teens. According to family accounts, as a young girl she was singing one day on her way to the well to draw water when she was overheard by Francesco Barili, a "composer of merit and the author of fine masses," as well as a vocal teacher. He began giving her voice lessons and then married her when she was fifteen. Francesco's instruction apparently did much for Caterina's voice as she soon began attracting attention with her singing. After Francesco's death (1829), she used her impressive talent to support their four children, Antonio (1826-76), Clotilda (1827-56), Nicolo (1828-1878), and Ettore (1828-85), the youngest, who was born on 5 November 1828 in Rome. All would become distinguished musicians.[6]

Caterina impressed Donizetti with her voice, so much so that he asked her to introduce the role of Isabella in his *L'assedio di Calais* for its premiere at the Teatro San Carlo in Naples 19 November 1836. He wrote three days after the performance: "*L'assedio di Calais* went well. I was called out six times . . . . It is my most carefully worked-out score. Barroilhet, la Manzocchi, la Barili, Gianni, everyone applauded." Caterina likewise sang the Naples's premieres of Elvira in Bellini's *I Puritani* (1836), Donizetti's *Gemma di Vergy*

(1837), and Pacini's *Valerie ossia La Cieca* (1838) in addition to the demanding role of high priestess Norma in the opera of the same name. She reportedly outshone the celebrated Giulia Grisi so during one performance that Grisi refused to appear on stage with her again. The colorful nineteenth-century pianist Louis Moreau Gottschalk, who knew the whole family, said that Caterina "was a fiery lyric tragic actress . . . .still celebrated in Portugal, Spain, and Naples . . . ."[7]

While singing in Naples, Caterina Barili met Salvatore Patti, leading tenor of the company with which she was working. Considering the dates of Ettore's birth (1828) and Amalia Patti's (1831), Caterina and Salvatore must have been married sometime near the end of 1830. Salvatore Patti was born to Pietro Patti and Concepcion Marino in Catania, Sicily. By the 1825-26 season, Patti, a *tenore robusto,* was singing at the Teatro Carolino in Palermo where Gaetano Donizetti—not yet thirty himself—was musical director. That season, which extended from May to February, proved trying for everyone because of personnel intrigues, mediocre musical quality, jealous singers, and financial problems, all of which forced the house to close on 19 February. Despite these problems, Donizetti managed to stage a number of admirable productions along the way. Patti sang Pipetto in Donizetti's *L'ajo nell'imbarazzo* on 5 September to good reviews for everyone; early the next year, on 7 January 1826 he created the role of Ismaele in the premiere of Donizetti's *Alahor in Granata.* This performance also enjoyed a positive reception. After marrying Caterina he appeared at other theaters in Sicily, Italy, and Spain. In 1836, for the Teatro Valle, Rome, he sang Ugo in Donizetti's *Parisina* as well as other roles. One listener described him as "a respectable tenor singer, with a smooth, soft, piping voice, a correct style of singing, and very good stage manner." Even though his roles consisted of supporting tenor parts, Patti was lauded as a competent singer, good actor, and solid musician. His handsome, strapping physique likewise added to his stage presence.[8]

After their marriage the couple continued singing across Europe. Their first child, Amalia, was born in Paris in 1831; Carlotta in Florence in 1835; and Carlo in Madrid in 1842. The year 1843 found Caterina and Salvatore in Madrid, where she sang Elena in Donizetti's *Marino Faliero* on 31 January. Contrary to the numerous legends, anecdotes, incorrect dates, and downright fabrications circulated since then, she did not complete the taxing role of *Norma*, walk into the theater's green room, and deliver her next child. Nor was the child then wrapped in the leading tenor's cloak. John Cone has put the record straight, finally, in his distinguished biography of the most illustrious star in the entire

Barili-Patti family. Adelina [Adela] Juana Maria was born ten days later on Sunday afternoon 10 February 1843. Within six weeks she was baptized at the nearby church of San Luis by the vicar Jose Losada. One of the greatest sopranos of all time had arrived.[9]

Soon, the entire family—parents, Barili and Patti children— returned to Italy. With her nervous, difficult nature, Caterina's stormy temperament often kept the household emotionally charged. When she was frustrated she could break out into rages, showering whoever had crossed her with torrents of invective, or even physical abuse. She was known to seize fire tongs to threaten her victim, should he or she show any independence from her fierce will. Perhaps this highly volatile atmosphere encouraged musical sensitivity, or at least compelled everyone to seek refuge in music from the tempests, for the children prospered musically. Clotilda was showing the same vocal precociousness as her mother and would make her singing debut at age nineteen. Her brothers were also developing into fine young musicians and singers, as were the Patti sisters, all of whom blossomed in the rich musical milieu.[10]

The family life in Italy continued for the next two years without much professional change. With that amazing amount of talent under one roof, however, in an era when the popularity of Italian opera was increasing daily, it did not take a prophet to predict that something would soon happen. First, it was clear that Clotilda stood ready for her musical debut at any time. Her splendid voice was maturing quickly. Moreover, her three step-sisters Carlotta, Amalia, and Adelina showed even more promising vocal talent. Also, few other families had a mother still holding the musical reputation of Caterina, married to someone with the operatic experience of Salvatore Patti. Stir in the impressive vocal talents of the older boys, Ettore and Nicolo, in addition to the instrumentally skilled Antonio and Carlo, and you have much more than simply a family—you have an opera company. That's exactly what Antonio Sanquirico realized when he met them.

Basso buffo Sanquirico had first appeared at Palmo's Opera House in New York on Chambers Street 29 April 1844 as Don Bartolo in *Il barbiere di Siviglia*. This was the first of a number of successful performances. Shortly thereafter he returned to Europe where he intended to stay, until he met the Barili-Patti family in the summer of 1846. The encounter was propitious for both sides. Sanquirico undoubtedly recognized the untapped goldmine onto which he had stumbled. Caterina and Salvatore, realizing that their own singing careers had all but run their course in Europe, likewise saw that they could extend their performing pursuits in America. Moreover, they thought that there might be riches ahead by becoming opera impresarios and presenting their talented brood to adoring American audiences. Encouraging their decision were the glowing reports brought back by European vocal stars touring the United States in the 1830's and early 1840's. With few brilliant native singers to entertain them, American audiences had developed insatiable appetites for European stars. Foreign singers of any merit could earn respectable, if not large sums by touring. New York was especially ravenous for dramatic lyrical entertainment. Italian opera was just twenty years old in the city, the Garcia family having introduced it in 1825 with *Il barbiere*.[11]

Seeing an opportunity, Sanquirico decided to take his chances managing an opera troupe. He obtained by mail $3,000 from 100 subscribers in New York and announced a new season of Italian opera at Palmo's intimate opera house. The enterprising troupe, which included the Barili-Pattis in addition to F. Beneventano, a *primo basso assoluto*, and tenor Sesto Benedetti, all under the direction of Sanquirico, Salvatore Patti and one C. Pogliani (who would subsequently disappear from the scene) left Liverpool for America in November 1846 on the *Caledonia*, arriving in Boston 5 December. Their reputation preceded them. On 21 November 1846 the New York *Spirit* reported that Sanquirico had assembled "a remarkably fine troupe," an assessment that, if anything, proved an understatement. Clotilda, just nineteen, was the prima donna and would quickly win over her audiences with her youthful beauty and angelic voice. The tenor, Sesto Benedietti, was soon proclaimed "the best tenor we have heard in America."[12]

It seems that neither Caterina, Nicolo, nor Ettore Barili—Alfredo's father—accompanied the family to the United States on this trip. Ettore's name disappears from the record until 1854 when he brought his wife and young Alfredo to New York to join the rest of the Barili-Pattis. Unsure of the success of the new venture, Caterina had chosen to remain in Italy with Ettore and the three younger Patti sisters. When Salvatore returned in the spring 1847 for a second recruiting trip, Caterina and the girls came to the United States, leaving Ettore behind in Europe. Nearly twenty, Ettore was able be on his own. As the young lady he would marry was from Barcelona, one can conjecture that he continued travelling and singing on the continent. He met Antoinetta Sampo (1839-1893) and they were married in Spain about 1853. Alfredo was born in Florence the next year and shortly afterward the young family emigrated to America and joined the others on East Tenth Street.

The Barili-Patti house, next door the Max Maretzeks, was one of the musical centers of New York. Visitors streamed through continually, enchanted by the precocious voice of young Adelina. The vocal stars Marietta Alboni and Henriette Sontag came by and heard their future competition. Richard Grant White, one of our most important sources for operatic history in New York, later recounted his visits when Adelina skipped in an out of the room chirping and singing until Caterina told her to be quiet or leave.[13]

The efforts of Sanquirico and Patti to mount a new opera season at Palmo's marked "a watershed in the annals of Italian opera performance in the United States." Up to this point operatic performance in this country had been a hit-or-miss affair, with few companies lasting longer than a single season. The longevity of opera companies would change following this new effort, which began brilliantly at Palmo's on 4 January 1847, with the American premiere of Donizetti's *Linda di Chamounix*. Italian opera had been absent from the United States for the previous two years. With its reappearance in New York, audiences stormed Palmo's on opening night and for the rest of the season, which ran until late March. Three family members performed throughout the run, Salvatore, Clotilda, and Antonio, "*maestro* attached to the company," who was in charge of the chorus as well as the orchestra. Sanquirico also sang. But it was "La Barili" who became the "toast of New York," captivating the critics with her "beautiful dark and flashing eyes, well formed mouth, and teeth of the most dazzling whiteness." Richard Grant White (*Courier & Enquirer,* 5 January 1847) had some few reservations about her singing, but, overcome by her beauty, declared she sang like an "angel." The troupe's second production, *Lucia di Lammermoor*, proved spectacularly popular. The reviewer for the *Herald* found the audience "music mad. Never in this city have we witnessed a more complete triumph." George Templeton Strong, curmudgeonly diarist of the city's social caste, finally exposed himself to Italian opera when he attended *Lucia* on 25 January. Though he thought it "a weak affair" he hoped that "it may bear fruit in a new opera house. The little Chambers Street concern is quite too small. 'Twas more than full last night. The aristocracy were present *en masse*. Washington Irving, among the rest . . . ." The troupe's victory demonstrated that opera could be an ongoing enterprise in America. As the critic for the *Albion* noted: "The success of this undertaking is now placed beyond a doubt, for the house is crowded to suffocation nearly every night. *Lucia di Lammermoor* has now been played four times, and its extraordinary attraction continues unabated." The company boldly strode ahead with two more firsts: on 5 February, *Nina, la pazza per amore* by Piere Antonio Coppola (in which Salvatore Patti made his New York debut); and 3 March, *I Lombardi* by Giuseppe Verdi. This was the first opera by Verdi presented in the United

States. By June the Sanquirico-Patti Company had produced eight different operas, including three American premieres. Clotilda enjoyed continued adulation in *Lucia* and as Griselda in *I Lombardi*. Unfortunately, the second season that opened in March was not as successful. Plagued by illnesses among the singers, a lack of stellar vocal stars, and competition from the large, celebrated touring Havana Opera Company, the season for the troupe ended as a financial disaster on 26 May. One benefit concert for Antonio Barili was presented on 7 June, but after that the company, in a distressingly familiar pattern for Italian opera companies, disbanded.[14]

The troupe left another legacy, however, in addition to permanently establishing Italian opera on these shores. Impressed by the initial success of Sanquirico and Patti at Palmo's, 150 well-to-do New Yorkers decided to establish yet another Italian opera association in the spring of 1847. They then re-engaged singers from their previous season, including "la Barili" (Clotilda), G. F. Beneventano, S. Patti, A. Sanquirico, and Antonio Barili. The three musically precocious Patti girls were already attracting attention as well. Amalia, a mezzo-soprano and only fifteen, had already been billed as a *"prima donna assoluta"*; twelve-year old Carlotta and four-year-old Adelina were not far behind.[15]

The directors of the new opera association also decided to build a new opera house on Astor Place. When it opened in 1847 the 1,500-seat house was the largest theater in the country. The location of the Astor Place Opera House and formation of a new company represents, as Katherine Preston aptly describes, "yet another in a continuing series of attempts by New York's *bon ton* to commandeer Italian opera for themselves. This time, for a variety of reasons, their efforts met with a great deal more success than had previous ventures." For one thing, the house's then uptown-Manhattan location at the triangle formed by Astor Place, Eighth Street, and Broadway was rather distant from the general public, who lived lower on the island, and clearly suggested to all New Yorkers that it was reserved for the city's wealthy and educated elite. For another, the fifty-cent admission was steep for common theater goers; even those who could afford it gained admission only to "the amphitheater" section, "the most uncomfortable and ill-contrived place imaginable." A stiff dress code made things even more difficult by adding to the evening's expense. Finally, for those few average folks persistent enough to show up anyway, the critic for the *New York Herald* in his review of the 23 November 1847 opening night bluntly removed any doubt as to who was welcome: "The fashionable world is now completely organized—the opera is successful—white kid gloves are all the go—and the *canaille* must keep themselves a respectful distance from Astor Place hereafter. Read and obey."[16]

Richard Grant White lauded the fashionable enterprise later in his accounts of opera in New York (published in the *Century Magazine)* as "the musical event of the first importance" for the city, which "has not been seen since." He praised the exclusive nature of the enterprise, which he felt had succeeded. "It may safely be said that there was hardly a person present who was not known, by name, at least, to a very considerable number of his or her fellow auditors . . . . Rarely has there been an assembly . . . with such a generally diffused air of good-breeding." His aristocratic prejudice caused him to miss the considerable number of general public that filled the audience of about 1,500 that opening night on Monday evening, 22 November 1847. The critic for the *Sunday Age,* who was more democratic in his assessment, reported that the "very hotbed of Upper Tendom exclusiveness" were seated below the "vulgar wretches, low creatures, [and] *canaille,"* some five hundred of them "piled up [in the third balcony], one above the other, and striving in vain to catch a glimpse of the stage."[17]

The opening production of Verdi's *Ernani* received generally positive reviews, though the critics disagreed on the merits of specific singers. George Templeton Strong delayed his appearance at the new Astor Place House until 1 December when he attended the troupe's second production of Bellini's *Beatrice di Tenda.* While he liked the opera house, he stayed true to form and sneeringly described the work as "stupid and silly and the poorest, weakest, shallowest, and most wearisome production I ever was bored by. Perhaps I did it injustice, but I think not, and I won't undergo the dose again." Soprano Teresa Truffi's debut brought sensational reviews, especially from White, who admired her regal bearing, expressive vocal sentiments, tragic demeanor, and long blond hair. But he thought Clotilda, the former toast of New York, as Beatrice, miscast. While "charming and sweet as ever," her angelic, small voice lacked the vocal depth and volume necessary for the star role. Even worse, she possessed "no dramatic power to supply her vocal deficiencies." The role of Beatrice, White thought, should have been sung by her mother Caterina, who, even though her voice was not as fresh, still could produce a "splendid and truly imposing display," and "certainly even in her decadence [was] one of the finest singers in the grand style heard in this country."[18]

The same production of *Beatrice* also introduced sixteen-year-old Amalia to New York in the role of Agnese. "Her voice is very fine, her style good," the critic for The *Albion* wrote. He predicted that "when she gains confidence we shall have a good deal to say in her favour." She sang one other role later that season: Fenena in the American premiere of Verdi's *Nabucco* (1848). By the end of the first six-week season, the company had produced (in addition to *Beatrice*) *La sonnambula, Lucia,* and *I Puritani,* in which Clotilda sang Elvira. Everyone now agreed, the Astor Place Opera season had been a complete success. The critic for the *Spirit* held high hopes for the troupe. "If none of those unfortunate disagreements, which have heretofore occurred in connexion with every Italian company in this city, should occur with this [troupe], we feel assured of its undoubted success."[19]

Alas, this was not to be the case. As in some fate-filled Greek tragedy, Sanquirico and Patti were destined to see their initial success start flagging, just as the first company's fortunes had declined the season before at Palmo's following its auspicious beginning. *Lucrezia Borgia* opened on 12 January and enjoyed a modestly successful run at the Astor Place Opera House. But then things went downhill. Even the introduction of new works for the second season did not help. Bellini's *I Capuletti ed i Montecchi,* enthusiastically received the September before, was now "heavy as lead" and sank like a stone. Caterina Barili-Patti made her New York debut in the performance on 28 January 1848, playing Romeo to Clotilda's Juliet. Unfortunately for the company, even with her impressive stage presence and strong deportment, she was past her prime. The critic for the *Albion* admitted that her voice once must have possessed beauty and power, but now lacked depth and splendor. The *Herald* meanly wrote the next day that "Madame Patti makes an elegant looking young man, performs tolerably well in the old style, but her voice is a mere wreck—a ruin." The *Mirror* (1 February 1848) reported that the second and final performance on 31 January drew the worst house yet seen at Astor Place. Even the American premiere of Mercadante's *Il giuramento* (which Strong surprisingly found "worth all the operas they have produced in Astor Place knocked into one") on 14 February did little to help; by the middle of the month the company had serious financial problems. Poor management, flaring tempers and jealousies so rife in Italian opera companies all contributed, causing the singers to become ill—or so they claimed. Bickering by the vocalists sabotaged the operas, the performances deteriorated, the audiences stopped coming, and by early March the unfinished season ground to an inglorious halt.[20]

The directors of the opera association announced that the company was taking only a two-or three-week break and dispatched the troupe by train south to Philadelphia in search of an audience. Once again the season opened successfully at the Chestnut Street Theater where the company's run involved twenty-one productions of *Lucia di Lammermoor, Lucrezia Borgia, Ernani,* and *Il giuramento.* For the first three weeks, Sanquirico and Patti's ensemble filled the house, but by the fourth week the company "went broke" according to one account and returned to New York. Phoenix-like, a "second season" of thirty opera nights was announced for 27 March. Nothing much changed, however. Beset by cabals, bickerings, and "sudden" illnesses which forced last-minute schedule changes, the listing operatic ship began taking on more water. Even the presentation of the North American premiere of Verdi's *Nabucco* on 4 April (1848) did little to help. Soon Sanquirico and the Barili-Patti clan jumped ship, leaving the three remaining stars at the helm, which, as one critic observed, lasted only *"trois jours."* Aspiring impresario William Niblo assumed the lease of the Astor Place Opera House and presented a remarkably successful summer series beginning in June.[21]

The failure of the Sanquirico-Patti operatic enterprise typified the fate of so many Italian companies. Financial and administrative management was sufficiently incompetent to guarantee failure, something that was roundly pointed out in the press. The singers received astonishing salaries, which was not surprising, given that the manager and two of the lead singers belonged to the same family. The *Democratic Review* (March) reported that "La Signora Patti was engaged for a month at $800, sings twice and refuses to sing again. Mlle. Truffi is paid $600 a month, and is obliged to take all the leading parts and sing every night, week after week, without rest or relief. Mlle. Barili is paid $500 a month, engaged for the whole season, and has not appeared over four or five times in all." No one was really in charge, either, as the critic for the *Spirit* protested. "The management is conducted by too many, and authority [is] exercised by persons having no idea what they were doing." Moreover, he pointed out, "there were too many stars, and too little brilliancy. The materials were possessed but so badly put together that there was discord behind the scenes and grumbling before them. The great variety that could have been presented was neglected, and two or three operas forced upon the subscribers. The *bon ton*, or the *dilettanti*, or both, were *ennuied* to death."[22]

With the collapse of the second company, the Barili-Patti family members turned elsewhere for work. Antonio remained popular as a pianist, vocal teacher, and conductor. Richard Grant White thought him "an excellent *maestro*, and for some fifteen years he was a teacher of singing in New York, and there could hardly have been better." On 22 June 1848 he assisted Maurice Strakosch— recently arrived from Europe—with a concert at the Tabernacle in New York that also included Caterina, Amalia, and the German violinist Henry Schriever.

Salvatore soon returned to the stage at the Astor Place Opera House, where he sang supporting roles for two years, one being di Fieschi in the American premiere on 10 December 1849 of Donizetti's *Maria di Rohan*. In March 1848 Clotilda married the son of a wealthy New York Colonel Thorne and formed the Barili-Thorne Opera Company. They later appeared in San Francisco during December 1854 where they remained for almost a year while performing. *Dwight's Journal of Music* reported that they left California en route to Peru "with the design of making a professional visit to all principal South American cities." The next year, 1856, Madame Clotilda Barili-Thorne died in Lima in August or early September. Amalia appeared frequently at Astor Place in both leading and secondary parts, sometimes with her father. Caterina sang her last complete lead role there for three performances of Norma in February 1850, with Amalia as Adalgisa. "The audience was taken by surprise by the excellence of the performance," the *New York Evening Post* observed (18 February 1850). "Madame Patti, who it was understood had retired from the stage, on the contrary, acted and sang the part of *Norma* with an energy, a feeling, and a correctness that created more enthusiasm than we have seen evinced for a long period." It impressed Richard Grant White as well, who remembered years later that "It was the last time that the grand old Italian style of singing was heard in America; —that large simplicity of manner, severe and yet not hard; that thoroughness, that constantly present sense of the decorum of art, died out before we, who were brought up on Donizetti and on Verdi, came to the enjoyment of operatic delights."[23]

* * * * * *

Even though the second season of the Sanquirico-Patti company fell apart, it did not signal another dry spell for Italian opera in the United States. As Katherine Preston has so splendidly summarized in *Opera on the Road* (pp. 141-48), 1847 was the pivotal year for Italian music in America. From that point on, Italian opera was firmly established on these shores, something the Barili-Patti family did much to bring about. As the country recovered from the disastrous financial Panic of 1837, businesses began growing, employing more citizens, cities grew and flourished, and theaters reopened. In contrast, the political and economic situation in Europe continued to deteriorate, growing more unstable, until it erupted in the revolutions of 1848. As a result, more musicians, unable to find work, immigrated to the United States in the late 1840's. The Barili-Patti family, encouraged by Antonio Sanquirico, came in the early stages of this movement, and subsequently played a decisive role for Italian opera's success in America.

As the population of singers and instrumentalists began arriving in the United States grew, it became unnecessary to send to Europe for entire companies. The lure of financial riches from an American tour had done much to attract many musicians. By the 1840's this country had gained a reputation as a gold mine for European artists, sending many vocal stars home far richer than when they arrived. Tours during the 1840's by virtuoso instrumentalists such as Henry Vieuxtemps, Ole Bull, Leopold de Meyer, and Henri Herz had brought them monetary windfalls. Undoubtedly the prospect of financial success played a major role in convincing the rest of the Barili-Patti family to pack up and come to the United States in 1847. (For a while this strategy worked because Caterina and Clotilda earned magnificent sums). But, as many journalists began pointing out during the 1850's, the frequent failures of Italian companies often resulted from the exorbitant salaries which the European operatic stars demanded—and got—whether they warranted them or not. The *Musical World* in 1852 insisted "The people of the United States cannot afford (and ought not if they could) to pay the . . . exorbitant and unjust . . . sums which are nightly expended, often on an ambiguous Prima Donna or an ordinary Tenor." This is exactly what bankrupted Sanquirico and Patti's operatic enterprise. Even full houses could not sustain such high fees.

Italian opera in the United States also benefited from the vigorous economic growth of the time. As prosperity returned, the transportation system expanded as well, especially the railroads. This encouraged cities and towns to expand in size and number. The increasing number of interior cities made it possible to support more visiting troupes. Atlanta by the 1850's was fast becoming one of the important inland cities because of her expanding rail connections. As soon as the city recovered from the Civil War, traveling opera troupes began visiting regularly and frequently. Before that, by the early 1850's, Italian companies had penetrated much of the country.

Growth in the population gave added support for traveling opera companies. Leading much of this increase was a growing middle class, boosted by large numbers of German immigrants, who settled in towns and cities after fleeing the political repercussions from the failed 1848 revolutions. Between 1840 and 1850 the American population increased by a third and yet again by the same amount between 1850 and 1860, when it reached thirty-one million. The widespread growth and economic prosperity of these middle-class citizens gave them the leisure time and the financial resources to support the theaters and concert halls that featured European musicians. Two places specifically served as home bases for these traveling troupes: the Academies of Music in New York and Philadelphia. With the collapse of the Astor Place House in 1852, the Academy of Music, which opened in 1854, became the east-coast headquarters for many companies. Philadelphia followed suit three years later with its own Academy.

Finally, one last factor in the growth of Italian opera in America was the appearance of operatic and concert impresarios, three especially: Bernard Ullman, Maurice Strakosch, and Max Maretzek. Each of these impresarios would exercise a decisive influence on the cultural life of the United States.

Bernard Ullman (1817-1885) forged the basic operating model for the impresario in nineteenth-century America. He reoriented the profession of musical performance from an aesthetic pursuit to a musical business, where marketing techniques overshadowed artistic concerns in promoting artistic enterprises. He appeared in this country sometime around 1842 and by 1846 was managing the tours of the celebrated European pianist Henri Herz. By 1852 he directed opera troupes connected with the German soprano Henriette Sontag and then those of French coloratura soprano Anna de la Grange. During the late 1850's he was overseeing a number of other artists, including the pianist Sigismund Thalberg, as well as his own Ullman Opera Company. Ullman also worked with Maurice Strakosch in joint enterprises such as the Ullman and Strakosch Celebrated Italian Opera Company, most of which were associated with the Academy of Music. Following the partnership's financial collapse Ullman returned to Europe in 1862.[24]

Max Maretzek (1821-97) was born in Moravia and conducted at Drury Lane and Covent Garden in London before coming to the United States in 1848, where the manager of the second Astor Place Opera House company Edward Fry secured his services as conductor. By 1850 he had succeeded Fry in the management of the opera house, and began a distinguished thirty-year career as an operatic impresario in North America. He was reportedly the first manager in this country to conduct his own operatic performances, a talent that would serve him well. In early 1851 Maretzek took the Astor Place Opera Company on tour, most importantly to Charleston and Augusta, which offered the finest and most extensive opera performances the two cities—or any southern town outside of New Orleans—had ever seen. Later in the decade his own Maretzek Opera Company toured widely in the United States, Mexico, and Cuba. He continued touring and conducting until 1878 when he retired from active management. On 12 February 1889 the Metropolitan Opera House staged a benefit for Maretzek in honor of his fifty years as a conductor. His two volumes of memoirs, *Crotchets and Quavers* (1855) and *Sharps and Flats* (1890), provide a witty and valuable account of musical life in this country during the middle third of the century.[25]

Maurice Strakosch (1825-87), thought by many to be a Russian or Pole, was in reality, like Maretzek, a Moravian. Trained as a pianist, he made his debut at eleven years of age, and won a reputation throughout Germany and Austria. Billed as the "Pianist to the Emperor of Russia," the handsome and flamboyant Strakosch not only became one of the most important impresarios in nineteenth-century America but also played a major role in the lives of the Barili-Patti family. He had met Salvatore Patti in 1843 when Patti's step-daughter, Clotilda Barili, sang in a concert with Strakosch in Vicenza. Upon arriving in America, he sought Patti out and the two became reacquainted. Following Strakosch's spectacular debut at Niblo's Astor Place House on 10 June 1848, he enlisted the aid of family members Caterina, Amalia, and Antonio in his next concert at the Tabernacle later that month on the 22nd. Antonio conducted, Maurice played, and mother and daughter sang the duet from *Norma*. Unfortunately, Maurice's musical charm ran out the following September when his gala concert flopped; one reviewer declared that each member of the orchestra must have had a different part, "for nothing but a mistake of that kind could cause a party of New York musicians to make such a hideous discord." Seeing the handwriting on the wall for his success in the city, Strakosch organized a concert troupe and toured throughout North and South America for two years.[26]

By 1851 he was back in New York working with Maretzek at Astor Place. On 15 July the *Message Bird* announced that later in the year the company would give the world premiere of Strakosch's three-act opera *Giovanna Prima di Napoli*, on a libretto by Agostino Pendalo. According to the published libretto, Strakosch composed it "expressly . . . for the Italian Opera Company of New York, Under the Management and Direction of Max Maretzek." The 6 January performance brought general approval from the critics, even if many of them did find the work derivative, as the writer for the *Message Bird* pointed out (1 February), "of course it is not to be disguised, that some of [its] themes are first cousin to something, *somewhere* heard before . . . ." One report praised Strakosch, assuring him that he had "done himself great credit" with his first opera. Another lauded the minimal amount of "those dreamy desert patches of monotonous and meaningless recitative which disfigure most . . . contemporary Italian Operas."[27]

Later that year on 8 May 1852 Strakosch married Amalia Patti, which made him an official member of musical America's most celebrated family. It is fitting that a person who came from another artistically significant family enterprise, the "Strakosch Arts Management," and who would play a critical role in the shaping of America's musical life, should marry into a household even more musically celebrated in this country. The marriage completed the cast of America's most eminent musical family. All the roles were now filled: impresarios, pianists, conductors, composers, and spilling over the floodlights, singers—singers everywhere. From Caterina, whose reputation still lived on in southern Italy and New York, through her Barili daughters who were still holding the boards, on to her Patti daughters, one of whom already enjoyed celebrity status, few families in this country's cultural history have ever been so active in so many arenas of its musical life. During the 1850's in the Northeast, where our musical institutions took firm shape, one could not listen, perform, or read about music very long without running into a Barili or a Patti. And had the Barili-Patti-Strakosch clan produced no further notable musicians, these achievements alone would have earned them lasting esteem. But there was *more* to come. Younger Barilis and Pattis were waiting in the wings, ready to step onstage and bring even more prominence to a remarkable family.[28]

At the end of that year another Barili showed up on the New York operatic stage. Nicolo Barili had been born in early 1828 and like his brother Ettore, had remained in Italy when his mother and step-father Salvatore Patti emigrated to the United States. By the early 1850's he had established himself as a *primo basso* of some distinction and was recruited there by one of the era's most distinguished singers, Marietta Alboni, for her opera company. She became an instant sensation at her first appearance in this country on 27 December 1852 at the Broadway Theater as the lead in Rossini's *La Cenerentola* with Nicolo as Alidoro. Even her stout figure—one critic later said she looked like Falstaff in petticoats—did not mar the accolades. The critic for the *Albion* (1 January 1853) wasted no time in dismissing every other contralto from the stage: "Queen of contralti, perhaps *the* great contralto, who is destined never to be rivalled or eclipsed . . . we could go on with *ad libitum*, as others have done before us; but to what end?" On 16 January at Metropolitan Hall she sang Rossini's *Stabat Mater*, which included Nicolo Barili, and by the end of the month she had added *La figlia del reggimento, La sonnambula,* and *Il barbiere di Siviglia* to her American roles. Nicolo is cited specifically as Rodolfo in *La sonnambula* and possibly appeared as well in *La figlia* and *Il barbiere*.[29]

By 1852 the youngest of the Patti sisters (she was nine at the time) was also singing in public—to unrivalled praise. Adelina, already billed as "the wonder of the age," sang in a "Grand Vocal and Instrumental Festival" at Metropolitan Hall on 5 May 1852. "Little Patti, or *La Petite Lind* gave the Nightingale's 'Echo Song' with wonderful effect," the *Mirror* reported (6 May 1852), "and the tiny *prima donna* was the star of the evening. She was encored with a *furore* that we have seldom witnessed at a concert." Caterina sang in the concert as well, and also impressed the *Mirror*: "Signora Patti, the mother of *La Petite* and of several full-grown *prima donnas*, sang a cavatina from *Gemma di Vegy* with exquisite taste, and with a freshness of voice that gave no evidence of decay. It is to be regretted that we do not more frequently hear this accomplished artiste on the stage or in the concert-room. Signora Patti and '*La Petite Lind*' are, in themselves, attraction enough to fill the largest Concert Hall in America."[30]

For the next two years few Barili-Pattis participated in the New York musical life, largely because the core of the family was out of town on tour. Salvatore, pressed by financial reverses in 1852, began planning a tour that fall for his youngest daughter, nine-year-old Adelina, whose concerts in the city had proven very successful. With the assistance of Maurice Strakosch and his wife Amalia (Caterina appears to have remained in New York), the troupe set out in the fall of 1852, traveling first to Connecticut (New Haven and Hartford), Massachusetts (Springfield), Philadelphia, and Baltimore, where the *Sun* (13 October) reported that "the most prominent prima donna might take a lesson in style and execution from the exquisite warblings of this gifted child." As fate would have it, the Norwegian violinist, Ole Bull, whose playing had earned him world-wide renown, happened to be in Baltimore at the same time as the Pattis. Sensing a ripe financial opportunity, he contracted with Adelina and Maurice to join the troupe. Their travels for the next two years took them as far south as New Orleans and west to St. Louis and Chicago. Already Adelina's willful ways kept the troupe stirred up. Years later she said of Bull, that he had been "a gentle, kind man, and like a mother" to her. She continued, "What a little child I was to be going about with only those men! Not a woman . . . only papa—poor papa!—and Maurice and Ole Bull, and I was a little tyrant, I dare say, to all three of them." By the beginning of 1855 the group was back in New York where Adelina sang on 20 and 27 January and 27 February. Not to be missed was the fact that the Pattis—Adelina and Salvatore—were richer by $20,000.[31]

By this time Ettore had arrived in New York from Florence with his eighteen-year-old wife Antoinetta and their six-month-old son Alfredo. Antoinetta Sampo had been born in Barcelona in 1837, where Ettore probably met her on one of his singing tours. They could not have been married long when she gave birth to Alfredo Riccardo Paolo Barili on 4 August 1854 in Florence. According to the certificate still in possession of the family, he was either baptized or registered—it is not clear—on 31 October at the Opera di Santa Maria del Fiore. The couple embarked the next month for the United States.[32]

Ettore hoped to establish himself in this country as an opera singer, which seemed viable considering the prominence of his first role here, that of the lead in the American premiere of *Rigoletto*. In January Ole Bull, Strakosch, and Maretzek had joined together to try their hands at managing the new Academy of Music. Open only since October, the beautiful new house had already gone bust, and now only four months later had new management. Its gala inauguration had been on 2 October 1854 when the two biggest superstars in Italian opera, soprano Giulia Grisi and her companion, the celebrated tenor known simply as Mario, opened the city's resplendent new opera house at Irving Place and Fourteenth Street with *Norma*. Since September they had been performing in New York, when they had made their debut at Castle Garden on 4 September in *Lucrezia Borgia* with a cast that included Amalia and Salvatore. Grisi had premiered both the roles of Adalgisa in *Norma* and Elvira in *I Puritani* in Italy and was the current reigning diva in the operatic world. She would prove to be a model for young Adelina, who undoubtedly heard their premiere.[33]

Few houses in Europe surpassed the opulence of the New York Academy of Music. Seating some forty-six hundred people, the main auditorium reached up eighty feet while facing a stage forty-eight feet wide and seventy feet deep. The walls shone with luminous mythological figures lit by gas, while the first two tiers of boxes rested on regal pillars topped with busts. Framing the gilded proscenium were eighteen luxurious boxes crowned with statues holding trumpets. As if the magnificent visual aspects were not enough, the house possessed superb acoustics. Grisi and Mario continued their season throughout the fall with *Lucrezia Borgia, I Puritani, La sonnambula,* and finally *Il barbiere;* in February they sang farewell to America at the Metropolitan Theater.[34]

By January 1855 the Bull-Strakosch-Maretzek trio had taken over management of the Academy. Strakosch had been dispatched to Europe in search of vocal leads, while Bull made grand plans for a festive reopening of the house on 19 February 1855 with the eagerly anticipated newest work from

Verdi, *Rigoletto*. When it became clear that Strakosch would not make it back in time with his vocal stars, Bull filled the male leads with two young unknowns: Beagio Bolcioni, a new tenor, as the Duke of Mantua, and Ettore Barili for Rigoletto; Amalia was also cast as Maddalena. The capable orchestra and chorus totaled 100 performers and was conducted by the impresario Max Maretzek, the "Napoleon of Conductors." For some reason Verdi's orchestration was not used, possibly to escape copyright or rental fees. The instrumentalists played from an orchestrated piano score by a local German opera conductor and violist Julius Unger. Because of this, the *Times* claimed it could not make a judgement on the instrumentation as it had "been vamped up from a piano-forte partition by some enterprising instrumentalist of this City." While the orchestrator showed some ability, the reporter rightly wondered if "is it not going a *little* too far to take these unnecessary liberties with a living composer?" But, he did like Verdi's new opera "rather better than we have had lately from his pen." And both male leads did well: "For a first appearance both these gentlemen may congratulate themselves on a good reception." Beagio Bolcioni impressed William Henry Fry with his "clear, muscular, and manly tenor *robusto*." However, Ettore seems to have made a better first impression on the *Times'* critic. He proved to be "a good baritone, highly cultivated, impressive and finished." Ettore brought a dramatic intensity to the role, but had a little trouble with ensemble work: "If he would avoid dragging the time, and resist the temptation of a *crescendo* or *diminuendo* occasionally, (he can execute these things very well, though) he would be much more enjoyable. The upper part of Signor Barili's voice is exceedingly clear and powerful; he phrases well, and possesses some dramatic ability."[35]

The *Message Bird* (24 February) also thought the opera was "admirably put upon the stage." It backhandedly referred to the clamor for operas sung only by stars, bluntly pointing out that for people who just enjoy the music and "are content to forget stars of the first magnitude and be satisfied with simply good singing" the evening was a success. Dramatically, the writer preferred Barili's "supple and adroit" acting to Bolcioni's.

The public reaction to Verdi's new opera did not help Barili's musical aspirations, however. Its fiercely intense and sometimes brutal plot, based on Victor Hugo's 1832 play *Le Roi s'amuse*, put off audiences accustomed to the more genteelly tragic outcomes of *La sonnambula, I Puritani,* and *Norma.* By the third and fourth performances (23 and 25 February) attendance had dwindled to a disappointing 400 to 500 each night. Even though the *Times* found the work increasingly attractive after repeated hearings, Richard Grant White snapped: "Verdi's *Rigoletto* does not prove a favorite with the public, and we are not surprised. Much as we clamor for novelty, mere novelty without merit will not charm us into giving our dollars or our time. *Rigoletto* should be withdrawn as soon as possible."[36]

Things only went downhill from there for Bull and Maretzek's season at the Academy when *La favorita* succeeded *Rigoletto* on 28 February. The stockholders had hired the soprano Vestvali as Leonora over the objections of Maretzek, a move that proved toxic for everyone. Vestvali was not up to it, either vocally or personally—"Suicidal" was the word used by the *Albion* (3 March). To make things worse, Bull showed little talent for operatic management and the new season started sinking financially. Not surprisingly, the whole affair collapsed within two weeks with the artists fulminating on the integrity of poor Ole Bull who wisely abandoned further opera production for the safer world of violin performance. Incredibly, the Academy was to see a new try at opera sprout almost immediately. Yet *another* group of directors formed an association and launched a new season on 16 March with *Lucrezia Borgia,* featuring the "*primo tenore Assoluto*," Pasquale Brignoli, a recent arrival from the Paris opera. *Maria di Rohan* followed on 23 March and a week later *Rigoletto* was repeated with the same cast (including Ettore Barili), excepting the Duke, who was sung by Brignoli.[37]

By this time Ettore, Antoinetta, and young Alfredo had settled in with Caterina, Salvatore, and the two young Patti daughters at the residence at 170 East Tenth Street next to Third Avenue. In the 1850's the area was an exclusive part of town, near such New York landmarks as Grace Church and St. Mark's in the Bowery, as well as tempting ice cream and candy stores. Unfortunately, the neighbors were not at all pleased to see immigrant Italians move in, and musical Italians as well, something they made clear to the Pattis and Barilis. Soon thereafter the family decided to move to what is now the Bronx. In May 1855 Caterina bought land near the city of Wakefield in Westchester County for $625 with money that Adelina had made on her tour. Salvatore and Caterina built the first brick house in the area, which is now at the address of 4718 Matilda Avenue. They would remain there until May 1867.[38]

During this period when the extended family lived together, Ettore offered an invaluable service to twelve-year old Adelina by giving her vocal instruction. As Adelina matured and became increasingly popular, various other instructors appeared, claiming to have taught her. Although she sang privately for many people along the way, many of whom undoubtedly offered her suggestions and comments such as Antonio Barili and Eliza Valentini Paravelli, the only person she ever credited with giving her the vocal foundation and knowledge that served her so well was Ettore. As she told the *Saturday Evening Post* in 1903 (8 August, p. 3): "It was my brother, Mr. Ettore Barili, who laid the foundation of my singing and his method is taught by my nephew Alfredo Barili. My brother-in-law Mr. Strackosch, taught me certain embellishments and cadenzas, but it was to Ettore Barili that I owed the foundation as well as the finish of my vocal development." According to her, Ettore taught her the strict discipline so critical to any artist's development. He structured lessons on a systematic basis that over a period of time allowed her to shape and develop her voice without undue strain or damage. In another article she added: "It was he who saved my voice. He never forced it; he never permitted me to strain it. And yet he taught me all that could be learned in the Italian school of singing."[39]

Alfredo later recounted these childhood years: "Adelina was only eleven years older that I, but when we lived in New York I was frequently under the care of my young aunt. Often she would sing to me under the trees . . . , and very often, they say, as soon as the grown-ups were out of sight, she would eat the porridge she had been told to feed me." She briefly attended school in Wakefield and played on the banks of the Bronx River. In early 1856 Salvatore decided that she was ready for another tour and planned to travel to Cuba with Ettore, pianist August Gockel, and violin prodigy Paul Julien, whose mother went along as well.[40]

The troupe travelled through New Orleans, arriving in Cuba on 7 April 1856. Seven days later Adelina created a sensation singing the aria "Ah! non giunge," the air "La calesera," Eckart's "Echo Song," and a duet with Ettore. Following a second concert 18 April, in which she offered "Casta diva" from *Norma* and "Una voce poco fa" from *Il barbiere*, the critic for the *Prensa de la Habana* declared that she would become the world's greatest soprano. The company performed seven more concerts before the cramped proximity of the group inevitably ignited the fiery temperaments (so the story goes). Some incident sparked the conflagration and with a flash the tour collapsed into two factions, both of whom abruptly packed up and separately retreated to New York, Salvatore and his clan first, followed by Gockel, Julien, and his mother.[41]

Meanwhile in New York, Ettore's older brother Nicolo continued his successes on the stage. When Maurice Strakosch once again took over management of the Academy for a short operatic season on 21 January (1857) he introduced to the city the celebrated Teresa Parodi as Violetta in *La traviata*. Two days later the troupe presented *Il trovatore* again with Parodi as well as Nicolo Barili in the cast. On the 28th Cora de Wilhorst made her New York debut in *Lucia* with Barili as Raimondo. Parodi reappeared 2 February with *La favorita* and on the 11th in *Ernani*, which ended the season. The shadow of the coming Panic that year was already disrupting many financial plans. Undaunted, Strakosch launched another season on 23 February with Cora de Wilhorst again for a repeat of *Lucia,* including Barili. With the desperate economic times Strakosch feared straying from the tried and true, so he once again dragged out *Il trovatore* with Parodi and Barili, joined by his step-sister Amalia as Azucena. The season at the Academy finally closed after 20 March when Strakosch presented a benefit performance of *Don Giovanni* in concert form with Parodi as Donna Anna, Amalia as Elvira, and Thalberg playing the piano.[42]

Later that year (1857) in September, Strakosch joined with Bernard Ullman in a partnership that would serve as an important "milestone in the history of American musical culture." The formation of their Ullman and Strakosch Celebrated Italian Opera Company led the way in which musical entertainment was packaged and presented in the United States. Theirs was one of the first musical troupes in the country to hold together for three successive years. Most opera companies dissolved after one season, if they even made in that far. By lasting three years the group demonstrated that a company could develop and maintain a viable existence as a musical and financial institution. This extended and *successful* life span offered a much-needed model of how to operate an artistic company on a stable business foundation. In addition, the way in which the two musicians assembled the company established precedents for the American musical manager. Unlike opera management up to that point, which generally consisted of throwing singers and players together willy-nilly at the last minute, Ullman and Strakosch's struggles mark one of the first major attempts by "American impresarios at deliberately pooling initiative, effort, and resources on a voluntary basis for the advantage of the individuals involved, without being forced into doing so as a result of financial stress." The two managers carefully conceived, planned, and operated their company using modern business methods, then proceeded to secure the available artists they thought would prove popular. Finally, the result of this work did much to establish the basic operating format for arts' management in the United States. Between 1857 and 1860 American impresarios came to realize that the presentation of music was a business venture first. No longer would art for art's sake do as the standard for organizing a company. Financial reality must determine the final profile of any season. Opera in America had finally found a firm footing.[43]

The success of their first season, which opened on 7 September at the Academy of Music, showed that they knew what they were doing. Bellini's *La sonnambula*, a mainstay of the operatic repertoire, was finally produced with the forces necessary to draw a full house—a daunting challenge given the financial Panic that had broken out only one month earlier. Ullman and Strakosch had procured outstanding singers for the leads, a sizeable chorus, and an enlarged orchestra directed by the country's most outstanding conductor, Theodore Thomas. Even the deepening economic storm would not cloud the opening of this season. To keep the momentum up, they continued a parade of new and established stars guaranteed to offer enough variety to keep audiences coming back while presenting some of their favorite singers. New on the stage was Erminia Frezzolini, one of Europe's celebrated sopranos. Anna de la Grange, whom Ullman had successfully sponsored in 1855, returned. As a familiar anchor Ullman and Strakosch presented Straksoch's popular wife Amalia Barili in addition to Carl Formes, the German dramatic bass, and French baritone Edouard Gassier. To balance this formidable array of vocal talent they shrewdly imported the German operatic conductor Karl Anschutz for subsequent productions.[44]

To provide a financial safety net, Ullman continued sponsoring other artists in concerts, such as Sigismund Thalberg, whom Ullman had presented the year before. He joined him with famed Belgian violinist Henry Vieuxtemps and his ever-faithful wife Amalia at Niblo's on 19 September. They spent the remainder of the fall playing various concerts around New York and Brooklyn before departing for a tour of the South in January and February. This tour provided one of Atlanta's first professional musical concerts. While in New York they also played between acts of the operas at the Academy, which much increased the draw. By May 1858 they completed their final appearances in the United States, concluding a concert season in which, for them ". . . dollars fell as thick as hail." By spreading his management umbrella to include these concerts Ullman was able to cover the deficits of the opera company. Moreover, Strakosch's demand for the use of "Star casts" meant that they had a stable of singers who not only could perform opera but also sing other solos and oratorio as well. They could also offer "Grand Concerts" with low overhead and thus derive enough receipts to help support the opera endeavor. Finally, to help pull the season out of the financial hole, Ullman imported the celebrated composer Musard from Paris and his "Imposing Orchestra Force of One Hundred Performers." This concert series, which opened on 12 April at the Academy, included along the way all the other stars gathered by Ullman and Strakosch for the season. After numerous other concerts, the remarkable season came to a close in early August 1858. Alfredo Barili was four years old.[45]

Given the worsening financial situation throughout the country, it is startling that Ullman even considered a second season. But he opened it on 20 October with a brilliant new star Marietta Piccolomini, in the opera Verdi wrote expressly for her, *La traviata*, to an "uproarious" reception. From a noble family and blessed with talent, youth, and beauty, Piccolomini filled the house—early, something rare with chronically late New Yorkers. Ullman continued sponsoring her in other operas and places such as Philadelphia and Boston, followed by a country-wide tour. Unfortunately, financial reverses in New Orleans put the whole enterprise in danger and Piccolomini joined Strakosch's small opera company currently in Pittsburgh. Ullman found himself once again hard pressed, but managed to pull things out of the fire and embarked on an astonishing third season with Max Maretzek on 12 September at the Academy of Music. The company featured the popular Italian tenor Pasquale Brignoli, French baritone Edouard Gassier, and the perennial contralto Amalia. By the end of the first season on 31 September, Strakosch and Maretzek had managed to present seven different operas.[46]

For the second series of the season, Ullman revived the Celebrated Italian Opera Company with Maurice Strakosch and opened on 17 October with *La traviata*. Ominously, lead soprano Speranza fell ill and her last-minute substitute Crescimano flopped. Even worse, tenor Amodio collapsed in the first act and had to be replaced in the second. By the middle of November the company teetered on bankruptcy. Desperate, Ullman finally relented and agreed to present a young newcomer urged on him by Strakosch, a move that would cement Ullman's name forever in the annals of opera.[47]

At their 343 West Twenty-Second Street residence, Maurice Strakosch had overheard the coaching sessions between his sixteen-year old sister-in-law Adelina Patti and Muzio, the principal conductor of the Academy and a pupil of Verdi. Ullman had severe reservations about the young singer's acting ability, as she related later, "He objected to allowing a beginner like me to come out in a leading part in New York; and I would not listen to anything about secondary parts." But desperation can breed good fortune as well as disaster and Ullman took a chance. To hedge his bets, Ullman introduced her as *Lucia* on an "off" evening—Thanksgiving night—24 November 1859, sandwiched between performances on the 23rd and 25th of *The Magic Flute,* and to a non-subscribing audience. The evening made operatic history. Odell recounts in his *Annals of*

The New York Stage: "Almost from that night, Adelina Patti, then a trifle over sixteen years old, was the reigning queen of song with none to dispute her sway; furthermore, her reign lasted for at least thirty years and possibly more. The history of opera shows nothing like it."[48]

With her extraordinary debut, Adelina Patti lifted the family reputation to the pinnacle of fame in the musical world. The group of relations into which Alfredo Barili had been born five years earlier now assumed an even broader renown and esteem. With all that talent rushing at him from nearly every blood line, he could hardly have escaped developing his exceptional musical ability. In fact, after seeing the incredible musical fortunes of Caterina, Ettore, Nicolo, Amalia, and now Adelina (and shortly Carlotta), Alfredo's impressive talent would almost have been expected. His father would certainly push him as if he were working a mine where gold had been found before. Nor would they have to wait long to see that talent emerge.

Patti's debut that Thanksgiving only served to confirm brilliantly for her generation what previous generations of the Barili-Pattis had been demonstrating since Caterina had similarly impressed Donizetti and his audiences nearly thirty years earlier. The *Tribune* (25 November) reported "her voice is clear and excellent; the brilliant execution which she begins with at the outset of her career . . . ranks with that where the best singers end." It also lauded her succeeding on her own merits, and as "an American without a transatlantic puff" that accompanied so many *debutantes*. The *Herald* (25 November) pointed out how she sang a difficult cavatina "perfectly, displaying a thorough Italian method and a high soprano voice, fresh, full and even throughout," which finally "increased the enthusiasm of the audience to a positive *furore* . . . ." The *New-York Illustrated News* critic proclaimed that "the most fastidious could find no flaw" in her voice and that "the most experienced could remember no superior." Even with her young age and initial dramatic reticence, she "took the house by storm; she not only sang as only she can sing, but looked lovely and acted well. Though a little timid at first, she displayed her great dramatic powers in the Mad Scene," as the *Musical Courier* observed.[49]

Adelina Patti's success lay first in her ability to perform the most difficult passages brilliantly and effortlessly. She dashed off the most daunting and challenging vocal roles with little apparent effort. Nor did it matter how high the parts ranged. She took E-flats and Fs above high C with abandon, while dispatching staccato passages and trills almost as afterthoughts. The purist critics attacked her for her musical liberties; everyone else just applauded louder. Also contributing to her extraordinary success was her thorough musical training. "To a pure soprano voice of rare flexibility has been added a solid education based on the grandest and best schools of Italy," the *Times* (28 November 1859) observed. "Hence it happens that at the present moment she is as finished artist, a most brilliant vocalist, better in some respects than any other in America. Her powers of execution and her voice, both in compass and quality are of the first class . . . ." She also possessed a keen ear, something indispensable for a professional singer, and something more rare than one would expect. Finally, Patti, like much of her family, was very bright. She learned roles at an unbelievable rate; e. g., she performed Leonora in *Il trovatore* after only eight days study. Moreover, she then went on stage and performed virtually without a misstep, thereby keeping "her performance almost free from fault," as the *Times* continued. One never reads reports of her stumbling in performance over words or music. This brightness also imparted to her a very credible acting ability, especially in the more lighter, elegant or humorous roles.[50]

On 1 December Patti added the role of Amina in *La sonnambula* to her success in *Lucia*. The *Herald* critic saw a new star rising on the horizon, "Her singing was so perfectly good as to leave no opportunity for the most captious critic to pick a flaw." And later, "Miss Patti performed the most difficult vocal feats with the utmost ease, and sang the brilliant music better than any of her predecessors in this *role* within our remembrance." For her subsequent European debuts she inevitably picked Amina, a role she thought displayed her abilities singularly well. On 3 January she sang Zerlina from *Don Giovanni* at the Academy of Music. In Boston she repeated the roles presented in New York and acquired two new ones as well, Rosina in *Il barbiere* on 17 January and Elvira in *I Puritani* eight days later. After returning to New York she increased her repertoire by five additional roles at the Academy of Music: Harriet (*Martha*), Norina (*Don Pasquale*), Anaide (*Mosè in Egitto*), Violetta (*La traviata*), and Linda (*Linda di Chamounix*). Appearing alongside her in some of these productions were tenors Brignoli and Errani; baritone Amodio; and bass Carl Formes. Some of the operatic evenings became virtual family reunions when Adelina was joined variously by Amalia, Ettore, and Nicolo Barili. In total, from her debut on 24 November 1859 to her final New York performance on 8 October 1860, Patti performed an astonishing ten leading roles. For a young girl sixteen and turning seventeen during the process this was nothing short of miraculous.[51]

After the close of the spring 1860 season Salvatore, Adelina, and Maurice toured the eastern seaboard, including Philadelphia, Boston, Baltimore, Washington, and Montreal, where Adelina honored the visiting Prince of

Wales—later King Edward VII—by ending the concert at 1 A.M. with "God Save the Queen." December found the trio in New Orleans for a three-month stay, which would include the roles she had previously sung as well as four successive new ones: Leonora (*Il trovatore*), Gilda (*Rigoletto*), Valentine (*Les Huguenots*), and Dinorah in the American premiere of Meyerbeer's *Le Pardon de Ploermel,* a feat that few other singers in the history of opera could duplicate. In a city steeped in opera and operatic heroines, she topped them all, as the *Daily Picayune* noted. Most Italian operatic engagements had never lasted longer than ten or twelve performances, even under the most advantageous circumstances, "But M'lle Patti, for three months and over, has been the leading and most compensating attraction at our Opera House, giving nearly forty representations . . . ." She reportedly made $10,000 for the run, a portent of the immense sums she would command during her lifetime. "All things considered," the writer observed, "we think we may safely say that the annals of the lyric drama do not furnish so remarkable and triumphant a success as this." On 23 March 1861 Patti, Salvatore, and Maurice sailed to Havana from New Orleans, where she sang three programs with scenes from *Lucia, Rigoletto*, and *Il trovatore.* On 7 April the triumphant trio embarked for London, where Adelina made her European debut on 14 May as Amina in *La sonnambula.* Before the final curtain fell the audience was hers, and Patti's twenty-five year reign at Covent Garden had begun. After a tour of the British Isles, she sang in Berlin in December 1861, and in Brussels the following February, then in Amsterdam and the Hague. In November 1862 thrilled Viennese opera lovers heard her for the first time. She had conquered two continents in as many years.[52]

* * * * * * *

Adelina Patti became Queen of Song for nearly half a century—longer than any other soprano of her era. But the Barili-Patti family story does not stop with her. Yet *another* soprano destined for world-class renown stood right behind her. Three weeks after Adelina finished her first run of appearances in New York, her older sister Carlotta made her concert debut at Dodworth's Hall on 25 October 1860. Born in 1835, Carlotta Patti, like her future nephew Alfredo Barili, had studied piano first, under the renowned virtuoso Henri Herz, but had abandoned the keyboard after her younger sister had achieved such vocal fame.[53]

A Mr. Frederick Gye, hearing of Carlotta's successes in the United States, hit upon the idea of bringing her over to England and profiting from the continuing sensation generated by her more famous sister. He contracted with

Carlotta for a year and presented her on 16 April 1863 at a concert at Covent Garden following the opera. Carlotta sang gloriously, brilliantly demonstrating her amazing range—up to G or G-sharp above high C—and rich quality. One reviewer, commenting on the Queen of the Night aria she performed during the concert, declared "The *staccato* passages we have never heard surpassed in clearness, crispness, and purity of intonation." Unfortunately, London was not big enough for both Patti sisters and the late concerts at Covent Garden did not draw well; with the completion of her year's contract she began touring on her own, inaugurating a successful seventeen-year concert career. In 1879 she married the celebrated Belgian cellist Ernest de Munck, retired from singing, and subsequently taught voice in Paris for ten years until her death there in 1889.[54]

No less a musical journalist than James Huneker, one of the leading music critics of the early part of this century, recounted hearing Carlotta sing the Queen of the Night at the Academy of Music (Philadelphia) in 1869. "Never shall I forget the prima donna who limped down a 'practicable' staircase to the footlights and then showered on our delighted ears a cascade of dazzling roulades. There was no doubt about her F in altissimo, clear, round, and frosty. She was a cold singer, the very timbre of her voice was icy when compared with the warmer, richer organ of her more celebrated sister, Adelina. But Carlotta was the more brilliant of the two, an incomparable coloratura singer."[55]

Another contemporary writer thought even more highly of Carlotta's talent. He speculated about her career, arguing that if she not been handicapped by lameness, caused by a childhood accident, "she would have eclipsed Adelina's fame in opera. She was the more beautiful of the two—indeed, she was the most beautiful member of a very handsome family. Her voice was as rich in quality as Adelina's and its range even higher. Her technical accomplishments were fully as wonderful. She delighted in singing music written especially to show off the violin technic. In all these respects she was as bountifully equipped for the operatic stage as her sister . . . ."[56] Herman Klein, it appears, put his finger on the subtle but important difference between the enormously talented sisters. Adelina possessed the entire range of talents in complete degree for success on the operatic stage. Moreover, she had a magnetic charm that Carlotta lacked. Adelina's charisma, combined with her effortless virtuosity, appealed directly to her listeners' emotional side, which then compelled them to respond to her. Carlotta, on the other hand, sang brilliantly—maybe even more so than Adelina—but impressed *her* listeners more with her technical brilliance than by her seductive presence. This difference could also account for the opposing followers that each enjoyed. One group enjoyed music primarily through their intellect while the others delighted in a more emotionally rich experience. More incredible than accounts of each is that two of the greatest singers of the age were from the same family.[57]

* * * * * *

By the time Carlotta was making her debut in London (1863), Ettore Barili had established himself in New York and continued singing to support his young family. The family by this time included Ettore and Antoinetta, Alfredo, Enrico (1855-?), and Armando (1856-1912). Ettore performed supporting roles for a short opera season managed by Jacob Grau that ran for only a month. It opened on 10 November 1862 with Barili reported in *Il trovatore* and *Un ballo in maschera;* he likely sang in some of the other productions as well. He showed up a year later in another cast assembled by Grau, who produced *La favorita* and *Lucia* in November 1863. The next April he and three of his students participated in a benefit at Irving Hall for the Italian Benevolent Society. He sang in another concert at Niblo's Saloon shortly after the New Year, 1865. In March Ettore, Theodore Thomas, and others assisted the Ladies' Fund for the Freedmen at Dodworth's. Finally, on 7 April, he and his brother Antonio presented ten-year old Alfredo to the world at Irving Hall.[58]

Young Alfredo impressed the audience at his debut, as the *Herald* noted the next day. The careful preparation and elegant execution that would characterize his playing throughout his life were already evident. He had been studying with his father since age six (Ettore must have resisted learning English as Alfredo had also been serving as his interpreter). The same systematic, meticulous, and thorough instruction which Ettore gave to Adelina as a young girl he imparted to his son as well, who "played two selections with much earnestness and effect, evincing in his delicacy of touch and expression, the evidence of careful and thorough training." Like so many members of his family, his impressive talent was clearly present at this young age, as the reporter observed: "It is not too much to say that great things may hereafter be expected of this boy in the fields of music should he persevere in them." The *Sunday Times* (9 April) agreed: "his proficiency as a pianist is really wonderful; he received a double encore." And yet one more voice joined in, when the *Evening Post* (10 April) declared "Master Alfred Barili, a boy of ten years, showed an ability as a pianoforte player which promises to lead to something first-class." That final phrase is telling because it is one of the first descriptions that comes to mind when discussing Alfredo Barili: "first-class"—first class in his teaching, repertoire, performance, demeanor—nearly everything about him. The next month the two Barili brothers, Ettore and Antonio, presented yet another concert for the Italian Festival. The *Herald* (15 May) dismissed any need to introduce them as "The Signori Barili do not need any ordinary praise, for they are too well known as masters of high standing in New York." Alfredo's playing of a fantasy "charmed the audience."

For the next months Alfredo continued his lessons with his father, who apparently could be quite demanding, insisting the young pianist practice long hours daily. "I was always the first one up in the house," he later told Cherry Emerson. "I would go downstairs to practice in a room which was under my father's bedroom. Sometimes I would get sleepy and stop playing. My father would then start banging on the floor of his room with his cane, which would awaken me and return me to work." Ettore inculcated into young Alfredo the same severe discipline that he had taught Adelina.

Another pervasive family trait was one of unrelenting perfectionism. In music this did much to account for the family's professional excellence, generation after generation. Ettore possibly inherited it from his overpowering mother and bequeathed it to the succeeding Barilis and Pattis. One sees virtually every one of them obsessed with faultless performing, which many in the family amazingly achieved. Accounts of nearly every Barili-Patti performance from Caterina through the next three generations (even on to Alfredo Barili, Jr. who studied architecture in New York) relate how doggedly they worked in preparing their music. The press accounts, from whatever source, continually talk about their "old world training," or in the style of the "grand old masters," "faultless performance," or "undisturbed elegance," which seems to point, in part, to this passionate commitment to perfect their preparation. For each member it was simply assumed that you left no stone unturned in laying your musical groundwork. The Barili reputation for consistent musical excellence (in addition to his considerable talent) is what clearly elevated Alfredo above nearly every other southern musician when he moved to Atlanta in 1880.

Randy Barili Harris (great-granddaughter) recounts how this perfectionism continued into her father's generation (Alfredo III). He, like his great-uncles, was an artist and was obsessed with painting something perfectly; he refused to show his finished work to anyone until he took it to the art show. She tells how he would find some minor flaw and rip up the entire work. In her great grandfather one can see this perfectionism in his handwriting, which is as nearly flawless as possible and still human. His dress, too, as reflected in photographs and reports, is described as "immaculate."

This perfectionism also accounts for another marked Barili family trait: obsession with secrecy. Barilis did not want the world to know any unattractive family problems; they must appear to be perfect. Again, Randy tells how the prevailing sentiment in her home as a young girl was the admonition, "Don't tell anybody." It was imperative to showcase only the finest side of their home life. Her father would insist that any less-than-flattering issue could not be mentioned. Victorian society encouraged family secrets, but the Barilis seemed to have raised it to a high art. Louise Barili (Alfredo's oldest child), who lived for nearly thirty years after her father's death, shared only certain, favorable family stories with her younger relatives. This explains why the research for this book produced a number of stories that surprised Mary Barili Goldsmith and Randy Barili Harris. Louise must have avoided talking about most family issues for fear of putting anything in a bad or poor light.

A secrecy about family problems explains the absence of certain things in the fairly voluminous family record that exists in other areas. Since Louise became the family archivist, she made sure—she thought—that nothing unflattering would remain for posterity. The family albums have pages with pictures or articles ripped out, suggesting that she changed her mind later about including them. Discomfort with family secrets probably also accounts for no mention of Alfredo's two brothers being made in the family materials, anywhere. These archives stretch back more than a century and a half, and include nearly every positive sentence ever written or published about the Barilis. Nevertheless, the existence of Enrico and Armando was uncovered quite accidentally. It appears that both brothers had socially unacceptable life styles, which would explain why the family wanted as little recorded connection with them as possible. One published source (1947), perplexed at who they were, mistook them to be sons of Nicolo Barili.

Family secrets might also explain another obscure matter. In 1867 Alfredo, Ettore, Antoinetta, and the other two sons made a surprising and puzzling move to Montgomery, Alabama. This relocation took on an even more mysterious air when Alfredo returned south in 1880 to Atlanta. Why would the baritone who premiered *Rigoletto* in the United States with his remarkable prodigy of a son move to such a small and artistically unimportant city as Montgomery? And then, thirteen years later, why would this child, now grown into an extraordinary pianist, move south again to Atlanta? America had only taken its very first, fragile steps towards establishing even the most basic musical institutions, and these developments were rare outside of Boston, New York, and Philadelphia. Any serious musician who sought to launch a career and make a living would almost be forced to locate in one of these cities. That Barili father and son (age thirteen) decided to move to Montgomery, Alabama is nothing short of astonishing.

After considerable discussion with current family members, Cherry Emerson, members of the History Department at Georgia State University, and reading in the Medical Library at Emory University, it seems that the only explanation for these moves is one of health. Mention of Alfredo's health problem occurs sporadically throughout the record, but not one syllable describing a specific ailment ever appears. Northern cities would have had the best medical care available. So, why the move south? In conversations with Mr. Emerson, Barili's granddaughter, Mary Barili Goldsmith, and Randy Barili Harris, it seems that Alfredo suffered from some kind of respiratory problem, probably asthma. As a young girl, Mary Goldsmith remembers seeing him use a medicated atomizer in his dressing room. Cherry Emerson likewise remembers Barili showing the atomizer to him. Mary Goldsmith's father, Alfredo Barili, Jr., and her aunt Viola both were plagued by sinus infections, Viola even having to undergo surgery for her condition. Mary Goldsmith feels that this could have been an inherited condition. Randy Barili Harris also states that both her grandfather and father had asthma. So, it seems that asthma/respiratory illness could have been an influence in the decision of Ettore to take young Alfredo with him as he embarked on a new career of teaching now available to him in the South.

So, father, mother and son came to Montgomery, where Ettore had obtained a teaching position; it is quite likely he secured it before leaving New York. They had settled in the Alabama capital at least by the beginning of 1867 for their first reported concert is reviewed in the Montgomery *Daily Mail* of 30 April. Ettore had taken a position as music instructor at a private girls' school, Hamner Hall. As he would have needed at least three or so months to prepare his young charges for their April recital, he, along with Alfredo, undoubtedly was in town by first of the year. The writer for the *Daily Mail* (30 April 1867) was delighted that the city has found a music teacher with the "unequalled abilities of Ettore Barili" which resulted in "a vast improvement in the musical abilities of the scholars." Reading between the lines one sees again the perfectionistic thoroughness of his instruction, "The most difficult, scientific and operatic pieces were well executed by the ladies." Ettore's preference for Italian music was reflected in programming, "the master compositions of Verdi,

Rossini, Donizzetti [sic], and others, being sung in Italian in the most harmonious and faultless manner." Alfredo of course performed: "He executed on the piano one of the most difficult pieces, in truly artistic style, without hesitation or a single mistake, clearly indicating a rare musical talent." Like the New York reviewers, the Montgomery critic realized that here was serious talent: "Master Barili will some day astonish the world by his musical performances."

The record is silent for a year, though Ettore stayed musically active, as the 27 May (1868) article reports Ettore's "charming concerts" and assumes that the readers are acquainted with his work, "The mere mention of Signor Barili's name is enough to satisfy all who are familiar with artistic excellence." At least five newspapers announced a concert given by Ettore and his students on Friday night the 28th (May) for the benefit of Bishop Cobb's Orphan Home. Once again the accolades pour forth. One critic assured his readers that those attending "will receive an ample remuneration for the small sum spent." Alfredo, for his part, had not been heard publicly in a year. It appears that after introducing him to the city, Ettore wisely refrained from pushing him to perform, insisting instead that he concentrate on solidifying his technique, as this would certainly prove critical for his correct musical development. Any musician at certain stages in his or her development must retrench and do this, just as Adelina Patti seems to have done shortly after Ettore arrived in New York and began teaching her (she was also about Alfredo's age at the time). One reviewer may have heard Alfredo before the concert as he reports that "He has made great progress since that time, and all who attend will be not only delighted, but astonished at the performances of little Alfredo on the piano." The hard work apparently paid off. It seems from a later notice that he played "The Banjo" of Gottschalk along with the virtuostic—and popular—Grand Fantasie on Rossini's *Mosè in Egito* by Thalberg, works that demand a sure-fire technique. Another critic wrote afterwards that "The difficult piano performances of Master Alfredo Barili showed correctness, which could only be attained by constant practice and diligent instruction."[59]

Even with these successes Montgomery undoubtedly proved too small an artistic pond. At the close of the school year (1868) Ettore decided to return north. One newspaper regretted "to announce the departure from our city of Prof. Ettore Barili, who . . . *cannot be replaced*, and with him we also lose our young friend, Master Alfredo Barili." By early summer the family had moved to Philadelphia. Exactly why the Barilis chose Philadelphia remains unclear. Antonio had relocated there as a voice teacher and quite likely invited his brother and nephew to come. The city, along with New York and Boston, possessed the richest musical culture in the country. Moreover, Philadelphia maintained a fairly strong artistic bond with the New York musical community, facilitating easy artistic exchanges between the two. Most singers and instrumentalists premiering in Manhattan also appeared in the other city as well. Philadelphia's Academy of Music rivalled the one on Fourteenth Street in New York, and provided a homebase for a number of opera and instrumental companies.

Ettore lost no time in introducing the Barili family to Philadelphia. At a concert the first week of July, Ettore sang, accompanied by his brother Antonio, while fourteen-year old Alfredo dispatched the brilliant fantasy on *Il trovatore* [Thalberg?] and Gottschalk's "Banjo." Typically, his playing combined "firmness and delicacy of touch with precision and evident feeling." The next week the troupe appeared in Germantown at Town Hall, where Alfredo made the same impression with his restrained but passionate playing, marked by "feeling, ease, precision, and taste." Once again the paper compared him favorably to Liszt and Thalberg. In Philadelphia Alfredo had become a pupil of Carl Wolfsohn (1834-1907), who came to the United States in the first wave of German immigrants who would much enrich American musical culture. Wolfsohn had studied with Aloys Schmitt in Frankfurt and lived in London briefly before coming to Philadelphia to teach in 1854. Wolfsohn became one of the city's leading musicians, doing much to encourage the growth of Philadelphia's musical institutions as well as introduce most of the romantic chamber, piano, and orchestral music repertoire. He was instrumental in presenting Beethoven's piano sonatas in this country as well as the complete piano works of Chopin and Schuman. Wolfsohn had become a highly respected teacher by the late 1860's and would do much for young Alfredo's musical growth.[60]

By the end of 1871 Wolfsohn must have decided that Alfredo was ready to move to a higher professional level and spotlighted him on the fifth of his series of orchestral concerts on 28 December at the Academy of Music. The program shows Wolfsohn's sure sense of programming as well as his German artistic preferences:

Symphony No. 8 in B Minor, "Unfinished"	Schubert
Polonaise (Philadelphia premiere)	Meyerbeer
Piano Concerto [Number unreported]	Mendelssohn
Alfredo Barili	

Waltz "New Vienna"	Strauss
Turkischer March (Philadelphia premiere)	Mozart
Overture *Pique Dame* (Philadelphia premiere)	Suppé

The critics again lauded Barili's performance, commenting on the elegant precision and musicality of his playing. He had that elusive skill of executing difficult passages passionately and calmly, sought by so many pianists , "He evidences remarkable facility and ease of execution," and he "possesses the true artistic feeling." The critics in Philadelphia also noted Wolfsohn's role in Barili's development: "Master Alfredo Barili's performance of Mendelssohn's Concert [sic] was excellent. He played with care, self-possession and grace. He has a good, firm touch and considerable expression. In this latter respect he evidently follows his teacher, Mr. Wolfsohn, closely. He has not yet a decided style, nor the brilliancy that comes of long practice, but there seems no reason why he should not in the future add his name to those already of note in the family of Patti and Barili." The following year (1872) Alfredo played again to excellent reviews, though one writer noticed a "perceptible inclination to hurry," that was attributed to his youth."[61]

Ettore must have decided that Alfredo was ready for his formal introduction to the musical world, meaning New York. He scheduled a series of four Saturday-afternoon matinees for his son at Chickering Hall on the northeast corner of Fifth Avenue and Eighteenth Street in Manhattan beginning on 20 April 1872. At an out-of-town run Ettore presented Alfredo first on a concert of his singing pupils in Philadelphia at Musical Fund Hall on 12 April in which Ettore sang himself, accompanied by his brother Antonio. The performance opened under a cloud as a patron had collapsed from a heart attack in the hall just before the concert began; nor did the half-filled house help spirits (or profits). The gloom "disappeared to a great extent, however, when the singing began . . . ." Ettore's pupils reportedly sang well, as did he. The critic found him "in fine voice and displayed unusual power, vim and clearness of tone." Antonio was up to fine form as well. The writer declared him "one of the best accompanists we have heard for a long time." He well supported the vocalists musically, "free from embarrassing annoyances to singers, too often given by incompetent performers." Alfredo distinguished himself with his Fantasy and Variations on *L'elisire d'amore* (Donizetti) by Thalberg and Weber's *Polacca Brillante*, op. 72 in the arrangement by Henselt. After praising the remaining student singers, the writer applauded Ettore for his fine instruction.[62]

Alfredo was fortunate that he did not have to debut in New York as an unknown. Few names in the city's musical world were better known than Barili—"fine musical stock" as *Watson's Art Journal* put it when it announced Alfredo's debut series. Ettore had shrewdly invited one music critic to visit the family at home for an introductory *soiree* the Tuesday before. This helped to spread the word; both *Watson's* and the *Sunday Times* announced the concert. In the fashion of the day, the Saturday matinee presented a combination of various musical selections:[63]

Duet, *La favorita,* Eliza Mooney, Ettore Barili	Donizetti
Cello solo, F. Bergner	[Unnamed]
Cavatina, *Saffo*, Eliza Mooney	
"Dreaming at Midnight," E. Guy, F. Bergner	[Unnamed]
Romanza, Ettore Barili	[Unnamed]
Trio, *Attila*, E. Guy, Eliza Mooney, Ettore Barili	Verdi
Fantasy and Variations on *L'elisire d'amore*	Thalberg
Polacca Brilliante, Op. 72 (arr. Henselt)	Weber
Alfredo Barili	

"A new Barili star has risen," the *Evening Post* announced. The writer briefly summarized the immediate musical family for his readers, pointing out how Ettore Barili had premiered *Rigoletto;* Antonio Barili was a composer and able conductor; and Nicolo Barili was well known to opera goers. Even though the reporter did not know other family members, he understandably concluded that there had to be others, that "undoubtedly, there are collateral Barilis of equal merit scattered throughout the world generally." Now the new young star demonstrated his "genuine ability." In his playing "he manifested taste and judgment, and showed delicacy of touch as well as brilliancy of execution." *Watson's Art Journal* gave him the most extended coverage, declaring the debut "a gratifying success," and predicting for him a "very brilliant future." Firmly in place were the impressive musical qualities he would exhibit throughout his life—his elegant, sensitive, and polished performances. Repeatedly, writers comment upon his artistic feeling, musical insight, and careful preparation: "He executed both pieces fluently and brilliantly, phrasing them with exactness, and giving cleanness to every point and passage. His technique is excellent; his touch is light, and firm; and his power is wrist power." His ease in playing rapid sections, "combined with his good phrasing, secures a clearness of form to all passages, however complicated." Perhaps most importantly (and astutely), "he has, we think, nothing to unlearn." Ettore and Carl Wolfsohn had indeed taught him well. The writer finished by asserting that if Alfredo keeps on this path, "the front-rank among pianists is within his reach."[64] The *New York Times* (23 April), *Sunday Dispatch* (21 April), *New York Evening Express* (24 April), and *New York Evening Mail* (24 April) reviewed the concert as well.

The favorable impression Alfredo created must have spread far. That August one of the most popular journals of the day, *Frank Leslie's Illustrated Newspaper*, ran an impressive article (and picture) on young Alfredo and his "distinguished family." It briefly recounted his European birth, travel to the United States and study with his father. The critic again praised his clear, powerful playing. "His execution is brilliant and rapid, combining clearness and accuracy, exhibiting great muscular power, while the touch is deliberate and effective."[65]

Alfredo Barili had arrived. Before he was eighteen years old, he had become an extraordinary professional pianist, and had been acknowledged as such by the leading musical critics in the country. But this was only the beginning. His father and Carl Wolfsohn had guided his impressive talent, led him in securing a formidable technique, and encouraged him to mature artistically. Now it was time for him to solidify and build on this foundation. The United States offered no place for intensive professional training in music at the time, forcing Barili, along with other serious American musicians, to travel to Europe for further study.

If Barili wanted to succeed professionally in this country, he had virtually no other choice than to study abroad. Not only were there no major musical institutions available in the United States for musical education, but nineteenth-century Americans continued looking to Europe for their cultural validation. "In their obsession with good taste, with elegance, with gentility," Gilbert Chase observes, "cultivated Americans sought, like the colonial gentry, to imitate or import the products of European culture." Indigenous folk and popular music, such as the spiritual, gospel song, and jazz, gradually emerged out of the American experience, deriving only their most basic musical structures from European art music. Classical music, however, had no serious roots in this country; thus to acquire more substantial artistic fare, "European musical culture, with much of its apparatus and its standard repertoire, was transported to the United States and superimposed upon our social structure." The actual whole of European civilization was not imported to the United States as complete culture is inseparable from its geographical origins. Rather, the outward trappings of continental musical art—the structures, techniques, and repertoire—were translated here. Only after these musical materials and methods had taken firm root was there any lasting interest in using them in developing an organic *American* music.[66]

* * * * * * *

In the fall of 1872 the family packed Alfredo off to study at the Cologne Conservatory, accompanied by his aunt Carlotta, who likely paid for the enterprise as well. After coming together in New York during the 1850's and early 1860's, the family was fairly scattered again. Back in Philadelphia Ettore resumed his teaching and choir directing at St. John's Church. Antonio shortly returned to Italy, somewhat bitter at the slow growth of American musical tastes and institutions. Adelina did not return to this country for nearly another decade; Amalia continued touring for some time with her husband.

The Cologne Conservatory was not twenty-five years old when Alfredo arrived there to study. It had first opened as the Rheinische Musikschule in 1845 and under the directorship of Ferdinand Hiller (1811-85) became a conservatory in 1850. Hiller reorganized the musical school along the lines of the Leipzig Conservatory, securing outstanding musicians as faculty and increasing the number of students. He played an important role in organizing the Rhenish music festivals and conducted many of the performances. Gradually he developed an international reputation with his numerous concert tours and compositions. By the last years of his life he had become one of the most highly respected, if somewhat conservative, leaders in German music. Barili studied piano, harmony, and composition with Hiller and undoubtedly used Hiller's own textbook, *Übungen zum Studium der Harmonie und des Contrapuntkes* (Cologne, 1860). The book consists of increasingly difficult exercises, beginning with simple chord progressions and moving to harmonizations of Bach chorales. It then proceeds to examinations of each chordal function and possible resolution; melodic harmonizations; use of different clefs; harmonizing bass lines; and much more.[67]

The composer of the popular opera *Hansel und Gretel*, Englbert Humperdinck, was a classmate of Barili's at Cologne and took composition lessons with him. For one lesson Humperdinck brought in a waltz in 6/4 time (instead of the requisite 3/4, the factor that defines a waltz), which caused Hiller figuratively to pull his hair out in frustration. Afterward, Barili walked home with Humperdinck, who wondered, "Well, why not a waltz in 6/4 time?"

Two things suggest themselves in examining Hiller's harmony text. First, it accounts for the contrapuntal clarity and solid structure of Barili's own compositions. They reveal the thorough grounding he had in the fundamental constructive processes found in traditional western art music. Second, it is astonishing how close the theory training practiced in today's music schools remains to the model established by Hiller and others. Translate his book into English, give it a flashy cover, simplify it somewhat, and you have essentially the same textbook found in most theory classrooms today. Students like Barili, John Knowles Paine, Dudley Buck, George Chadwick, and many others learned their theory through German textbooks such as Hiller's, which was used widely. When they returned to this country, they led the way in music education and, not surprisingly, imitated those models when they wrote the textbooks from which they taught. Their students did the same. Thus, here at the end of the twentieth century, we still find ourselves much indebted to these German musicians of the nineteenth century for our models.

The faculty of the Cologne Conservatory during the 1870's included some of the finest younger-generation musicians in the world. A number of them had studied at Leipzig, which had been founded by Mendelssohn in 1843 and had featured some of the brightest names in German romantic music such as Ignaz Moscheles, Moritz Hauptmann, and Ferdinand David. Mendelssohn's school formed the model for professional musical education in the nineteenth century. Soon it was being emulated across Europe when Cologne, Frankfurt, and other German cities founded their own music conservatories. Students from across the west, including numerous Americans, flocked there. They returned home with the highest levels of music training available. Barili's student years coincided with the recent arrival of brilliant new faculty members, which soon raised the esteem of the conservatory throughout much of the world. Friedrich Gernsheim (1839-1916) was one of these new additions who had studied at the Leipzig Conservatory with Ignaz Moscheles before further work in Paris. He joined the faculty at Cologne in 1865 as a pianist and conductor. Gernsheim was a friend of Brahms, whose music he favored in his conducting. Barili studied piano and probably conducting with him. The young American also took piano instruction with Hiller, who had been a student of Johann Hummel, one of Mozart's pupils. Barili's elegant, refined, and supple piano technique reflects this unbroken artistic heritage handed-down from Mozart. Barili would in time pass it on to his pupils well into the twentieth century. Barili studied piano also with James Kwast (1852-1927), who came to the conservatory in 1874, two years after Barili's arrival. Percy Grainger studied with Kwast as well. After earning a widespread reputation at Cologne, Kwast taught at Frankfurt and then Berlin.[68]

Barili excelled at the conservatory. He was much esteemed by faculty and students alike during his two years there. For a typical "Music Abend" at the conservatory on 10 December 1874 he played the concluding work, Chopin's dazzling Scherzo in B minor. When the Empress Augusta, wife of the reigning German Kaiser, made an unannounced appearance at the conservatory one day, Barili was immediately selected on the spot to perform for her. He was likely chosen because the faculty needed a student that they knew would not fail to impress the Empress. He acquired the nickname of the "Dark Pianist" after the lights went out during a concert and he continued playing his Chopin nocturne undaunted. Barili also reportedly performed later for Liszt and Brahms.

Barili's personal life also took a major step in Cologne. There he became much better acquainted with someone he had probably known back in Philadelphia, Emily Vezin, who had been sent in 1866 by her father from Philadelphia to live and study in Germany at the home of her aunt. Emily had been born on 9 February 1856 to Charles and Lina Vezin. The titled French family ancestors had owned lands in the Champagne region. When the Edict of Nantes was revoked in 1685, the Huguenot family leader Pierre de Vezin fled to Hanover where he served as Konzertmeister in the Duke of Hannover's opera orchestra. Pierre's great-grandson Charles Vezin (1782-1853) returned to Bordeaux and clerked for ten years in a commercial house before emigrating to the United States during the War of 1812. Unfortunately, he took passage on an American vessel, was captured by the British, and imprisoned for three weeks before being exchanged (and deprived of the sizeable savings he had amassed); he landed at Baltimore, penniless. Undaunted, he started over and became prosperous by importing German, Belgian, and French textiles. At age thirty-nine he married Emilie Kalisky (1803-1858) who was a native of Magdeburg, Germany. She and two daughters were later lost at sea in 1858 when their ship, the SS Austria, sank.[69]

Their third child, also named Charles, was born in September 1827 and married Caroline Kalisky (1832-64) on 4 August 1854. Their first child, Emily Vezin, was born two years later in Philadelphia. Her father had served as American consul to Germany. Both parents were singers with good voices and as a child of eight young Emily accompanied them on the piano. Emily possibly studied piano with Carl Wolfsohn, who was the leading piano teacher in Philadelphia. Shortly following her mother's death in 1864 her father sent her to Eringhausen, Germany to live with her Aunt Louise , who had married Ernst

Hasenclever. Emily continued her music studies in Eringhausen; after her marriage later to Alfredo Barili, they named their eldest daughter Louise in honor of this aunt. Emily continued to live and study in Eringhausen until the age of eighteen (1874) when she too was admitted to study at the Cologne Conservatory. This fateful move subesquently brought together the Vezin and Barili families.

Like the Barili-Patti clan, talent coursed through the Vezin veins. Hermann Vezin (1829-1910), Emily's uncle, moved to England and joined the theater, where he "was probably the most scholarly and intellectual actor of his generation." Oscar Wilde studied elocution with him before his celebrated tours of America.[70] Emily's two brothers went on to distinguished careers in art: As a young man, Charles Vezin (1858-1942) became a member of the distinguished Art Student's League in New York before developing into a landscape painter of note; Frederick (1859-1843) achieved recognition as a portrait painter after returning to Germany, where he joined the Academy of Art in Dusseldorf. At death both were members of the Royal Academy of Art. Not surprisingly, Barili's son (Alfredo II) and grandson (Alfredo III) both displayed considerable artistic talent. Alfredo, Jr. became a respected architect in Atlanta, and his son later won a number of prizes for his art work during his lifetime.

In Cologne, Emily and Alfredo must have hit it off together right away. Alfredo was not yet twenty, Emily barely eighteen. But the couple seemed delighted with each other and the relationship blossomed. Two of the few extant letters by Alfredo come from these student days. They both are written to Emily, which she saved and are currently in the possession of Mary Barili Goldsmith. Examining these with the other materials we have concerning Alfredo's life reveals, or perhaps better said, confirms a number of things. First, the handwriting reveals the same kind of exquisite care he brought to his playing. It is elegant and precise, almost sculpted in polished perfection. It is also refined, restrained, and miniature in size. The handwriting immediately reflects his personality, which was precise, flawless, controlled, and unruffled. Let me quote the first one in full:

> This morning my little friend came to my room while I was practicing and said that Emmie was down stairs. It seems you accompanied Mr. Biggs home, you little *rogue* why did you not whistle ? I should have come to the window.
> This morning I received a letter from Auntie Carlotta who is not so angry after all with me, she has only given me a little lecture about writing so seldom.

I shall not be at the music abend. I am very sorry but it cannot be otherwise.

I hope you sit on the same bench Tuesday, as you did last time. I am sure you will do me this favor. As I think my letter already too long I close; with thousand kisses I remain always your affectionate Alfredo Barili.

The letter shows Alfredo much the way others knew him later in life. While he was clear, articulate, and warm, he used words sparingly and efficiently ("I think my letter already too long"). Moreover, he could be confident and certain, but without becoming dogmatic or defensive: "I shall not be at the music abend. I am very sorry but it cannot be otherwise." This would serve him well during his life. He kept that rare balance between asserting his view on an issue, while not growing intolerant with a different belief, nor insisting that the other person adopt his opinion. In short, he knew his own mind. He also possessed personal warmth and compassion. But in typically Victorian fashion, he refrained from excessive emotional display. His sense of humor comes through the second letter as well, in which he relates how he kept Emily's umbrella and took it home with him. "I had quite a conversation with the umbrella last evening when I reached home," he wrote. "The above named article told me you flirted terribly while you were away, but I did not believe it . . . ." Alfredo also had internalized the Barili obsession with relentless perfection. He could be quite demanding of himself, as he would be with his students. It goes without saying that few artists attain any degree of professional achievement without this single-mindedness, if not fanatical dedication, to their art. Alfredo learned much of this from his demanding father. Of course Ettore's unswerving insistence on excellence forged Adelina's natural talent into the flawless voice of the century. And, not surprisingly, Alfredo played—from the beginning—faultlessly. Throughout his life this excellence pervaded everything he did: his conducting, his music manuscript, his teaching, his personal conduct. The remarkable thing is how he came to soften this harsh professional side when dealing with people. Few great artists arrive at this enviable position. But it seems everyone loved Alfredo Barili: children, students, family—Adelina called him "my dear little nephew"—friends old and young, and colleagues.

Emily certainly did. Barili loved her as well. He ended his second letter to her, "Your photograph receives a kiss every morning and night. I have it near my bed evenings while I go to sleep. I must now give a lesson so good bye now—write soon. Addio mia cara con mille baci, il tuo Alfredo." Whether the two became formally engaged or simply made a verbal commitment is unclear. Whatever happened, it alarmed Aunt Carlotta, who had sent Alfredo to Cologne to study, not get married. She likely summoned him to Paris in hopes of his forgetting about Emily. He continued his studies there with Theodore Ritter (1841-86), one of Liszt's pupils and a friend of Carlotta's. But he refused to budge concerning Emily, who remained in Cologne to complete her studies. In desperation, Carlotta offered him 20,000 francs—an enormous sum—to end the affair. In true romantic fashion, love triumphed; Alfredo persisted, declined the money, finished his studies, and returned home to Philadelphia sometime in late 1875. After finishing at Cologne, Emily briefly returned to Eringhausen before departing for Philadelphia, where she and Alfredo completed plans for their marriage.

They wed on 23 November 1877 in Newark, New Jersey on Wycliff Street, where the Rev. Isaac See officiated. Alfredo then opened his piano studio on the third floor of a building at 1126 Chestnut Street in downtown Philadelphia. Fees for twenty-four lessons at the office were $86.00; for the same number at private residences it was half that. He did not give single lessons: "Signor Alfredo Barili will not make any engagement less than one Quarter; that is to say, 24 lessons. Each half Quarter will be paid for in advance," as he firmly stated in his brochure announcing himself. James Huneker, who would become one of the country's most renowned music critics, was a young man at the time and took lessons with Alfredo. He later recounted: Alfredo "was a finished pianist of the French school. When he first played Chopin's B minor Scherzo for me, it acted like catnip on a feline. I rolled over the floor. The music made my nerves naked. I play the tragic, morbid composition now—yet can never rid myself of the initial impression." Barili "made a prediction that came true when he assured me that I would never become a pianist worth hearing." He and Alfredo became close friends.[71]

Years later (1919) Huneker wrote Emily. The deep affection the three shared shines through his tender memories of those good days nearly half a century earlier. Alfredo's affectionate, genuine friendship left a deep mark, as Huneker related to Emily: "I felt my eyes wet when I read your lovely letter for it brought back to 1877 when you and dear old Alfredo—he will always be young to me—used to walk down Chestnut St., a newly married couple, and drop in at Dutton's piano warerooms corner 13th St. where Wanamaker's now is. Oceans of memories! Alfredo was always good to me, and he predicted that I would *never* make a pianist. It has proved true." Huneker reminds Emily of his final scene in 1878 with Alfredo. Romantically obsessed with seeing Paris (can anyone blame him?) and idolizing Liszt, who had become a musical icon in the United States, Huneker impetuously decided to run away from Philadelphia. Early on the morning of 25 September 1878, he waited until he was leaving the house to awaken his parents, who, seeing his resolution, gave him their blessing (and financial support it turns out). A few friends and his brother accompanied Huneker to the station, where he took the train to New York to catch the French steamer Canada, which sailed that afternoon. "Alfredo came to the old Penna. RR Station at 31st and Market. He was very kind."[72]

Alfredo and Emily must have also been entertaining thoughts of leaving Philadelphia at the time. They had a child that same year (1878), Charlotte May, but she died the next year. Whether Alfredo's teaching prospered we do not know. But his asthma was apparently causing problems. As Philadelphia grew it became more industrialized, which increased the pollution considerably. After the baby's death, with perhaps a disappointing number of students and difficult health problems, the young couple made plans to move. Alfredo seems to have secured a position with Mrs. Ballard at the Atlanta Female Institute before he made the final decision. With that in place, one of the country's promising young musicians packed, went to the station with his wife, and departed for a city barely older than himself, Atlanta.

2 MUSIC FROM THE ASHES: ATLANTA CONCERT LIFE 1860-1880

When Alfredo and Emily moved to Atlanta in 1880 they found a bustling, vibrant city of nearly 40,000. Atlanta had not only recovered from the devastation of the Civil War, but stood poised to assume leadership in the "New South" of which Benjamin Harvey Hill and Henry Woodfin Grady spoke so eloquently. The remarkable physical expansion that Atlanta would see during the next decade—flanked on one end by the 1881 International Cotton Exposition and by the 1889 Piedmont Exposition on the other—was accompanied by a gradual refinement of musical life. With the improvement of economic conditions, and its place as capitol of the South assured, conditions in Atlanta began encouraging more artistic activity. The confident atmosphere also attracted important artists such as Barili, whose arrival marked the beginnings of professional musical leadership for the city.

* * * * * *

When one considers the numerous barriers that stood in the way of real cultural development in Atlanta it is surprising that someone of Barili's stature would move there in 1880. The conditions under which the city had begun and grown worked against the establishment of a serious concert life. Unlike many American cities, which developed naturally around waterways or trading routes, Atlanta was arbitrarily established as a rail junction. As trade increased, the city thrived. Between 1850 and 1855 the population nearly tripled, from 2,500 to almost 6,000. But missing from the growth was the class of elite, landed aristocrats that gave other southern towns their distinctively genteel, settled, cultured atmosphere. Most of the constant influx consisted of new workers and farmers—uneducated, often garrulous, and fiercely independent. Of course

51

this unfettered climate, lacking the restraint of an older landed gentry, also accounted for much of Atlanta's economic vigor. Atlanta champions made it clear that all men were welcome in the city, "free from the domination of *caste*— objections being made only to *drones*." Well-bred gentlemen, relying solely on their pedigrees would find no automatic rank and station in Atlanta. Only talent, ambition, and relentless toil would earn the newcomer a good living and prominent place. "These men can sell their goods cheaper," explained the *Atlanta Constitution* in 1879, "than merchants [in the established southern cities] who come to their houses at 10 a.m., in a fine carriage, smoking an elegant Havana cigar . . . .[who] go home about four in the evening . . . spend the balance of the day at dinner, where they entertain a fashionable visitor [with] a full description of the age of the city, and the pure blood of their ancestors . . . ."[1]

Unfortunately, the absence of a class of educated, settled citizenry made it difficult for any social institutions, cultural ones especially, to gain a secure foothold in the young city. Truthfully, the future leading city of the South had more in common with the rough and primitive towns emerging on the western frontier than the older southern towns such as Charleston, Savannah, Mobile, New Orleans and Richmond. Edward King, traveling throughout the South in the early 1870's observed: "From the ashes . . . has sprung up a new, vigorous, awkwardly alert city . . . . There is but little that is distinctively Southern in Atlanta; it is the antithesis of Savannah." He was stuck by the newness of the place: "Atlanta has an unfinished air; its business and residence streets are scattered along a range of pretty hills."[2] This resulted not from her size, as most of the major cities of the Deep South were larger, nor the composition of her population, for Atlanta had a smaller proportion of foreign-born people than much of the South. Racial issues were not the cause either; she had a similar mix to that of Augusta, Savannah, and Mobile; and Charleston and New Orleans had an even higher percentage of African-Americans. As the editor of the *Daily New Era* observed in 1870 "The results of this rushing together of men of varied characters and origins is a community *sui generis* in many of its features." He saw Atlanta as "a city cosmopolitan in degree heretofore unexampled in the history of any Southern town."[3]

What gave Atlanta its distinctive and culturally resistant *un*southern heritage was the nature of her development. The swift urbanization indeed had brought prosperous economic progress but concomitant disorganization and social problems as well. Too-frequent changes of government—mayoral terms were only one year until 1874—and an ineffective program of law enforcement prevented the establishment of a solid community base. Moreover, the haphazard spread of the city streets, built with little organization or planning, gave Atlanta a feel of physical disarray as well. Large numbers of poor, especially after the war, only added to the difficulty of building a successful city, earning Atlanta the unpleasant reputation as "Poor House of the State."[4] Sanitation treatment was virtually non- existent, resulting in appalling civic health problems. These factors together gave the city a lawless, disorderly environment which made solid artistic development almost impossible.

In spite of these difficulties, Atlantans enjoyed a striking diversity of popular entertainments in the decades before the arrival of Alfredo Barili. At the most common level, anything that promised to astonish and amaze was sure to fill the house. Panoramas such as "Waugh's Italia and the Italian Fantocini—A Panoramic Voyage from Boston to Rome and Naples and New York" fascinated the *Daily Intelligencer* as "the most elegant, interesting, sublime exhibition ever presented to the American people" (7 November 1857). Circuses like Dan Costello's Model Circus visited, bringing along a South American hippopotamus, a two-humped Bactrian camel, and four-horned Patagonian sheep. Daguerreotype demonstrations brought responses from audiences as well. Outside, balloon ascensions, accompanied by rousing band music, drew enthusiastic participants and spectators. Minstrel shows proved enormously popular. From the earliest years into the end of the century troupes such as the Bill Power's Minstrels, the Campbell Minstrels, the Empire Minstrels, starring R. H. Sliter, "Champion Dancer of the World," and Old Joe Sweeney's Great Burlesque Opera Troupe never failed to enjoy sizeable audiences.[5]

Music and the legitimate theater offered the city a higher class of entertainment, as the *Daily Intelligencer* applauded in an 1869 editorial. It disapproved of "a large number of entertainments now filling the country," insisting that corrupt amusements must be avoided in favor of "such as will be wholesome. The enjoyment of harmless entertainments causes us to forget our pains, invigorates our systems, and prolongs our lives."[6] As time passed, however, the hope for a higher level of entertainment would swell to a general tone insisting that music and theater concern themselves only with virtuous and noble themes. For now, though, they could get by as long as they avoided the cheap, vulgar, and indecent.

Atlanta theaters before 1880 offered a striking array of musical entertainment, ranging from variety shows of songs, skits, and dances, to burlesque opera, concerts, operetta, and full-scale opera. And though there was a surprising amount of local activity for a city of its size—the population would not reach 22,000 until 1870—professional quality productions had to wait until touring companies staged them. For the decade from 1860-1870, Atlanta saw nearly 140 serious music performances of opera, opera concerts, and general concerts, along with the more standard fare of burlesque operas, minstrel shows, and varieties acts. Predictably, concert life slowed considerably into 1863 as the war reverses mounted, and all but stopped the next year. Only one amateur concert is reported for 1865. The next two years saw constant growth in musical performances, including an appearance of the first opera troupe in 1866. By 1870 musical life, while not back to the levels of a decade earlier, was showing vigorous growth.[7]

Owing to its youth, adequate facilities for musical and theatrical events proved a major problem for Atlanta. For years, performers played wherever they could manage to secure space: in large rooms, halls, and churches. The city's first hall with seats was quite likely Parr's Hall, built in the early 1850's at the southwest corner of Whitehall and Alabama Streets, and located on the third floor of a commercial building. In 1854, a prominent produce dealer, Mr. J. E. Williams, built the first hall specifically planned as a theater. Mr. Williams would later serve as mayor in 1865 during the difficult days following the War. Williams worked in partnership with Mr. William H. Crisp, an English actor who had performed throughout the Northeast before moving to Atlanta in 1854. When Williams was planning his second warehouse on the north side of Decatur Street between Peachtree and Pryor, Crisp convinced him to design the second story as Atlanta's first theater, the Athaeneum. The Athaeneum was so called because the exterior of the building consisted of a row of white-fluted classical columns which extended from floor to the ceiling. On 16 February 1855 the City Council, at the application of Mr. Crisp, awarded him a license to stage theatrical productions.[8] Apparently Crisp found little support for musical theater in Atlanta and soon departed for New Orleans where he was contracted by the owners of the Gaiety Theater to take over management of that house, which opened in November 1856 as Crisp's Gaiety.[9]

Constructed ninety-feet long and fifty-feet wide, with a gallery on three sides, the Athaeneum seated about 700 people and had a stage at one end with small, plain dressing rooms and the first greenroom in the city. William Barnes, an active enthusiast in Atlanta's amateur theatrical life until the end of the War (when he moved away) described the theater upon his return in 1888. "The entrance was very narrow. Up a short flight of steps you went from the street, and when you reached the top the little box office faced you . . . ." The actors had to make their first and last exits through the back entrance up "a long ladder, the top of which rested on one of the dressing room windows . . . ." Nevertheless, "the old Athaeneum—a primitive place in those primitive times— was a good little playhouse, the best, perhaps, all things considered, that the town has ever had."[10]

Musical entertainments in Atlanta at the Athaeneum reflected the tastes and preferences of American audiences at mid-century. As the city was culturally behind the other major southern cities—it was not even a decade old the year the Athaeneum was completed—Atlanta lagged behind the current musical fashions that had been standard fare for years in cities like Charleston, New Orleans, Richmond, Savannah, and Augusta, something the *Daily New Era* realized: "cultural entertainment in Atlanta . . . never attained the level achieved in those Southern ante bellum cities [where] wealthy classes . . . patronized the concert hall and theatre".[11] While Atlanta did manage to maintain an impressive concert life into the first years of the Civil War, entertainments by the summer of 1863 quickly declined as the Confederate economic, military, and political situation grew increasingly desperate. The Federal occupation and burning the next year devastated the city, bringing everything to a grinding halt. And though Atlanta quickly restarted itself with amazing resiliency, the promising musical entertainments that had sprouted by the late 1850's had been unable to establish themselves securely. The best way to gain a clear picture of Atlanta's musical life at the time of Barili's arrival in 1880, then, is to examine briefly musical concert life in the South during the decades before the Civil War.

CONCERT MUSIC IN THE ANTE BELLUM SOUTH

It is not surprising that among southern cities Charleston achieved a high level of social and cultural activity by the middle of the ante bellum period. This achievement was supported by a broad base of economic and social activity in the years soon after Charleston's founding. Perhaps more than any other American city, Charleston had most completely transplanted its English heritage of customs, social graces, and entertainment tastes to these shores. So, early on in 1736, the city's first theater opened on Dock street.[12] Later, an Englishman, Thomas Wade West, worked as one of the early leaders in establishing theater in the South. In 1793 West started a new theater in Charleston, known later as the Old Charleston Theater, which remained open until 1833. When the number of French immigrants began increasing during the 1790's, Alexandre Placide, a French immigrant dancer and composer, decided to build a theater catering to their tastes. In 1815 Charles Gilfert, a talented German musician, assumed management of the Charleston Theater. Under his tenure Charleston's theatrical life flourished, earning him considerable respect and affection until he left the city to manage the "New Theater" in Richmond before moving on to the Bowery Street Theater in New York.

In 1833 the Charleston Theater was sold. This forced theatrical entertainments to move to the Queen Street Theater or other unsuitable places. Four years later, the New Charleston Theater opened, bringing the total number of theaters to five.[13] Constructed in the Greek revival style fronting a portico of Ionic columns, the new theater held 1200 seats and proved a boon to Charleston's theatrical and musical life. The theater's first manager, William Abbot, not only proved an effective administrator, but he also inaugurated the opera seasons that would prove immensely popular until the Civil War.

Music in Charleston, like most ante bellum American cities, was an integral part of many theatrical entertainments. An evening at the theater typically included an extensive opening piece, either a spoken drama or, later, an opera, followed by a shorter, lighter work, often a musical farce, comic opera, burlesque, or pantomime. Inserted between these events would be popular songs or dances such as hornpipes. Charleston holds the distinction of staging the first opera and the first song recital in America. In the Charles Towne Courtroom on 18 February 1735 *Flora, or Hob in the Well* by Colley Cibber was presented. Two years earlier, on 26 February, the first song recital, consisting of English and Scotch songs, was performed.[14]

Two of the most popular singers to visit Charleston in the antebellum period were Jane Shirreff (1811-83) and John Wilson (1801-49), who sang at the Charleston Theater from 14-27 December 1839. Both had begun their careers in Great Britain before moving to the United States. Wilson was a Scottish tenor with a "pure, sweet, vigorous, and highly cultivated voice" who likewise sang at Covent Garden. His singing of national Scottish song earned him the reputation as one of the century's most successful Scottish singers, something he drew upon for his 1842 *Wilson's Edition of the Songs of Scotland*. For their 1839/40 tour they performed concerts and popular operas in English from the current repertory. In Charleston they presented ten performances of *La sonnambula, Fra Diavolo, Cinderella, Rob Roy,* and Henry Bishop's *Native Land* before moving on to Augusta and Savannah and then returning to Charleston.[15]

In March 1851 one of the most important American travelling opera troupes visited Charleston for almost three weeks. The troupe was managed by

Max Maretzek, the Moravian mentioned in chapter one, who had come to New York in 1848. He served briefly as music director before assuming control, at the request of the management, of the Astor Place House and its dormant opera company. He subsequently managed several Astor Place companies, one of which he took on the road to Boston, Charleston, Augusta, and (again) Boston from mid February to the end of May 1851. The troupe—designated only as "Italian opera" in the playbills—arrived by boat from New York on 18 March. Newspaper reports credited the Astor Place Company with some seventy performers, including "upwards of forty persons" in the orchestra and chorus. Maretzek wisely programmed a variety of eight different operas over the three-week stay: *Ernani, La favorita, Parisina, Lucrezia Borgia, Il giuramento, Norma, Lucia di Lammermoor,* and *Il barbiere di Siviglia,* giving two performances of four: *Ernani, La favorita, Lucrezia Borgia,* and *Norma.* The company seems to have enjoyed a successful run. Descriptions suggest full houses; one commentator noted that the theater was "crowded from pit to dome" on the last evening.[16]

Incredibly, Maretzek's Astor Place Company found itself facing serious competition during their Charleston stay, and not just from one other corner. Just three days before Maretzek's group appeared, two important contemporary singers had given a concert. Caroline Vietti and Fortunata Tedesco gave a grand concert on 15 March, drawing many of the same listeners that Maretzek hoped to attract. Even worse, an operatic concert company, boasting of better known singers, arrived on 1 April, having come by steamer from Wilmington, North Carolina. Maurice Strakosch's touring group included two well known and celebrated singers, Teresa Parodi and Amalia Patti, as well as Salvatore Patti. Much earlier, the Astor Place Company singers had scheduled two concerts, one of which conflicted with the scheduled opera evenings. To avoid a conflict detrimental to both groups, Maretzek attempted to move the date of the production, only to be thwarted by the prima donna's illness, which delayed the opera one night. Nevertheless, both performances drew large crowds, as the critic for the *Mercury* joyfully noted on 7 April. "It is a gratifying evidence of the musical taste of our City, that it can furnish in one night two such audiences as that of the Opera and that of the Concert, and equally gratifying that Charleston can attract the musical talent to furnish forth two such splendid entertainments."[17]

Jenny Lind captured the hearts of Charlestonians on 26 December 1850 as she did everywhere she sang. Adelina Patti, only ten years old at the time, was not far behind when she first appeared at the Charleston Theater in 1853.

Sigismund Thalberg, along with Henry Vieuxtemps, presented a series of piano and violin concerts in January 1858 on a tour that took them to Richmond and Atlanta. And the even more well-known violinist, Ole Bull, made at least four celebrated appearances in 1844, 1853, 1854, and 1856. In 1854 Charleston heard one of the most well-trained orchestras of the period conducted by Louis Antoine Jullien (1812-60). His renown only increased as he programmed works like "Quadrille National, the 'American,' which contained all the principal National Melodies." Just before the war, in 1860, Patrick S. Gilmore brought his "celebrated band" for a concert in April 1860.[18]

Richmond also had a rich concert life by the turn of the nineteenth century. By 1820 the city had two theaters (one with orchestra), a number of temporary spaces, and several circuses. A concert at the Eagle Hotel in 1823 contained instrumental works by Haydn, Rossini, and Mozart in addition to the vocal numbers. Rare was the major dramatic piece, tragedy, melodrama, or comedy that did not include singing and dancing, usually between works, and often concluding with a short farce. If the event was billed as an opera, comic opera, or musical entertainment the audience could expect even more songs.[19]

The quarter century before the Civil War saw an increase in the number of concerts, both by touring artists, and local musicians. In 1848 the first touring opera company, the Sequin English Opera troupe, brought Balfe's *The Bohemian Girl* and *Fra Diavolo*. They returned the next year and added *Maritana, Cinderella,* and *Norma*. The Pyne and Harrison English Opera Troupe played twice, performing much the same repertoire, with the addition of *Daughter of Regiment* and *The Barber of Seville*.

Italian opera sung in Italian was first heard in Richmond in 1849 at a concert at the Exchange Hotel, followed two years later by a complete performance by Max Maretzek's company, which staged *I Puritani* and *La favorita*. Steffanoni's Opera Troupe presented the second acts of *Norma* and *Lucrezia Borgia* in Italian "plus popular and sacred classical combinations" in 1853. The next year saw the "New York celebrated Italian Opera Company" of "over forty performers . . .under the direction of Signor L. Arditi" present *Lucrezia Borgia, Lucia di Lammermoor, Norma, La sonnambula,* and *Belisario*. Altogether, visiting opera troupes offered nearly twenty separate operas in Richmond in the years 1848-60.

In the decade before the Civil War Richmond concert goers regularly heard European and American touring artists. The most frequent visitors were members of the Alfredo Barili's family: Maurice Strakosch, Amalia Patti, Adelina Patti, and the singer Teresa Parodi. About Parodi, the *Richmond*

Dispatch observed that although she "has sung here at least a dozen times, there has been, from first to last, no abatement of the desire to hear her . . . ."[20] Other relatives of Barili appeared as well, including Antonio Barili, Nicolo Barili, and Alfredo's father Ettore. Instrumental groups such as the Germaina Band and Jullien's orchestra brought a higher class of music to Richmond. Along with quadrilles, waltzes, polkas, and gallops Louis Jullien presented Beethoven, Haydn, and Mendelssohn. Solo performers also drew enthusiastic audiences. Luigi Elena and Ole Bull played the violin to packed houses while Henry Vieuxtemps and Sigismund Thalberg presented a violin and piano recital together on their southern tour in January 1858.[21]

New Orleans early on enjoyed the distinction of having the richest concert life in the country, beginning in 1792 when the first theater opened on St. Peter Street on 4 October.[22] By the 1820's New Orleans, with a population still under 30,000, had two French opera companies, one of which could boast of an impressive troupe of twenty-two French actors, musicians, and a *corps de ballet*, recruited from France by theater manager John Davis. On 4 March 1823 they presented Rossini's *Barber of Seville*, only seven years following its premiere in Rome and three years before it played in New York. In the nearly five years from 1821-25, the two theaters—the Orleans and St. Philip—gave 464 performances of 150 operas by 50 composers. James Caldwell, who had been renting the Orleans Theater on nights when the French were not using it, opened his new theater New Year's Day, 1824, on Camp Street to present productions more distinctly American in flavor.

In order to make ends meet during the torrid Louisiana summer, when the theaters were closed, Davis sailed with his company on 12 June 1827 to New York. On Friday 13 July it played in the celebrated Park Theater, offering a double bill of French operas.[23] All-in-all, the New Orleans troupe made six summer tours north, adding Boston, Baltimore, and Philadelphia to its itinerary. Along the way they presented an assortment of sixty-one different operas by twenty-four composers for an extraordinary total of 251 opera performances, including works by Auber, Weber, Herold, Grétry, Méhul, Rossini, Spontini, and Mozart. Not only were most of these operas heard for the first time in the Northeast, but they also constituted the first regular opera offerings in Boston, Philadelphia, and Baltimore. Even more incredibly, add to this that during their regular seasons home at the French Orleans Theater, from fall 1827 through spring 1833, they staged 367 performances of eighty-five different operas by thirty-two composers. No fewer than twenty-seven of these were new operas, introducing twelve composers new to New Orleans.

French opera was more popular than ever, as the *New Orleans Bee* pointed out in 1836: "Spectacles and operas appear to amuse our citizens more than any other form of public amusement—except balls."[24] By that time New Orleans had three active theaters serving a population of 60,000. In 1835, James Caldwell, flushed by beating the French to the punch with his production of *Robert le diable*, sought a different challenge by building a magnificent new theater on St. Charles Street, on which he would spend more than $325,000. With its two-ton chandelier, and seating between four and five thousand, it was the largest in the United States when it opened on Monday, 30 November 1835. Season boxes cost an incredible one thousand dollars, more than the average yearly income of most Americans. The Orleans Theater had the largest orchestra, followed by the twenty-nine players at the St. Charles, consisting of ten violins, two violas, three cellos, two double basses, two trumpets, one trombone, two clarinets, two flutes, two horns, and one oboe, harp, and bassoon. Both theaters supported two of the five largest theatrical orchestras in the country at the time, including the Tremont (Boston), Park (New York), and Chestnut Street (Philadelphia).[25]

By the end of the season in 1840 the three theaters had presented an astounding repertoire. The French company at the Orleans Theater had given 364 performances of sixty-five operas by twenty-seven composers, including sixteen premiers. The Brichta and De Rosa Italian opera companies totaled fifty-four Italian offerings in 1836-37, of which seven were premiers. As Auber was the most popular composer of these years, English companies at the St. Charles played him frequently. In addition, the company presented Halévy's *The Jewess, La sonnambula, Cinderella, Barber of Seville,* and *Marriage of Figaro.* During these five years New Orleans enjoyed an astonishing number of opera performances, nearly 550! When you add to this a large number of ballets such as *La Sylphide* and *L'Hirondelle,* and even more English musicals, many with music by Sir Henry Bishop, you have a wealth of musical entertainment that no other American city remotely equaled.

By the middle of the next decade—the 1850's—interest in opera was growing enormously not only in New Orleans but across the country. This popularity was accompanied by a growing call for opera in English. In spite of the subtle pressure to be "cultured" and stylish that attending opera in Italian supposedly bestowed upon the listener, more and more Americans found themselves uncomfortable with the emerging association of Italian opera with elitist entertainment. Adding to this distaste for opera in another language was the reputation which the foreign singers had earned over the last decade for being difficult, temperamental, and "high-class." As one music critic astutely remarked in 1857, "a good English opera is, after all, the only one which can give entire satisfaction to the great mass of our people." The expanding demand resulted in an increase in the number of touring troupes that performed opera in English. Of these, the Pyne and Harrison English Opera Company proved the most successful English troupe in North America during the 1850's.[26]

The Pyne and Harrison Company arrived in New Orleans in late January 1856 to find the city ecstatically awaiting them. On 25 January the *Daily Picayune* crowed: "The lovers of truly good music, rendered in the vernacular have now a 'feast of fat things' provided for them, in the engagement of the Pynes and Messrs Harrison and Stretton, at the St. Charles theatre. Never, since the days of the Woods, have we had so perfect an English troupe of opera singers as this." The company filled the house "pit to ceiling" with their performances of *Cinderella*, which saw six stagings, *The Crown Diamonds*, *Maritana, The Bohemian Girl, La sonnambula,* and *The Daughter of the Regiment.* The resident company added its expected farce to each evening's presentation.[27]

In November of that same year at Crisp's newly organized Gaiety Theater, a stock company appeared, composed of singers probably enticed away from New York to form an ensemble. They played in various musical works as well as operas such as the ever popular *The Bohemian Girl,* and *Der Freischütz.* They also worked with the resident dramatic members in performing such works as John Brougham's burlesque *Pochahontas.* Between 1857 and 1859 the troupe, working as the New Orleans English Opera Company, travelled widely over the South, playing in Richmond, Baltimore, Charleston, Savannah, Macon, and Columbus, before ending up as the house company at Maguire's in San Francisco.[28]

CONCERT MUSIC IN ATLANTA 1860-1880

While these southern cites were enjoying a rich concert life during the 1840's and 1850's, Atlanta put most of its efforts into simply establishing and defining itself. Led by an energetic middle-class of business men, many of whom were northern transplants, Atlanta showed little resemblance to the southern culture supported by a landholding aristocracy. The city's age, upcountry location, and commercial economy gave it a thoroughly different social profile from that of the plantation South. In Atlanta, planters and slaves were the exception—the 1860 census reported that only 0.3 percent of the city's working population listed their occupation as planters and 1.4 percent as farmers.[29]

Even so, the citizens of Atlanta did take time for social diversion and amusement. During the earliest years, state fairs, circuses, various traveling acts, and especially minstrel shows such as the Campbell Minstrel's and Brass Band in 1857, or LaRue's Famous and Original Carnival Minstrels, Brass Band and Burlesque Opera Troupe offered popular entertainment. One of the most fascinating events in the ante bellum years featured the Blind Tom Meefie, an eight-year old slave who toured the South, first playing in Atlanta in 1857 and returning five times during the 1860's. He possessed what must have been nearly total musical recall. Otherwise impaired mentally, he awed his audiences with the most astounding musical skill at the piano. After one hearing "The most difficult and lengthy pieces are performed by him . . . His fingers move with the rapidity of the wings of a hummingbird; and what is more surprising than all, he never makes a mistake."[30] Magic shows proved similarly popular, such as that of M. Leo Taylor, "The Great Oriental Wizzard [sic] and Ventriloquist" who appeared in 1857 and 1859.

Ante bellum Atlanta did see some local musical activity during the 1850's. A Mr. Guilford brought the first piano (Denham & Sons) to the city in 1849, where he and his son taught on it for more than twenty years. Herman Braumuller opened what was surely the city's first music store in 1852; he sold sheet music, instruments, and piano fortes. His wife, Mrs. Braumuller was likely Atlanta's first art teacher. In 1857 Mrs. J. A. Wright opened a school for young ladies where music was taught. Carl Barth began giving music classes as well. He also joined with a partner to form Barth and Nicolai to sell pianos and string instruments. Local citizens taught music and dancing, and private schools as a practice included music and art in their curricula for an additional fee. Mrs. Cunningham's "Young Ladies Seminary" offered music instruction for $12.50 as well as drawing and painting "in all its varieties" at the lower cost of $10.[31]

Following the completion of the Athaeneum in 1854, and now that railroad travel made the city accessible, touring companies that had routinely played southern cities on the eastern seaboard began adding Atlanta to their itinerary. Sigismund Thalberg, on tour through the South in 1858, brought his Grand Concert to Atlanta on 4 February. Though he probably did not think about it at the time, he quite possibly inaugurated Atlanta's professional concert life with this appearance. He had played in Richmond on 8 January before traveling to Charleston for five concerts, finishing on 2 February. Assisted by the celebrated violinist Henry Vieuxtemps, Mme. Bertha Johanssen, and Miss Annie Kemp, Thalberg presented what was basically an operatic concert. By this time he had earned a world-wide reputation as a dazzling performer as well as arranger of operatic melodies and well-liked songs. His remarkable keyboard skill, combined with the widespread passion for opera music, made his American concerts among the most popular of the day. Though we do not have the specific program he presented at the Athaeneum in Atlanta, we can determine the repertoire he drew upon from the available Charleston programs. Thalberg, et al., knew what audiences of the day wanted to hear, and it was Italian opera—they filled their programs with virtually nothing else. Thalberg undoubtedly opened his Atlanta concert, as he did all five of the Charleston performances, with at least four brilliant Fantasies on various operatic works, such as *La sonnambula, Norma, Don Pasquale, Lucrezia Borgia, Les Huguenots, Don Giovanni,* or *Lucia di Lammermoor.* Vieuxtemps then followed him with his own musical fireworks such as *The Carnival of Venice,* or a Fantasie on Verdi's opera *Ernani.* For contrast (and for some needed relief from the sheer sizzle of their playing), Miss Kemp and Mme. Johanssen sang songs such as "Thou art Lovelier," and "Ave Maria." Atlanta audiences, like those elsewhere, simply could not get enough, keeping Thalberg in demand almost to his last breath.[32]

By 1860 Atlanta found itself on the verge of becoming a significant commercial city. Situated on the dividing line between the Cotton Belt and the food-growing regions of the upper South, Atlanta increasingly earned the name "Gate City" owing to its centrality as a major foodstuff distribution point for the lower South. The city had made impressive strides in population, growing to just under 10,000 inhabitants at the beginning of the decade. Serious music still waited to secure a solid base, however. Records indicate few classical concerts during that year. One of the few listed gives a classical music soiree as presented by Madam Anna Bishop on 18 February. Legitimate theater had more activity with thirty-one productions.[33]

The next year, 1861, brought the southern secession and the outbreak of the Civil War. The attack on Fort Sumter forced the few southern theaters still operating to close, and with them, most musical activity ceased. With the theaters dark, touring companies disbanded, and most actors and managers fled North. By the fall however, music and theater began to rebound as the theaters reopened, such as the Concert Hall and the Academy of Music in New Orleans. The Richmond Theater also resumed operations, under its new manager, John Hill

Hewitt (1801-90), who would become the "Bard of the Confederacy." In Atlanta, too, concert activity reappeared, presented mostly by two organizations.[34]

The Atlanta Amateurs, a dramatic club, presented their first concert on 8 May 1861 before they officially organized themselves later that month to raise money for the war effort. Managed by W. H. Barnes, the Amateurs consisted of twenty-eight members, including five women. In less than two months the group raised more than $2,400 for the Confederate soldiery. By September they had performed in four other cities with their "Grand Medley Soirees" of "rollicking fun, nonsense by Mr. Barnes, and the delightful songs of the ladies" to packed houses. With their third, and last, anniversary "Soiree" on 12-13 May 1864, they had raised a total of $32,000.[35]

Atlanta also enjoyed the musical/dramatic presentations of the Queen Sisters during the war. The company, which also became known as The Thespian Family, consisted of father Alfred Waldron, Sr.; daughters Laura, Fanny, and Julia; and sons Alfred, Jr., Andrew, and Arthur. They had been in Charleston at the outbreak of the war, from which they travelled to New Orleans in April 1862. With the fall of the city later that spring, they toured through Mobile and Montgomery before appearing in Atlanta in July. They later settled in Augusta where Alfred Waldron took over management of the Concert Hall, in conjunction with John Hill Hewitt, who had moved from Richmond. On Tuesday Evening, 15 July at the Athaeneum they played, danced, and sang the musical farce "Loan of a Lover" along with patriotic songs such as "The Patriot's Appeal, and "Sweet Hearts vs the War," accompanied by the Palmetto Band. Their return engagement in October brought similar success.[36] Another touring southern troupe, Mr. Sloman and his daughters, travelled from Mobile, where the paper claimed that "Wherever *taste* and *cultivation* in this beautiful art [of music] are appreciated, they cannot fail to give delight." They played at the Athaeneum New Year's Eve, 1862.[37]

The growing desperation of the war finally took its toll on concert life during 1863. William Crisp, back in Atlanta with his touring company for a twelve-week dramatic run in the fall, found it increasingly difficult to hold things together. Large numbers of soldiers in the audience continually disrupted the plays with their loud and rowdy behavior and attendance began falling. Even worse, some of the dramatic leads were too ill to perform. By December the theater was closed—forever, as it turned out. July of the next year brought Sherman and the Battle of Atlanta. Finally, on 15 November, the Athaeneum, along with much of the city, went up in flames.[38]

* * * * * * *

As 1865 dawned, artistic life in Atlanta lay strewn among the rubble and ashes of Peachtree Street along with most of the city. "It would be impossible for me to give you a description of matters in that once flourishing city," penned former resident James R. Crew on 1 December 1864. One estimate put the number of buildings destroyed at between four and five thousand, including nearly all of the business district, railroad machine shops, mills, and foundries. All that remained, one visitor observed, "were a few battered brick walls, and an occasional chimney looking grim and gaunt."[39]

Atlanta was only bowed, however, not broken. Sherman may have obliterated the physical city, but he only interrupted the march of its spirit. Indeed, Atlanta's rapid recovery from the Civil War bordered on the miraculous. Even with the appalling devastation and lasting trauma, the war but briefly slowed Atlanta's progress and actually inflicted little permanent harm. Knowing full well the looming hardships, many citizens returned to the ravaged city with astonishing speed. "Everyone that can," O.S. Hammond reported after he had gone back in February 1865, "is returning as fast as transportation and the roads will permit." By 1867 more than 250 commercial buildings had been rebuilt and opened for business. Atlanta took off: its 1870 population of 21,789 was more than double that of 1860, and by 1880 the 37,409 inhabitants more than quadrupled the pre-war figure. Unlike most of the South, Atlanta—matched only by Richmond and Nashville—experienced major economic growth in the fifteen years after 1865.[40]

Artistically, the newspaper editors led the way in calling for a restoration of Atlanta's cultural life. In August 1865, even before the rubble was cleared, the editor of the *Daily Intelligencer* was lamenting the lack of suitable entertainment: "the want of a place of amusement is beginning to be keenly felt here. By all means, let us have a theatre!" In a little more than a year his wish would be granted. Dramatic activity was staged in thrown-together quarters at Broad and Walton Street, where Pratt and Carney produced the popular melodrama *The Drunkard, Or The Fallen Saved* in January 1866.[41]

In July 1866, S. H. Hubbard and A. J. Nelson leased a hall in the Bell and Johnson building for a year, planning to install a legitimate dramatic company. As was typical of the period, a total subscription of fifteen hundred dollars was raised to install a stage, dressing rooms, fixtures, and scenery. Seating six hundred and lit by four wax candle chandeliers, and with a small stage probably no more than fourteen feet high, the Bell-Johnson Opera Hall opened 18 October. Just as the physical and economic elements of the city had promptly picked right up where the war had left them, so would the inaugural post bellum entertainment return to its severed musical threads: opera.[42]

Max Strakosch, already well-known for his operatic management, resumed his southern tour as soon as it seemed feasible following the cessation of hostilities. He was scheduled along with the Ghioni and Sussini Grand Italian Opera Company to open the Bell-Johnson Hall at Broad and Alabama streets on 18 October 1866. The event soon generated enormous excitement in the city. For one thing, it marked Atlanta's first full operatic production. But perhaps more importantly, the visit to the new opera house carried immense symbolic import for a population that had seen little but death, defeat, and devastation for years. Even if the grinding hard work of rebuilding the city still had far to go, Atlantans could point to Strakosch's glittering performances with pride and assure themselves that some civilization and elegance, even if it seemed a little tattered and shaky, had at last returned, and that they could find some brief respite from the dirt, despair, and destruction all around them. While there may have been just a little over-confident boosterism in the comment by the *Atlanta Daily New Era* that the opera was a "commentary upon our refinement which is undisputable and undenied," one can sympathize with the editorial's relief at finding *something* of cultural quality to point to.[43]

The *Daily New Era* was not alone; it seemed that everyone was excited. The *Daily Intelligencer* seconded the *Era*: "it reflects great credit upon the refinement and civilization of our city." There was not the least doubt that "everybody will go to the opera tonight," and that "the audience will be brilliant, such as never before assembled in this city." Apparently, Atlantans did rise to the occasion, for "The applause was frequent, enthusiastic and critical, and we will guarantee that not a single fine point fell still-born upon the vast auditory." One reporter was much encouraged by the full houses, which showed that "a large portion of our people are at least devoid of that provincialism which is natural to a people who have not been educated to a just appreciation of the fine art."[44]

The Ghioni Troupe brought an incredibly large group—seventy-five artists, including orchestra. Strakosch featured Amalia Patti, sister of Adelina Patti, in *Il trovatore*. While the audience was disappointed to find that she did not sing in *Norma* on the second night, her appearance as Rosina the following evening in *The Barber of Seville* proved the hit of the tour. Of course, Strakosch added some popular frosting to the operatic cake by promising that she would insert "Within a Mile of Edinboro Town," "Kathleen Mavourneen" and "Comin' Through the Rye'" into the letter scene. He knew what he was doing "because the audience will stop the show until she sings 'Comin' Through the Rye," promised the editor of the *Intelligencer*.[45]

As far as concerted operatic music went, however, Strakosch had been beaten to the punch by the Pozonanski Brothers's Grand Concerts, which they had presented earlier that year at Orme's Hall on 16 and 17 April. Assisted by Madame Varian Hoffman, "The Celebrated Prima Donna," I. R. Pozonanski played the piano and brother Joseph played the violin, performing musical fare reflecting the programs that had been popular for years. Madame Hoffman led off with the stirring "Involami" from Verdi's *Ernani* before moving to "Thou Art So Near and Yet So Far." Brother Joseph played the Introduction and Variations on the Barcarole from Donizetti's *L'elisire d'amore* , followed by Chopin's *Fantasie Impromptu* and [Thalberg's] *Souvenir d'Amerique*, before closing with a Grand Duo for Violin and Piano.[46]

The popularity of opera music continued throughout the decade. Only one month after the Strakosch performances the Grover Opera Troupe staged an operatic concert. The eight artists presented highlights from *William Tell, Robert le diable, Bellisario* (Donizetti), *Ernani,* and *Lucia*, closing with the Grand Garden Act of Gounod's *Faust.* March 1868 brought the arrival of the Grau German Opera Troupe, which planned three evenings of complete opera stagings, opening with Flotow's *Martha* followed by *Faust* (the third opera remained unannounced). Their travails during this visit demonstrated just how precarious the whole itinerant opera business could be. When a critical singer became ill, Grau found himself forced to change the program, which seemed odd as the company supposedly had forty-two members. However, gone was a complete operatic evening. In its place, the audience witnessed the overture and first act of *Martha*, the second act of the comic opera *Stradella*, Schubert's solo song "Der Wanderer," the grand overture from *Marseniella,* rounded out by the last act of *The Magic Flute.* The next evening proved even more strange in its operatic hodgepodge, even for an era that liked operatic stews concocted from left-overs. Grau presented, to what must have been bewildered listeners, the scenery from the first and second acts of *Fra Diavolo* in costume, an aria from *The Prophet*, the "Grand Scene" and duet from *The Merry Wives of Windsor,* and acts two and three from *Faust.* After all this, why is it not surprising that no record exists of the third evening? It likely never happened. Moreover, the absence of reviews for any of the music clearly suggests how the press viewed the whole affair.

By February 1870 Atlanta had enjoyed three additional operatic appearances. The McCulloch Opera Troupe featured its lead soprano Miss

MCulloch in *The Barber of Seville* and *Don Pasquale* in May 1868. She possessed dual attractions for her southern audiences: an excellent voice and a southern pedigree from her Charleston origins. Her two-night performance brought rave reviews. A year later in April Signor Brignoli, supported by five secondary vocal stars, gave two successful operatic concerts. In March 1870 he joined forces with McCulloch to form a Grand Italian Opera Company, which staged *Martha, Lucia di Lammermoor,* and *Il trovatore* for three successive nights. The company drew a "large and intelligent audience" which, in the sometimes puffered prose of the Atlanta press, "created a *furore*, and the excited audience again and again broke out in rounds of applause." Even though the listeners apparently enjoyed the operas, they refused to let Signor Brignoli leave until he sang "Goodbye, Sweetheart, Goodbye." Brignoli and McCulloch apparently performed well, but the paper expressed concern over the lack of a "single encore during the entire performance . . . . The very difficult pieces that often prohibit this opera from being performed were excellently done, but only minimal appreciation was shown."[47]

Given the travails of the preceding decade, it is amazing that Atlanta witnessed any full opera productions during the immediate post war years. With the advent of Reconstruction, the daunting civil, political, and overcrowding problems, and the general disarray of the overall social structure, it is a remarkable credit to the citizens that any concert activity flourished. It also demonstrates the tenacious popularity of the music. Italian opera, whether in concert or fully staged productions, continued to draw large audiences. While other types of entertainments in total were more frequent, opera held its own. In the five years since the war, six complete operas were presented in twenty-two performances: *Norma, Martha, Faust, Il trovatore, The Barber of Seville,* and *Don Pasquale.* Two companies presented different productions of the last three operas.[48]

As the 1860's ended, Atlanta, like much of the country, began seeing a gradual change in the world of stage and concert music. The large tent designated "musical/theatrical entertainment," under which for decades the whole mixed assortment of musical enterprises in America had lived comfortably together, began to rip and tear. No longer did a musical or dramatic evening at the theater automatically interest Americans from all walks of life. Opera, while not completely separated from popular culture, "like Shakespearean drama, was no longer part and parcel of the eclectic blend of culture that had characterized the United States." One sees this menacing rift raising some concerns in the contemporary Atlanta press. The reviewer above regretted the "minimal appreciation shown" to Signor Brignoli and Miss McCulloch by the audience. A year earlier in May 1868, hints had appeared as well. The *Daily New Era* was glad to see the McCulloch's two opera performances: "Coming at this time, when there has been a dearth so long of anything like higher class entertainments, it will be like a refreshing shower of *eau de cologne* upon the atmosphere too long surcharged with sooty particles of penetrating dust and the odor of unfragrant tan bark. Happily our community is sufficiently divided not to present a serious conflict between the higher and lower grades of public amusements." These few comments point to a radical transformation developing in America's cultural life. Atlanta, as the capital of the New South, rode the crest of this change.[49]

As it had for decades in the South, opera in Atlanta remained popular entertainment into the 1870's; its music likewise formed a central part of everyday culture. But in hindsight, one can see subtle indicators of its changing status. By the 1880's, musical entertainment would find itself essentially redefined. As Katherine Preston points out, culture would slowly devolve into two divided camps. Certain types of entertainment continued to perform as "popular"culture, while the remaining elements became Culture, i.e. not "popular." The theater, which had for more than half of the century provided an eclectic blend of entertainment, was no longer the one place where everyone went to be entertained, ready to enjoy whatever fare the evening held—opera, minstrel show, Shakespeare, melodrama, or concert. Now, different playhouses assumed specialized functions, presenting varied types of entertainments to separate segments of society. "Drama, dance, farce, acrobatics, melodrama, and opera increasingly were viewed as unrelated and separate. Music, which once had subsumed under its umbrella all sorts of widely divergent styles, likewise was divided into popular music and art music. It was vernacular or cultivated, but rarely both."[50]

This specialization of Atlanta theaters into those presenting "popular" entertainment and those aiming to uplift society by staging only high Culture was well under way before the turn of the 1870's. In 1867 Larkin H. Davis erected a large, more permanent theater on Broad Street to rival the Bell-Johnson Hall. With 1,600 seats, "long pine benches with back rests", and kerosene lamps on the walls, the $40,000 brick structure opened 25 February 1867 with acts by a gymnastic troupe. Competition from Bell-Johnson Hall caused Davis to remodel in September 1868. Following a popular run of Bullard's Panorama of New York in April, Davis's new playhouse burned, taking with it the owner's adjacent residence and businesses on Fosyth and Broad Streets. Not to be defeated, he hired thirty workmen to construct a new 1,100 seat theater on Pryor Street to open with the Young Men's Library Association benefit concert on 3 November. Unfortunately, the variety shows of questionable taste appearing after the first of the year soon proved very popular—to the dismay of the city's more refined element.[51]

As it happened, circumstances intervened to provide a house suitable for proper Cultural entertainments. A wealthy Belgian immigrant, Laurent DeGive, at the urging of some prominent personages, decided to complete the unfinished building at Marietta and Forsyth Streets and turn it into DeGive's Opera House. It opened 24 January 1870 with Bulwer's *Richelieu,* produced by an acting troupe from Selma, Alabama. *Constitution* editor Isaac W. Avery, a first night-attendee, approved, making it clear what he thought of the fare at Atlanta's *other* theaters: "We are glad to see legitimate drama again being enacted upon the boards of our Southern theaters . . . " he wrote."We heartily commend this theater to the good people of this city as a source of *refined* [italics author's] entertainment." Its 1,200- chair upholstered and sloped seating, arched acoustical ceiling, and modern gas lights controlled from the stage indeed proved a great boon to Atlanta's musical concert life.[52]

By this time, the city had several theaters, including the Pryor Street Theater (and later another Academy of Music/Varieties Theater here), the Decatur Street Varieties Theater, the Academy of Music (Varieties Theater) on Peachtree Street, another Varieties Theater in Kimbro's Hall, and the new Cole's Opera House. The availability of houses increased the number of local amateur dramatic troupes, including the Concordia Association, the Histrionics and Benevolent Society, the Gate City Dramatic Club, and the German Theater Company. But DeGive's House towered above them all. It immediately joined the "circuit" for the finest theatrical talent in the country. Undoubtedly the *Constitution* editor was gratified to see one of the hallowed names in American theater make an appearance before the year was out. Opening Monday 5 December 1870, Edwin Booth graced the footlights on five successive evenings in *Viriginius, Richelieu, Hamlet, King Lear,* and *Damon and Pythias.* Later, Lawrence Barrett starred in *Hamlet, Romeo & Juliet,* and *Julius Caesar* (February 1873). Atlanta could judge itself as having arrived when the "Divine Sarah" Bernhardt expired for the umteenth time in the last act of *Camille.* Other celebrated touring companies such as the Fifth Avenue Combination of New York Actors, Ada Gray's Combination, and the Oliver Doud Byron Troupe found a gracious welcome also.[53]

As the city became familiar with the house, complaints about lack of safety, poor ventilation and limited seating increased. To forestall outside investors from erecting a competing theater, DeGive closed the house in the summer of 1873 for renovation. Criticism changed to delight when the new patrons beheld the newly remodeled Opera House in October. With additional seats it could now hold 2,000 patrons in cushioned chairs staggered and sloped to remove any obstacles to viewing the stage. DeGive put more than $60,000 into new decorations as well, including a new drop curtain painted with a radiant copy of "The Golden Horn" by Jacob, frescoed walls and ceilings, and other opulent accoutrements.[54]

Unfortunately, theater goers in Atlanta did not always exhibit the genteel manners appropriate to Atlanta's rising social status. An editorial in the 23 January 1869 *Daily New Era* reproached audiences for their automatic applause, predictable calls for undeserved encores, and uncouth "pounding of boots and canes upon the floor, and hammering upon the benches, and hooting and shouting as if a young bedlam were turned loose upon the community." Perhaps in places with only men in the audience, it would be acceptable behavior, but it was completely inappropriate when "sensitive ladies" were present. It apparently was quite a problem for the more refined, who found the typical audience reaction "an abomination and a nuisance," as another critic complained. "Whooping, snorting, shrieking, groaning, whistling, stamping, grunting . . . and bellowing out applause is in no wise gratifying." Little did the writer realize that some things are just not going to go away. More than a century later the same things continue to irritate theater goers. And, just as predictably, the *Atlanta Constitution* continues to harp about it—with similar results.[55]

* * * * * * *

Performances of opera in Italian symbolized the cultural change occurring in American concert life. The increased size and quality of the Italian opera troupes that began touring widely in the 1860's exerted a beneficial influence on English opera companies, which subsequently found themselves forced to match the Italian groups in size and polish. This rise in quality resulted in audiences becoming more discerning and sophisticated. Moreover, during the late 1850's the Covent Garden Theater in London, which still exercised considerable influence on opera in America, was turning to English opera. These developments broadened the appeal of English opera in this country, just as Italian opera was increasingly regarded by American audiences as highbrow entertainment for a privileged elite. The activity of these traveling companies did much to establish the growth of an "English opera movement in the United States—a movement that espoused 'opera for the people'" and one that comprised a significant portion of operas performed in this country during the last half of the century.[56]

The result of this change meant that in Atlanta during the 1870's opera performances in Italian dwindled and all but disappeared. Italian opera troupes became even more scarce, replaced by a succession of English Opera Companies, who presented a few of the stock Italian favorites in English: *Il trovatore, Cinderella, La sonnambula,* and *La traviata.* Typical of these were the three November 1871 performances of Rossini's *Cinderella, or The Lover, The Lackey, and The Little Glass Slipper,* "with all the original music," by the Worrell Sisters, Sophie, Irene, and Jennie, assisted by various other cast members, including the Leon Brothers. In addition to the opera, they enriched the evening with songs, comedies, and the farce "The Fool of the Family." A few months later, one of the increasingly rare productions of opera in Italian was performed, when the Mariotti Italian Opera Troupe presented *Il trovatore* on Friday evening 29 March 1872. They concluded the performance with the first act of *Il barbiere di Siviglia.* So as not to overtax the audience, the company returned to English the next evening with *La traviata; or, The Estray.* By this time, opera offered as a popular musical entertainment for all classes of listeners had about run its course. It would live on in English adaptations and concert programs, but would not hold a secure place on America's dramatic stages again until the end of the century when it resurfaced as a "higher" form of art, detached from any other entertainment and aimed at more cultivated and exclusive audiences.[57]

As foreign-language opera departed from the realm of "popular"music and ascended towards High Culture, the entertainments that replaced it fell into two broad types: those comprised of unrelated songs, dances, and skits; and those whose musical numbers and spoken dialogue were held together by some thread of plot, bare though it may have been.

Minstrel and variety shows (vaudeville) increasingly took on a life of their own, maintaining their popularity into the end of the century and beyond. The variety or vaudeville show actually derived from the minstrel show, which first appeared in New York following the Civil War at Tony Pastor's Opera House in the Bowery. Pastor abandoned most of the blackface skits along with the minstrel show format and replaced them with a succession of various acts comprised of singing, comedy, acrobatics, dancing, and pantomime. It quickly became popular and soon spread throughout much of the country. Pastor couldn't keep it from acquiring the tone of morally questionable entertainment, however. As soon as the first Variety Theater appeared in Atlanta in November 1868, the *Constitution* was immediately critical: "The question is, shall such an institution, such an insult to public morals, be permitted to continue in this city?" The minstrel show, since it presented less objectionable fare, was more acceptable though it was not viewed as *helping* uplift community morals. Even when it increased the scope of its productions, included more polished singing and dancing, and lost many of its African conventions, its basic elements remained unchanged. Neither vaudeville nor the minstrel show aimed at any extended dramatic unity or anything approaching serious music, factors which kept them both on the periphery of American musical theater.[58]

Towards the end of the decade English operetta appeared. Eichberg's *The Doctor of Alcantara* was produced in August 1877 in what appears to have been the second local production in a month. The writer for the paper well understood the work's appeal. He rightly observed "the intricate beauties of classical music" which along with the "simple airs and striking stage effects" please those who are not sufficiently cultivated to appreciate "the higher and nobler excellencies," and yet desire entertainment above that of the common variety and minstrel show. In March 1879 a new wave of operetta evoked unbounded enthusiasm in Atlanta: Gilbert and Sullivan's *H.M.S. Pinafore*. *Pinafore* had premiered in New York the year before in 1878 and within just a few weeks was playing across the country. These works subsequently took their place at the forefront of the American musical stage for more than a decade. The Atlanta production by Bartley Campbell's Pinafore Company involved "thirty-two people in the troupe, with twenty-two well-trained voices in the chorus," played for three performances, and necessitated special excursion trains to bring the excited listeners from out of town. The work found productions by other types of companies as well, including minstrel and burlesque troupes and children's "operatic" companies. Ford's Juvenile Pinafore Company brought about forty children—none over eleven years old—to the city for a remarkable performance in October of that year.[59]

By this time, staged foreign-language opera had all but disappeared from the Atlanta theaters, largely eclipsed by productions of French and English operetta. Italian opera music persisted vigorously, though, in concert form. Through the end of the decade, serious musical concerts in Atlanta typically consisted of musical selections and adaptations from Italian opera. In fact, a minimum of fifty percent of the programs consistently originated in music for the operatic stage, whatever their respective format. These concerts reflected those of other southern cities such as Charleston, New Orleans, or Richmond during the decades preceding the Civil War. In this respect Atlanta, damaged, but not permanently, by the Civil War, was simply continuing the concert life prevalent throughout the ante bellum South that had been interrupted by the outbreak of hostilities in 1861.

Max Strakosch, having enjoyed an enthusiastic reception when his troupe inaugurated the Bell-Johnson Opera House in October 1868, once again toured in March 1870 to present Carlotta Patti in concert. Patti had returned to America after the Civil War. Strakosch's insistence (and the promise of considerable financial reward) finally lured her back to the United States for this tour. As with all the Patti sisters, her reputation drove the prices of tickets to an unheard-of $2.50 per seat. Contradictory reports make it difficult to verify whether she sang to full houses. Nevertheless, it must have been successful enough because Strakosch surfaces again in 1871 and then two years later with Carlotta in tow.[60]

The years immediately following the end of the war saw the establishment of Atlanta's first resident musical organizations. The Mozart Club was quite likely the first of these. Started just after the war, by 1867 it sought members for its weekly meetings. These meetings aimed to encourage "not only entertainment of a most pleasing character . . . but an enthusiasm in the culture of music, . . ." Only two years later, Atlanta's earliest significant musical association began meeting in the office of the railway agent at the Georgia Railroad Office on Alabama Street next to present-day Underground Atlanta. Another group, the Beethoven Society, met every Monday evening on the third floor of the new building, where two of the rooms were combined to form a suitable concert hall. The society attracted the most talented citizens of Atlanta and would present impressive musical programs for some years.[61]

The completion of DeGive's Opera House in December 1870 brought the number of Atlanta theaters and concert spaces up to at least five, and in a town of slightly over 20,000 inhabitants. Relieved at the rapid progress in putting the trauma of the war behind them, the citizens of Atlanta began to avail themselves of an increasing number of theatrical presentations, operas, and concerts. In fact, it seems that after the war musical life in the city almost sprang to life full blown, making up for the lean years. DeGive's housed two striking concerts within a week of each other in the spring of 1871.

First was a concert benefit for the First Methodist Episcopal Church, South. The program, which drew upon some of the strongest resident talent, was apparently directed by one Professor Freyer, a violinst, who appears frequently throughout concert bills during the 1870's. The performance Friday evening, 28 April (1871) included a mixture of opera selections interspersed with some of the most well-liked music of the era. In addition to the overtures from *Tancredi* and *The Caliph of Bagdad*, the group presented (among others) two selections from *La sonnambula,* including the Phantom Chorus ("When Daylight is Going"), a *Grand Galop de Concert* (Liszt?) for piano, a violin arrangement of *The Carnival of Venice* and "Speed Away" by the Atlanta Quartette, before closing with the "Soldier's Chorus" from *Faust.*[62]

On the following Monday evening, 1 May, Maurice Strakosch reappeared "to announce to the public of Atlanta and vicinity, that Mlle. Christina Nilsson will give, in this city, Her First and Only Concert." To support her, Strakosch brought along the vocal stars (once again) Signor Brignoli, tenor, and Signor Verger, baritone, as well as the now-famous veteran on the circuit, the violinist Henry Vieuxtemps. The group apparently performed with orchestral accompaniment as one Signor Bosoni is listed as music conductor. Nilsson (1843-1921) was a Swedish soprano who sang leading roles at the Theatre Lyrique and the Opera in Paris and Her Majesty's Theater, as well as Drury Lane in London, before embarking on her first American tour in 1870. The sheer brilliance, spacious flexibility, and perfect evenness of her voice enabled her to maintain her position as one of opera's leading divas for decades. Perhaps most notable for the United States was her role in the inaugural performance of *Faust* that opened New York's Metropolitan Opera in 1883.[63]

February of the next year, 1872, brought to Atlanta the most important musical entourage yet to visit the city, led by America's leading musician, Theodore Thomas (1835-1905). Born as the son of a German *Stadtmusikus*, Thomas came with his family to this country in 1845, settling in New York. As a violinist Thomas was soon playing in opera and theater orchestras before joining the Philharmonic Society in 1854. He first conducted his own concert on 13 May 1862 at Irving Hall, after which he assumed the conductorship of the Brooklyn Philharmonic. His Irving Hall Symphonic Soirees marked a milestone in symphonic programming in this country. In these concerts, Thomas championed the giants of German Romantic music: Beethoven, Schumann, Liszt, and Wagner, doing much to hasten their absorption into the mainstream of America's musical life. In 1869 the Theodore Thomas Orchestra began the first of many tours over the "Thomas Highway" of the United States and Canada. He indefatigably performed great symphonic music from Maine to Georgia, New Orleans to most of the midwest, and as far afield as San Francisco.

While the impact of Thomas's first visit on Atlanta's musical life will never be known, it certainly encouraged local participation. Concerts by local musicians increased, as did the quality and extent of their programs. Fostering this cultural activity was Atlanta's thriving economic life. The Financial Panic of 1873 slowed this vigorous growth only momentarily; it resumed full-speed in only a few years. With the completion of the Atlanta & Richmond Air-Line Railroad to Charlotte on 5 September 1873, Atlanta had five main-line railroads. In little over a decade the city had completely overtaken the south's tidewater cities both in business and cultural activity. Visitors to Atlanta remarked on the difference they observed between the Gate City and "Augusta, Savannah, Mobile, and the rest of the sleepy cotton markets, whose growth, if they have had any, is imperceptible."[64]

In 1872 alone Atlanta had more serious concert activity than any year since the war. The newly established Beethoven Society was flourishing with forty-five members and planned what was probably the first local musical series in Atlanta's history. For this they decided to offer to the public four grand concerts in addition to monthly soirees each year. Season tickets were six dollars apiece, or two tickets for ten dollars. Their First Grand Concert that summer with Miss Annie Simon went well enough, but many felt it was under par "because some of the men and women are North visiting." They opened the season as planned with a musical soiree in early September. Their concert in October, however, made it clear they were serious about their musical efforts. They were able to form an orchestra capable of executing operatic overtures, and a choral group able to sing challenging choral literature. On 29 October the society presented this program in their hall in the Georgia Railroad Depot:[65]

Part I

Overture, Orchestra
"Lo, the Morn on the Mountains"   Donizetti (Beethoven Society)
Cavatina, "Infelice"   Verdi
Quartette
Vengine Waltz, Song
"Home Sweet Home," Piano
"Strike the Band," Chorus   Verdi (Beethoven Society)

Part II

Overture, Orchestra	
Aria, "Regnava ne . . . "	Donizetti
Quartette. Prayer.	De Roude
Ballade	Goldnoven
Overture, Orchestra	
Chorus. "Hallelujah" *Mount of Olives*	Beethoven

In 1872 Ferdinand Wurm organized his orchestra, which consisted of the professor and his four sons on first violin, second violin, bass, clarinet, and cornet. Wurm was a German immigrant who had taught at the University of Munich before coming to the United States. For more than forty years Wurm's orchestra played for concerts as well as weddings and other public occasions in the city.[66]

The New Year of 1873 opened brilliantly, with Maurice Strakosch returning once more with Carlotta Patti. Her audience had not dwindled: "Who can resist her notes?" the *Constitution* queried. "Song, melodious, heart-thrilling song is simply the natural language of this great artiste." Locally, the Beethoven Society continued to take the lead in musical programs for the city. They were well aware of the dedication it involved, as they made clear in a statement in the *Constitution* "The interest in this organization is but in keeping with the growing importance and progress of our city... We are gratified at the honest endeavors of the members by their readily sacrificing so much valuable time, and their diligent joint effort, and their enthusiastically attended rehearsals, to build a musical organization." The orchestra, under the direction of Prof. Freyer, seemed to prosper from the accounts, drawing on the best of Atlanta's musical talent. Their program on 12 April not only shows skillful planning and balance, but fit well the choral and instrumental talents of the society. Overtures opened both parts, one by Bellini and one by Suppé. Likewise, two choral works with orchestra appeared in each part, the second closing with Haydn's "The Heavens Are Telling." A trio by Donizetti and a baritone solo by Flotow balanced the two instrumental works, one a flute and clarinet duet and one a violin solo by Professor Freyer. Though the concert quite likely was performed well, the *Constitution* undoubtedly exaggerated again by confidently declaring the singing "faultless" and that "no city exceeds Atlanta in musical talent."[67]

The Society started 1874 with forty voices in the chorus and fifteen instruments in the orchestra. By the time of their concert on 17 February they had increased to twenty players. From the evidence of their program, they seem to have grown musically as well.

Part I

Wedding March, Orchestra	Mendelssohn
Chorus & Orchestra, *Robert le Diable*	Meyerbeer
Trio, Piano, Violin and Violincello	Beethoven
Duet, *Norma*	Bellini
Duet (two pianos) *William Tell*	[Rossini] Arr. Ascher
Chorus "Ave Verum" Chorus & Orchestra	Mozart

Part II

"Krolls Ball Klange" (Waltzes)	Lumbye
Duet "Vieni al mio sen"	Arr. Millard
Grand Duo, Piano & Violin	
La Sonnambula	Bellini
Solo (soprano) "Venzano Waltz"	
Barber of Seville	Rossini
Solo Piano Scherzo Fantastique	Willmers
Solo and Chorus - Finale, Act 3, *Ernani*	Verdi

For their April Grand Concert the Beethoven Society was joined by the Mozart Society, all under the direction of Prof. F. L. Freyer. After the opening overture from *Norma*, a violin solo by Freyer called the *Railroad Gallop* brought sustained applause. The program closed with Haydn's "The Heavens Are Telling" which "completely enchanted the audience." Professor Freyer joined the Mozart Society in a May concert that the *Herald* called a "brilliant success." Italian opera still held sway as it did for the June concert. The program of twelve numbers began with the overture to *La muette de Portici*, vocal music by Bellini and Rossini, and the brilliant "Ah, forse lui" from *La traviata*. The reviewer for the fall concert in October declined to say much "for the high order of musical talent possessed by each member is well known to them." Freyer's Orchestra participated in the 8 December soiree of the Society as well, performing DeBeriot's *Second Violin Concerto*. Professor Gnospelius made his debut as the new musical director of the Society at this concert.[68]

DeGive's Opera House continued to be the showcase theater for Atlanta. Even so, it did not limit itself to only refined and proper entertainment. The Denier's Pantomime Troupe's produced *Humpty Dumpty* in February 1875. Apparently they structured it differently, and, reading between the lines, a little on the racy side, because the *Constitution* wrote that some aspects of the program were "not so acceptable." The Beethoven Society gave an orchestral concert at the Kimball House in April, closing their season. The year ended with the Adelaide Phillips Grand Italian Opera presenting *Martha* in December. The eleven soloists and "Full Company of Grand Chorus and Orchestra" rendered the opera "superbly," but it was Miss Phillips singing the "Rose Bush Song" between Acts One and Two that "will be long remembered here."[69]

By 1877 the Beethoven Society had articulated its purpose by publishing its goals. Implied here is the emerging moral function which music increasingly assumed as the century moved forward: "The objects and business of said Society will be to increase the musical knowledge of its members, and afford them a rational and improving recreation, and to foster a correct musical taste in this community." It was taken for granted by now that there is correct music, fit for refined and proper people. And conversely, "incorrect" music must exist as well, music that is to be avoided if the well-bred and cultivated artistic community is to prosper. This move towards an unsullied musical art is clearly evident on the Society's programs, such as the 13 February concert. Italian opera continues to dominate, with selections from Meyerbeer, Mercadante, and Rossini (two). What is clear is the purging of any kind of musical offerings that would appeal to the tastes of a wide range of listeners. This is why for the last decade the reviewers invariably describe the audience as "fashionable," "glittering," "elegant," or "refined." And just to make sure that everyone understood whose music had ascended that artistic Parnassus, there was a large suspended sign on the stage reading "Beethoven" surrounded on each side with the founding date of the society "1871."[70]

On 25 June 1876 the Rossini Club was organized and soon boasted more than seventy members. For its third program it presented *The Bohemian Girl* on 29 November 1876. One member later recalled: "The Rossini Club was a wonderful organization. Atlanta was a small town then and we lived closer to each other, in spirit . . . ." She recounted how the members had to walk to rehearsals as there were no streetcars yet, "we just went as best we could to any social affairs to which we were invited."[71]

In 1877 the first spring concert of The Atlanta Musical Institute, directed by Professor and Madame Schultze, was presented. Schultze also assumed leadership of the Beethoven Orchestra, which gave a concert in July. Two major concerts closed the season in May, one by the Brass Band of the 2d Regiment Infantry and one by the Rossini Club. The influence on both programs of the popular lyrical style of operatic music on concerts is apparent. Out of the two programs, there is music drawn from only three non-operatic composers: Schumann, Gibson, and Bousquet (see Appendix A). The Rossini Club must have been prospering because it presented its fourth production of *The Bohemian Girl* in July. The next month they moved into new rooms on the corner of Whtehall and Peters Streets in August, and in September staged Gilbert and Sullivan's *Cox and Box.*[72]

By the last year of the decade Atlanta had established a secure concert life involving a blend of resident musical performances by groups such as the Beethoven Society and the Rossini Club, in addition to touring musical groups. The Mendelssohn Quintette from Boston played in February and again in April. One unusual concert was offered by the Swedish Lady Quartette. Their performance in Cleveland had received rave reviews for the four women "without any accompaniment or ever a tuning fork to fix the key-note, blending like the chords of a delicately tuned instrument, and singing with a unity and precision that defy the most critical ear to catch a single false or discordant note." In March three of America's leading musicians traveled the circuit through Atlanta: pianists Madame Teresa Carreño, August Wilhelm, and Walter Damrosch, the first two for their second appearances. While the *Constitution* may have lapsed into hyperbole once again, it could indeed have been true that "Never were artists so warmly received or persistently encored as were Herr August Wilhem and Madame Teresa Carreño."[73] Carreño became a good friend of the Barilis.

Atlanta stood ready to move forward musically. She could not have had better luck than to welcome Alfredo Barili to the city the next year.

PHOTOGRAPHS

Santa Maria del Fiore in
Florence, Italy.

Ettore Barili.

Alfredo Barili,
about age four.

Alfredo Barili,
about age ten.

ALMAN & CO.,   172 5TH AVE., N. Y.

Alfredo Barili in his early twenties.

*Alfredo Barili
in his thirties.*

The Hasenclever house in Eringhausen, Germany.

Emily Vezin (Barili) as a young girl in Germany.

Emily Barili in her early twenties.

Emily Barili shortly after the move to Atlanta.

Emily Barili.

Charles Vezin, brother of Emily Barili, noted painter.

Fred Vezin, brother of Emily Barili and noted painter, and his wife Ida.

Barili family, from left to right: Louise, Emily, Mary Hudgins, Alfredo, Jr., Sister of Mary Hudgins, Julien, and Viola.

Viola and Alfredo Barili, II.

Alfredo Barili, II.   *Viola Barili.*

Louise Barili.

Adelina Patti: "To my darling Louise. In loving remembrance of Adelina Patti Cederström 1906".

Adelina Patti.

Caterina Chiesa Barili -Patti

Miniature of Alfredo Barili as a young man.

Miniature of Emily Barili as a young woman.

Barili and the
Polymnia Club,
1886 or 1887.

Gravestones - Westview Cemetery.

3 BEGINNINGS - THE FIRST DECADE

When Alfredo Barili moved to Atlanta in 1880 he already possessed an impressive reputation as a pianist. His success at the Cologne Conservatory had brought him serious attention as a musician, something that only increased following his return to this country. Reviews of his playing in Philadelphia identify him as a singularly gifted young performer. With his distinguished musical talent, honed by a rigorously thorough musical education, he was arguably one of the best trained and most outstanding pianists of the day. That he chose to bring that talent to Atlanta in 1880 was phenomenal.

Not that the city failed to embrace new talent. It was newcomers like Barili who had helped Atlanta make such spectacular strides in the fifteen years since the end of the war. During Barili's first ten years it would move forward even more rapidly—the 37,409 citizens that Barili joined in 1880 would nearly double to 65,533 by decade's end. Only the southern cities of New Orleans, Richmond, and Savannah would remain larger than Atlanta in 1890. More importantly, not long after Barili's arrival, Atlanta would become nationally recognized as the capitol of the New South and its leading commercial and industrial center.[1]

These changes have persuaded some historians to mark the year 1880 as a watershed in southern history—the beginnings of southern urbanization and the subsequent rise of a new middle class. Much of this change came from the growing numbers of talented people like Barili who moved to Atlanta. The economic growth and the vibrant spirit of the city magnetically attracted a new business elite, and the many opportunities served to keep them there. By the early 1880's, nearly sixty percent of the leaders in Atlanta were new arrivals, which meant that they had no ties to the city's ante bellum past. This new generation of leaders proved adept at mobilizing capital and production, which further accelerated the city's economic progress and laid the foundations for its spectacular growth in the twentieth century. As A. K. McClure observed in his 1886 work *The South*, "There is nothing of the Old South about it . . . . The young men are not the dawdling pale-faced, soft-handed effeminates which were so often visible in the nurslings of the slave . . . . They bear unmistakable signs of culture, but it is the culture that comes from self-reliance, and it is valued because it cost them sacrifice, invention, and effort."[2]

The spirited atmosphere and untapped social resources did much to draw Barili to Atlanta. Given his apparent asthma/respiratory problems, which forced him to leave the North, he realized that his health would be much stronger in a warmer southern climate with little industrial pollution. As the aspiring capitol of the New South, with a new middle class enthusiastically seeking to better its cultural life, the city would offer him much more opportunity than other southern cities, most of whom would not fully recover from the Civil War until well into the next century. As the year 1880 opened, Atlanta gained one of the country's most gifted young pianists as a new citizen.

* * * * * * *

Alfredo and Emily, expecting their second child, moved to 173 Peachtree when they arrived in 1880. Both began teaching music almost immediately at the Atlanta Female Institute where Mrs. Ballard was principal. Barili would continue to teach there for six years before opening his own school in the fall of 1887. Mrs. Ballard had opened the Atlanta Female Institute and College in 1865 with eight pupils. Soon enrollment had grown to forty, necessitating a move to the basement of the First Presbyterian Church. When the public school system was established in 1872, she closed her school and taught for the city until 1876 when she resumed her own private instruction. After a number of moves she finally settled in 1882 into a five-story brick building with fifty-three rooms at 143 Peachtree Street. The ten faculty members taught an impressive curriculum by any standards: literature, spherical trigonometry and conic sections, intellectual philosophy, astronomy, universal literature, Latin, French, composition, penmanship, and music. By 1883 Barili had eighty-three students in the music department.[3]

Alfredo Barili was surely the first thoroughly-trained professional musician to move to Atlanta. By 1880 the city had a number of musically inclined citizens, but none of Barili's stature. They had been active, but like so many amateur efforts, they lacked sustaining power. The heartening promise raised by the performances of the Beethoven and Rossini societies earlier had proven premature, for both had stumbled and fallen by the wayside. The *Constitution* in May 1882 expressed "a regret to look back a few years and remember the advancement which had been affected in the city in the direction of musical art culture, and then to see suddenly a break up of every organization, and to witness such a calm in musical matters." Other musical organizations had subsequently tried to get off the ground, but with little success. Four years earlier the newspaper had found encouraging a rumor of one club starting, so that listeners could for a brief while be "disengaged from the vulgar objects of a life, and our passions and our cares lulled to repose." In 1880 a musical society sprouted among the members of the First Methodist Church, only to prove likewise stillborn. Professor Schultze, the German violinist, provided a couple of programs in January and November that same year but left little impact on the city's concert life. Discouraged by the scarcity of musical life, he and his wife eventually returned to Europe. In June the school board debated whether or not to offer music in the public schools. This apparently had no effect on the broader musical life of the city.[4]

By 1883 little had changed. The paper again reported on rumors of another planned musical society, only this time the writer penned his exasperation with the situation and what appeared to be another exercise in musical folly. "Cannot Atlanta have a first class musical society?" he pleaded. "Petersburg, Richmond, Norfolk, Charleston, Augusta, Huntsville, Nashville and other southern cities, have large choral societies, giving series of concerts, and some of them operas." How can Atlanta boast of being the first city of the South and "fall back in this matter of art and culture?" The writer well realized that Atlanta depended on outside forces to sustain its concert life, which largely consisted of touring companies. Talent was not the city's problem; Atlanta had no dearth of that. Nor was this talent just amateurish, but musicians who "can sing at sight . . . can accompany a singer and a solo player, with correctness and propriety . . . as a science—as and in the same way as do composers and teachers." The problem lay elsewhere, mainly in the petty jealousies and self- serving agendas of those who had purported to walk the high artistic road in the now-defunct musical organizations. Inevitably, the lack of serious commitment to the musical goals had undermined every group. If Atlanta was to have a thriving and *enduring* resident concert life, then "money and place must not be the motive—

but those musically inclined and who are desirous to form a society should band together, lay aside every personal consideration and honestly and cordially go to work." In other words, the city needed committed professional musical leadership. They were in luck; they had one in their midst.[5]

Soon after his arrival, Barili introduced himself to the city musically with his first recital on Friday evening 30 April 1880 at the home of Mrs. Ballard. His programming reveals a shrewd assessment of his audience:[6]

Melody	Pergolesi-Joseffy
Valse E Minor	Chopin
Fantasie Lucia	List [sic]
Menuet	Boccherini-Joseffy
Scherzo, B flat Minor	Chopin
Nocturne	Alfredo Barili
Mazurka, No. 1	Barili
Spanish Serenade	Barili

The works Barili played, in contrast to his recital that next fall, suggest that he intentionally programmed on the light side to gain his audience's musical trust. Atlanta had quite likely never had a serious solo professional recital by anyone, much less a resident. As chapter two points out, the "grand concerts" presented by various touring companies consisted of operatic pot pourris interspersed with vocal numbers. Those glittering melodic variations alternating with popular solo songs left little time or room for listeners to grow restless. That Barili played entirely alone was remarkable enough; that he presented music composed originally for piano signaled a new era for the city's artistic life. Now Barili was raising the stakes by insisting that his audience focus intently on one genre of music without the diversions to which they had been accustomed. To assuage the increased seriousness of the evening he played music stylistically derived from the world of Italian opera. That this was planned carefully is suggested by his overt inclusion of a work (and subsequent absence as well) from the programs of the grand concert touring pianists, the *Lucia* Fantasie by Liszt (few in the nineteenth century seemed capable of spelling the virtuoso pianist's name correctly, from the printer of the program to numerous newspapers and journals). The Chopin and Pergolesi works also find their stylistic origins in the music of Italian opera. Finally, Barili confidently closed the evening by playing three of his own works.

The *Constitution* revealed rare musical insight in its assessment of his "too short program." It measured the man as well. In fact, with Barili, like any serious professional virtuoso, the performance mirrors the personality as the musician matures artistically. In its review, the *Constitution* acknowledged (remarkably free of the boosterism and puffery that mar so many reviews) that nothing approaching Barili's sense of interpretation had been heard for a long while in the city. His lack of musical posturing and pretense—lifelong traits that would endear him to so many audiences, students, and colleagues—showed him to be the "true, sincere artist" that he indeed was. His personal modesty extended to his music as well, keeping his playing free from "bombast and clap-trap"; moreover, he "needs no false puffing and boasting to establish his right as an artist," something almost anyone could hear. Even more, the "purity and simplicity" of his playing exactly fit the genteel elegance of his music. Finally, in spite of his youth—Barili was only twenty-six—"we predict for him a brilliant future should nothing cross his path to darken his already bright career."[7]

Within two weeks of his first recital in Atlanta, Emily gave birth to their first daughter to survive, Louise, on 13 May 1880. She would become the only musician among the children. As a young woman Louise would join Alfredo and Emily in the music school. Gradually, she became the archivist for the family, collecting and organizing the considerable materials related to her father's career. Her close relationship with her famous aunt Adelina Patti would provide an important link between two eras, lasting until Louise's death in 1963.

The next fall Barili challenged his listeners slightly more aggressively with his program of 4 November. Emily joined him in the opening duet by Berthold Tours—"a bright pleasing work, but of no special depth"—after which he introduced Atlanta to Beethoven piano sonatas with the Op. 7 work in E Flat. Barili chose well as this is a work from Beethoven's first period, a more direct and classic sonata that would not overwhelm his audience. The paper applauded the "grand work, never heard here before, and played by Mr. Barili in an earnest and artistic manner . . . ." In this way he gradually gained his audience's musical trust, so that when he added more daunting sonatas from the Viennese master's later periods, they would give them a similarly thorough hearing. He also performed three popular Chopin works—a nocturne, the *Fantasie Impromptu*, and the D-Flat waltz—before closing with his own *Cradle Song* and a "Valse Caprice" by Rubinstein. And is it just coincidence that the very same evening, 4 November, Professor Schultze gave a program as well, one including a Beethoven sonata? Or that a month later on 2 December Schultze celebrated the composer's birthday with an entire Beethoven program? Why after all these years of no reported Beethoven piano or chamber music, suddenly, do we find an eruption of his works? Would it be unkind to wonder if perhaps some found Barili's arrival if not threatening, then at least a stimulus for increased artistic efforts?[8]

The *Constitution* pointed out Atlanta's good fortune in finally attracting a "true artist, what our city has so long needed . . . a great acquisition to the musical world of Atlanta." Philadelphia took notice too. While the *Evening Bulletin* was pleased with his "great success," the *Item* realized his stature and regretted that "Philadelphia is deprived of his services." These accounts underscore two things. First, Barili's talent. From the very beginning, the reviews consistently point to Barili's uncommon musical ability. From the early reviews in New York, then Montgomery, to his early successes in Cologne and on through the enthusiasm that greeted his playing in Philadelphia, one reads again and again of his exceptional skill, artistic sensitivity, and musical distinction. His listeners realized they were hearing something unusual, which leads to the second point: pianists of Barili's ability in post-Civil War America were still exceedingly rare. Playing piano as a professional in this country was still in its infancy. It had taken firm hold in the decade before, but remained enough of a novelty as to evoke awe and excitement still. Barili stood at the forefront of its development.[9]

He probably also brought the first solidly professional piano and choral teaching to Atlanta. Music instruction had resumed following the war, with various musicians. A Mrs. Mary Madden and Professor Schultze apparently offered some worthwhile music lessons early on. Mr. G. P. Guilford played the organ at Second Baptist Church, taught organ, and served as an officer in the Beethoven Society. One Professor Otto Spahr charged $4 per month for four lessons in 1880. By contrast, Barili was getting up to $2 per lesson in 1885. This fee demonstrated the esteem with which many held him. Some students at the Institute later described the genial good humor that balanced the musical rigor of his teaching. "He had a mighty good disposition to put up with us all," one former student still remembered after more than fifty years. At times, his affable humor became even more entertaining, always within proper tastes, of course: "Remember how he used to get in a dark corner and run a comb through his hair to let us see the sparks fly?" she added.[10]

In 1882 Alfredo and his wife were blessed with the birth of their second daughter, Viola, on 30 April. She would inherit her father's love of performance, but in theatrics. As a young woman she would become quite active in portraying children in local entertainments and for a while would study in New York.

By 1882 Barili had hit full stride. He had proven his ability as a pianist and as a composer of quality. Now he stood ready to share his musical expertise. On 7 June the second musical evening at the Female Institute demonstrated to an "overwhelmingly large" audience the fruit of Barili's labors. Two of his better students opened the program with the challenging duet from Rossini's *William Tell* for piano. Later, the *Lucia* Fantasy reappeared, played by Carrie Matthews. Matthews would soon become one of Barili's most prominent students. To complete the program the young ladies sang and played various works from the popular solo vocal and piano repertoire of the day, including a song ("Creole Lover's Song") by one of America's most important young composers, Dudley Buck (1839-1909). Buck, who presided over the music program at the imposing Church of the Holy Trinity in Brooklyn, was emerging as America's most important organ and choral composer. His solo songs enjoyed considerable vogue in American concert life into this century. The audience would not leave that evening, however, until Barili played two of his own works for them.[11]

Atlanta papers sensed that Barili brought something new to his teaching; this was something unseen in the city before. As the *Evening Post* astutely pointed out, "Atlanta has had music teachers before, good, bad and indifferent. Prof. Barili is more." The "more" well summarized his remarkable talent, refined by years of rigorous training. But Barili brought more than musical excellence to his work. He had that mysterious gift possessed by the greatest teachers: unflagging inspiration combined with relentless persistence. This means that the teacher neither overwhelms the student by insisting that he or she perform at an unattainable level nor permits the student to become lazy and slipshod. No, distinguished teachers have that uncanny ability to maintain the right amount of tension between pushing and supporting. One unidentified clipping observed pointedly: "The effect of Prof. Barili's training shines in his pupils." They loved what they were doing. But, he insisted that they earn it; absent from even the youngest was the "amateurishness so naturally to be expected. Under this gentleman's tutorage music is not a mere accomplishment—it is an art." This is his finest compliment. The *Constitution* chimed in also: Barili's "success in Atlanta has been most gratifying, and he now deservedly ranks as one of the foremost musical instructors in the state."[12]

Later that year Barili clinched his title as Atlanta's leading musician with two more piano recitals. With these, he established the romantic piano concert tradition in the city. He boldly seized the highest ground by opening both evenings with Beethoven sonatas. On 16 December the audience heard the *Sonata pathétique* first; on 6 January 1883 they were greeted with the *Moonlight*. Barili probably also introduced Atlanta to another critical facet of serious concert life: program notes. He was at heart an educator, both as teacher and conductor. While he performed superbly, his personality did not seem to need the limelight in order to prosper. Rather, he delighted in the wonder of discovery and accomplishment shared with other musicians, whether students or choristers. Here at the beginning of his career, he started educating those in his audiences. He undoubtedly realized that not only were his listeners unfamiliar with much of the literature he played, they also possessed virtually no background for understanding such sophisticated music. By the addition of concise notes and definitions, he enabled his audience to put what they were hearing into a context. Barili's final two sentences reveal his German romantic training: "Of his many compositions, he reached the climax in his gigantic Sonata Work. The Beethoven piano—Sonata—should be to every pianist like a musical Bible."(Do we detect a little, perhaps more than a little, Robert Schumann here?)[13]

The evenings contained other works that had long since been routine concert fare in other places: Mendelssohn's *Songs Without Words, Variations sérieuses,* and *Rondo Capriccioso*; two Schumann piano miniatures, *Novelette* and *Fantasy Piece,* and a nocturne, etude, and valse by Chopin. Not to leave the audience with too-serious a musical taste, he and Emily concluded each evening with Moszkowski's *Spanish Dances,* Books I and II, respectively.

Barili moved out into the wider Atlanta community for his next concert. In March, the *Constitution* notified its readers about an upcoming program by the Young Men's Christian Association. The writer, reminding his readers that Atlanta has not had a serious resident choral group in some time, asks "Who does not recall with pleasure the beautiful singing of the Rossini, Bethoven [sic] and Mozart clubs." Whether the chorus organized itself independently and subsequently chose Barili to conduct, or whether he brought the group together is not clear.

Whatever its origins, Barili's extraordinary talent again elecited the best possible music from the group. First, he ensured steady musical support for the chorus by having Emily accompany. Her sure playing would carry the group through any rocky places. Then he augmented Atlanta's talent by adroitly inviting the leading contralto from the Cincinnati Conservatory, Ethel Crippen, to sing an aria from Rossini's *Semiramide.* (As a conductor myself, I would propose an even more astute reason behind Barili's inviting Miss Crippen to sing. On the surface it appeared that she came to sing a brilliant operatic aria in the best touring company tradition. One wonders, however, if his invitation did not contain an additional, unstated motive. By having her sing with the chorus as well, which I suspect Barili may have done, she could have functioned more importantly as the vocal pillar of a possibly weak alto section. In this way, Barili could ensure a balanced strength in all four sections, but without raising any ire about hiring outside ringers, to which Atlanta would have been particularly sensitive at this time. The finished product would have produced a strong choral tone while allowing the Atlanta chorus to feel pride in its own accomplishment.)[14]

Aside from musical talent, the most critical factor in the success of a musical concert is the programming. Add to this the necessity of educating his listeners on almost every front, and one quickly gets a picture of exactly how precarious the balance was that Barili sought. Too many weighty classical works would lose his audience. Conversely, a program filled with hackneyed, vapid, and musical bon bons would have delayed further his hope of bringing some substance into Atlanta's concert life. He had already shown his deft handling of repertoire in his own performances. Now he faced a more difficult challenge, one which he handled superbly, as the *Constitution* noted: "the programe [sic] was just long enough to furnish a variety of gems, and yet not to weary any one." He framed the program with choral numbers, opening with Barnby's "Sweet and Low," whose familiar style would catch everyone's attention, and he closed with Robert Schumann's energetic "Gypsy Life." He launched the second half of the program with a Dudley Buck work, sung by a local tenor, M. J. Goldsmith. For added variety, Barili performed the dazzling concert paraphrase on *Rigoletto* by "Listz" (sic; at least his music was being performed even if the press could not yet spell his name) between the opening choral number and Miss Crippen's cavatina. He symmetrically balanced the opening section in Part II, playing his own "Introduction and Polonaise" right before Schumann's closing choral piece.[15]

As expected, the Atlanta papers applauded the concert heartily, lauding Barili's "excellent style" in conducting and the accompanying by his "accomplished wife." More impressive, however, was the notice which *Music and Drama* of New York took, describing it as the most "meritorious local concert ever given in Atlanta." The writer laid the responsibility squarely at the feet of Barili "for the tasteful manner in which the programme was gotten up."

And, unlike most local concerts, "was just long enough to furnish a variety of gems, and yet not weary any one." The paper noted as well Barili's effortless performing demeanor during the taxing Liszt paraphrase (New York seems to have understood how to spell his name). It also pointed out Barili's "great merit as both composer and performer."[16]

* * * * * * *

Other concerts in Atlanta presented by touring companies had continued at about the same pace as the decade earlier, though the production of operas continued to decline in the 1880's. Laurent DeGive had remodeled the opera house extensively to encourage concert life in the city. He increased the seating by adding a second gallery, bringing the total capacity to 2,000, and enlarged the exits. The interior finish was enhanced with added gilded frescoes on the walls, along with new busts of Shakespeare and other authors to set a suitably dramatic tone for arriving audience members. DeGive spent a good amount of his own money (which he probably never recouped) to improve the house, something the paper noted and hoped would "be fully repaid by a generous patronage." The paper also predicted the greatest dramatic and operatic season yet in the city, one which did not quite come off. The Rive-King Grand Concert Company presented an evening with "A Complete Ensemble of Lyric Stars" on 29 November, but the next month the paper was commenting on the short season of Italian opera, consisting of only Donizetti's *La favorita* in December before the end of the year.[17]

The next year, 1881, saw little improvement. In January the Mendelssohn Quintet Club returned followed by the Grand English Opera Burlesque Company's production of *Carmen*. In March pianist Teresa Carreño, supported by a quartet of vocal stars, offered a double bill opening with an operatic concert followed by the grand opera *Il trovatore,* which surely did not include the complete dramatic work, but selections. That fall different operatic companies presented concerts of rather varied musical fare, from the minstrel level all the way to serious scenes from Italian opera.[18]

As if to compensate for the dearth of serious concert fare the previous year, 1882 proved to be a rich feast. It began with Adelina Patti making one of her visits to the city to sing a Grand Operatic Concert on Wednesday evening, 25 January. Patti had returned to this country in November of the previous year (1881) after a two-decade absence. On 9 November, assisted by her current liaison, tenor Ernest Nicolini, she gave her first American concert in more than twenty years at Steinway Hall in New York. Unfortunately the exorbitant seat prices of $10 affected the size of the audience. The company, under the management of Henry Abbey, departed for Philadelphia in December before moving on to Cincinnati, Louisville, and New Orleans where, "the house was simply full and running over from bottom to top, with tickets sold at $5 each."

By the time she appeared in Atlanta, Patti had ascended to her status as the world's most celebrated diva. She had conquered nearly every major opera house in the years since leaving New York, making her European debut at Covent Garden on 14 May 1861 as Amina in *La sonnambula*. The next year she sang at Brussels and the Hague as well as the Thèâtre-Italien in Paris. In the winter of 1865-66 she toured Italy, appearing at Florence, Bologna, Rome and Turin. By the end of the decade she had spent the entire winter in Russia at St. Petersburg and Moscow, had premiered *Aida* for London on 22 June 1876, and made her debut at La Scala on 3 November the next year in *La traviata*.[19]

Three days before her concert in Atlanta the *Constitution* ran a lengthy article by Alfredo's father Ettore Barili, describing his early years with his celebrated step sister, whom he had not seen since she was seventeen. With its vivacious descriptions of her childhood premiere in 1859 as *Lucia* and subsequent fame, the article did much to arouse enthusiasm for her appearance. It needed to. The price of tickets was double the usual prices—admission was $2 plus another $2 or $3 for reserved seats. The evening consisted of a Grand Operatic Concert for the first part, followed by the third act of *Faust*. Patti was supported by a vocal cast of seven, including Signor Nicolini and a Grand Orchestra under Signor d'Auria. While Alfredo is mentioned briefly in the article he is curiously absent from any other journalistic mention in connection with the concert, though the association obviously enhanced his already strong reputation. By the time Patti and company returned to New York in April they had given thirty-eight performances and cleared, according to Abbey, $175,000.[20]

Locally, things were improving only slightly. The paper the year before had pled for a musical organization to replace the departing Fifth Artillery Band. In February 1882 some efforts were moving in that direction; by May the paper informed its readers that "a musical society has been fully perfected in the city." With regret, one could remember the growth in musical culture in earlier years, only "to see suddenly a break up of every organization, and to witness such a calm in musical matters." Not only that, high-quality music had suffered as well since these groups "created a taste for the higher and better class of music . . . and stimulated many in the city." Later in May the paper gladly announced the formation of a "military band, a chorus and an orchestra" to be capitalized with $5,000 worth of stock at $5 per share. In June the group, named the Atlanta Musical Union, was chartered to form a "first-class" band and to "secure a first-class orchestra and with the hope of organizing a large and magnificent chorus" in order to present musical festivals.[21]

Concert life picked up considerably in 1883. Henry Abbey, Patti's manager, returned with Christine Nilsson together with the Boston Mendelssohn Quintet Club in one Grand Concert on Monday evening 15 January. In March the Charles Ford's English Opera Company presented Gilbert and Sullivan's *Iolanthe*. And in August an announcement ran about plans for what would be Atlanta's grandest concert yet. The directors of the Musical Union approved the circuit entertainments for the upcoming year, including the visits of two major orchestral companies, that of Carl Sentz in November and of Theodore Thomas and his "Unrivalled Symphony Orchestra of Sixty Distinguished Artists" in December. While the other companies would cost about $300, Thomas would need $2,000 as a guarantee.[22] Together these would offer Atlanta its finest symphonic concerts yet.

As the capitol of the New South, Atlanta excelled in many economic and commercial arenas. In the arts, though, she continued to lag behind, something that increasingly concerned the city's leaders by the 1880's. "If you will think of it you will see that we have done very little in the last two years to draw the people to the city," one prominent citizen, C. M. Cady, told a *Constitution* reporter in August 1883. "It is time we should wake up on this subject" and have the people of Atlanta offer "some great musical attractions in the course of the winter." It apparently took little sustained effort to convince others, for by December Atlanta would have its first music festival and a second visit by Theodore Thomas and his orchestra.[23]

Music festivals were not new to this country. The Handel and Haydn Society organized the first one in Boston in May 1856, with 600 singers and 78 in the orchestra. For the next one in May 1865 the chorus grew to 700 and the orchestra to 100. Others followed, culminating in the World's Peace Jubilee and the International Music Festival celebrating the end of the Franco-Prussian War. Its two-week Boston run opened on 17 June 1872 and included a chorus of 17,000 voices supported by an orchestra of 1,500. Not to be outdone, Chicago jumped in with its mammoth Jubilee the next year with Patrick Gilmore as manager. Cincinnati presented its own festival in May 1873, drawn from the numerous singing societies in the region, and presented works such as Beethoven's *Ninth Symphony*, Haydn's *Creation*, and Handel's *Messiah*. Two years later a second festival, designated as the Cincinnati May Festival, inaugurated the yearly festivals continuing to this day. The centennial year 1876 brought the Philadelphia Centennial Exhibition, which opened with a monster concert on 10 May 1876 in front of President Grant and some 100,000 persons in attendance listening to an enormous choir, huge orchestra, military bands, and organ. By the 1880's the festivals had caught on, with New York presenting it first on 2-6 May 1882 with a chorus of 3,000 and an orchestra of 300. The following year Pittsburgh, San Francisco, St. Louis, and other cities joined in, including Atlanta.[24]

It was the visit by a noted impresario that provided the catalyst Atlanta needed to take the plunge with her own festival. Herr August Doepp had successfully managed a music festival in Charleston the previous November and decided to broach the subject to Atlantans. When questioned about the risks of such a festival, he immediately squelched any doubts by bragging that he had "too much confidence in the public spirit and liberality of the people of Atlanta to apprehend a failure." How could a city that had become the capitol of the South walk away from his proposal "to make it the grandest affair of the kind ever held in Georgia. . . .?" It was decided to stage the festival on 15, 16, and 17 November with Carl Sentz and his orchestra from Philadelphia providing the instrumental music and Barili directing a 300-voice chorus comprised of Atlanta citizens and others from outside the city.[25]

One reporter attended a rehearsal about three weeks before the first concert and remarked on how pleased Barili looked with the sound of the 300 voices. The reporter "sat almost spellbound when the bridal chorus from Lohengrin was rendered . . ." Also present was Herr Doepp, who gave pep talks during breaks in the rehearsal. He warmed up the group by relating his initial skepticism for accomplishing such an expensive undertaking in Atlanta. He doubted at first whether the city was really up to the task, but soon the vigorous spirit of the Gate City sparked his interest in the project. Then, as he talked to more citizens his enthusiasm mounted. He described to his choral listeners the considerable expenses incurred in staging the festival and exactly how these costs were to be met while keeping the tickets at a reasonable price of $1.50 to $2.50 per performance. With mounting fervor Doepp closed by appealing to their "earnest sympathy and hearty cooperation," assuring them all of "the effect the festival will have in creating a new and vigorous interest in music."[26]

As performance week approached the *Constitution* went into overdrive, boosting the festival, the city, the players, the composers, and almost anyone within earshot of anything connected with the upcoming musical event. It became virtually impossible to pick up an issue that did not carry some comment, interview, announcement, or discussion about the festival. Nearly every mention of the festival paraded Barili's name as the chief helmsman of the whole enterprise. Typical is the article a week before opening night describing, yet one more time, how the 75 tenors, 50 contraltos, 50 sopranos, and who knows how many others are "under the masterly direction of Professor Alfredo Barili, who has gone into his work with great enthusiasm." The writer points to "the genuine surprise" awaiting music lovers who attend full rehearsals. This comment, which is typical of many during these years, suggests the genuinely high musical level on which Barili worked. Aware of the very modest artistic leadership so prevalent in much of the country, not to say across the South, people expressed gratified amazement at seeing such excellence in Atlanta. Even if one discounts the boosterism that plagued much of the reporting, the remarks about Barili's rehearsal style ring true at a distance of more than century to anyone who has ever sung or conducted choral music. His singers were inspired as well as respectful, responding to his sure gestures "before a dozen measures had been sung." Moreover, the instrumentalists likewise responded as quickly and alertly as the singers—a telling compliment, as few orchestral players *ever* enjoy performing under a choral conductor's direction. Barili's reputation by this time had spread to other southern cities as well. Augusta's *Evening News* thought even more of him than Atlanta, if that was possible. Not only was he a "refined and elegant gentleman," but he is "becoming by far the best musician ever known in the south . . . ." His reputation for gentle firmness in his teaching was known, as well as the devotion his pupils kept for him.[27]

Opening night Thursday 15 November brought citizens from all over the region to hear the Sentz orchestra, "Prince of Cornetists" Jules Levy, sopranos Letitia Fritch and Bessie Pierce, and of course the Music Festival Chorus. The repertoire of each of the five concerts, as well as the timing in holding off firing the biggest musical guns, bear the stamp of Barili's sure hand behind the scenes. The opening program was bounded on both ends by overtures, starting with Weber's *Jubel* Overture and closing with Rossini's rhythmically infectious curtain raiser for *William Tell.* In between, Miss Fritch sang an aria from Verdi's *Sicilian Vespers* and Balfe's *The Bohemian Girl,* Mr. Levy played the "Inflammatus est" from Rossini's *Stabat Mater* on the cornet, and Wallace's unsinkable overture to *Maritana* sailed across the musical horizon yet once again. Barili assumed the podium for the Grand March and chorus from *Tannhäuser* for festival chorus and orchestra, at the choice spot of any two-part concert, the opening of the second half (to unrelenting applause necessitating an immediate repeat). The refreshing first for Atlanta came in the presentation of Schubert's *Unfinished Symphony.* At last the musical leaders, Barili among them, felt that Atlanta was ready for serious symphonic literature.[28]

The subsequent four concerts generally showcased the same operatic repertoire, but the musical substance of the programs increased significantly (See Appendix A). Each of the remaining concerts presented an important symphonic work: Haydn's B-flat Symphony and String Serenade, Beethoven's Second and Fifth Symphonies, and Mendelssohn's *Reformation Symphony.* As astonishing as it may seem, each of these performances, along with the Schubert symphony, was apparently an Atlanta premiere. If this is the case (as it seems to be), five of the core works of the entire symphonic repertoire had their first complete Atlanta performances in this incredible three-day period. Few cities in this country or even Europe ever witnessed such a condensed introduction to a group of masterworks at one time. Of course Barili and Sentz sweetened the weighty fare by slipping in things like Mr. Levy rendering "The Lost Chord," a rousing polka, and an aria from *Il trovatore* on the cornet, Barili's Menuet arranged for orchestra, and overtures to *The Magic Flute, The Poet and Peasant,* and *Rienzi.* Part II of the closing concert on Saturday evening provided a dazzling finale for the festival. It opened with Barili as soloist for Ferdinand Hiller's electrifying Concerto in F-Sharp Minor for Piano and Orchestra (Andante and Finale). After Schumann's song "The Lotus Flower" Sentz led the orchestra in Beethoven's Second Symphony. Finally, the festival concluded with Barili leading what had become the *de facto* national anthem of America's choral societies, "The Heavens Are Telling" from Haydn's *Creation.*

The 1883 Atlanta Music Festival was a milestone in Atlanta's cultural history. No matter what ups-and-downs marked the city's concert life in the ensuing years, for the first time great music, performed on a thoroughly professional level, had been planned, executed, and supported with critical participation by local musicians led by a resident professional, Alfredo Barili. The festival also transformed the way in which Atlanta music lovers conceived serious music concerts. Repertoire for important music programs moved away from an eclectic mix of disparate musical genres and incompatible artistic styles. Symphony concerts now began, as a practice, to build their programs around the masterpieces of the orchestral repertoire, performed in their original scoring and in their entirety, shorn of arrangement and shabby interpolation. Gone as well were the chamber music insertions and works so slight as to be musically incongruous. In short, we see in Atlanta a new standard for musical excellence, one which carried with it a new respect for a body of great music chosen, played, and heard with respect and deference.

Choral-music performance also moved to a new level. Even if the paper exaggerated their number, encores seem to have stopped the concerts almost at every turn, delaying the close of the first evening until eleven-thirty. Repeatedly, "the audience was wild with excitement and applauded so vociferously that the whole chorus was repeated." In fact, after the first evening the management added choral numbers to each of the succeeding concerts in response to the overwhelming demand. Carl Sentz, the visiting conductor, "when he heard the rehearsal singing, openly expressed his surprise at the wonderful training and power evinced, and said he had never heard anything in Philadelphia to surpass it." This might contain a whisp of puffery, but the jist of it corresponds with all the other reviews. Barili's training, preparation, and careful, detailed rehersals not surprisingly produced a previously unattained level of choral excellence. Little wonder that the *Musical World*, published in New York, assured its readers that "No one is doing more to create a better demand for classical music in Atlanta than Prof. Alfredo Barili." Unfortunately, the festival concluded on a sour financial note; expenses exceeded income. Barili rescued it by securing twenty contributors to pay off the debts.[29]

The applause had barely died away when less than two weeks later Theodore Thomas and his orchestra arrived in Atlanta for another visit. But now his arrival was almost anti-climactic. The great conductor had traveled once again on the "Thomas Highway," but this time he brought only soloists and players to join with local choral groups. Choral activity in this country had increased tremendously since the Civil War. Nearly every city of any size had a group, and the larger towns had numerous ones, inevitably including some titled Beethoven or Mendelssohn societies or Apollo Clubs for male choruses. Thomas apparently felt local standards of performance had matured to the point where he could add his players and soloists to a resident chorus without fear of disaster.

Barili once again prepared the ninety-voice Musical Union for the two performances on 1 December 1883 at DeGive's Opera House. Interestingly enough, in his programming Thomas displayed less resolution than Barili and Sentz two weeks earlier. Absent from either Thomas concert is a complete symphonic work; only the Larghetto from Beethoven's Second and the Andante from his Sixth symphony appear (see Appendix A). He did present two more contemporary works in the *Les Préludes* by Liszt and Saint-Saëns's *Danse Macabre*. The Choral Union joined with the "Nuptial Chorus" and "Hail Bright

Abode" from *Lohengrin* to close the matinee performance. That evening they repeated the two major hits from the music festival, the "Gypsy Life" chorus by Schumann and the indestructible "Heavens Are Telling." During these two works Barili received what was probably the supreme honor of his life. To the audience's amazement and delight, when Thomas reached the choral parts of the program, he stepped aside and handed the baton to Barili to conduct. Even after Barili's reputation had spread throughout the South and the east coast, even after he had been honored by some of the most important journals and musicians in American musical life, even after the accolades he had received in Cologne, this probably was his finest hour. Thomas was renowned for his absolute, demanding autocracy, keeping exclusive control of the podium, brooking no interference or assistance from less talented musicians. That he entrusted *his* musicians, *his* reputation, and great music to Barili put a stamp on the young pianist that never faded. In fact, the glow from this event flickers to this day, even in the 1990's. While interviewing people interested in Barili's life, the story is inevitably recalled. Alfredo Barili had arrived.

* * * * * * *

During the mid-1880's, Atlanta's concert life — supplied as it was by touring companies — changed little. The various musical offerings had virtually stalled, with the same operatic companies merely rotating reliable operatic works. The Emma Abbott Grand English Opera, Grau's English Opera Company, and Ford's Opera Company all made return appearances. Abbot's company offered *Rigoletto* the first week in January 1884 and *Il trovatore* and *Ruy Blas* in February 1888. March and October 1884 saw an addition to Atlanta's stage repertoire with the *Queen's Lace Handkerchief* by Strauss, offered by a New York Comic Opera Company and Grau's English Opera Company respectively. Both groups brought sizeable performing troupes, including soloists, chorus, and orchestra for their three-performance run. Grau's also played Lecocq's effervescent favorite *The Little Duke* that same year. In November the year concluded with Ford's staging of *Girofle-Girofla* one night and *The Orange Girl* (an adaptation of *The Chimes of Normandy*) another. In April 1888 they returned with *Girofle-Girofla*.[30]

The first week of February 1889 saw Atlanta's first week-long operatic festival. While the production by the Emma Abbot Company established an important precedent, it was not as remarkable as it may seem. This festival was simply an extension of the three-day runs that had become standard by the

1880's. Her company had completed successful presentations to full houses in Chicago, in Los Angeles for nine days, and for a reported four-week engagement to capacity crowds in San Francisco. Opening Monday evening, 4 February, the Atlanta week included the following operas:[31]

Monday	*The Rose of Castile*
Tuesday	*The Yeomen of the Guard*
Wednesday matinee	*The Chimes of Normandy*
Wednesday evening	*Faust*
Thursday	*Norma*
Friday	*Il Trovatore*
Saturday matinee	*Martha*
Saturday evening	*Yeomen of the Guard*

The week of opera proved important in more ways than just length. It confirmed Atlanta's position as a cultural microcosm of the change occurring in classical music throughout the country, particularly opera. As demonstrated in the city, opera was well on its path of upward evolution towards "higher" Culture, where the works were presented in their entirety as sacred art to a select and cultivated audience. The *New York Times* critic W. J Henderson articulated this for higher society by insisting that opera—whole operas—be performed with taste and discrimination. It was too weighty, too elevated an art form to be chopped-up into excerpts and "popular" favorites for the uninformed masses who could neither appreciate the story nor the refined and delicate musical subtleties of an entire production. A final element that was not quite in place was the demand for operatic performance in the original tongue. For Atlanta, this would occur by the time the Metropolitan Opera was visiting the city annually in the early years of this century. By then, opera had become, in the words of Ronald Davis, "more a symbol of culture than a real cultural force," and the opera house "less a center of entertainment than a sacred source of cultural enlightenment."[32]

In Atlanta as elsewhere opera increasingly attracted socially elite audiences. As it moved away from including extraneous musical additions such as farces and plays, opera stopped appealing to all types of American audiences. The listeners were much more homogenous and socially conscious than they were a generation earlier. In the Atlanta *Constitution*, as in other parts of the country, operatic accounts now described audiences as filled with "very many of Atlanta's most prominent people, as well as many from other cities of

Georgia," or, "It was an audience such as Atlanta is noted for, embracing the wealth, the beauty and the intelligence of the capital city of Georgia. The boxes presented a scene to be remembered, with their theater parties of beautiful women and handsome men . . . ." The reviews of the week's opera, like those that would follow for more than a century, included detailed lists of the most important members of the audience from Atlanta society. Also in place were the numerous opera parties that would come to mark the glamour of opera week in Atlanta.[33]

There was one other important element in this transitional period for opera. By the final decade of the century, the operatic repertoire presented in Atlanta, like the rest of the country, had all but petrified. As represented by the Abbot Company's opera week, the practice of simply rotating tried-and-true favorites was becoming standard. With companies growing in size, expenses mounted as well; thus even one night's disaster could threaten financial ruin. The landscape was already littered with the debris of many troupes whose engagements had misfired, leaving them financially bereft and marooned in some remote location. To avoid this calamity, companies relied on works that had filled the house the year before—and the years before that. While one cannot blame the struggling troupes, it is disheartening to realize that before Verdi had even concluded his life's work—*Otello* and *Falstaff* were yet to come—his sacred trinity of *Il trovatore*, *Rigoletto*, and *La trvaviata* had already seized the stage, crowding out most of his other works. And if the operatic canon had not quite yet frozen, the temperature was falling rapidly. Granted, Verdi was not completely alone—he had Rossini, Donizetti, Bellini, and Gounod to help him keep warm. But the freezer door was closing rapidly, and only a few other occupants, such as Mozart, Puccini, Wagner, and Strauss would scurry in before it slammed shut. Unfortunately for our century, even the strongest efforts to pry it open and admit more contemporary members have largely proved futile.

Light opera had fallen into the same predictable rut, with the expected works like Balfe's *The Bohemian Girl* and *The Rose of Castile*, Flotow's *Martha*, French operetta, particularly Offenbach and Lecocq, and the Gilbert and Sullivan fare dominating the stage. *The Mikado* made its first appearance in Atlanta on 12 October 1885, introduced with a rather large cast of soloists and thirty-voice chorus by the Ford Opera Company. Emma Abbot mixed the genres when her company played once again in January 1886, offering *The Mikado* on a bill with *Il trovatore* and Donizetti's *Linda of Chamounix*.[34]

By 1886 a local orchestra had come together under the leadership of Professor Wurm. The group accompanied vocalists at DeGive's Opera House the evening of 15 October 1886 as a benefit for the organ fund at St. Philip's Church (now Cathedral). Similar to what would be played by an ochestral touring company, the program consisted mainly of orchestral works and assorted excerpts from the operatic repertoire, along with popular songs such as "Father in Heaven". The program also included music from Rossini (*La gazza ladra* overture), the "Pilgrim's Chorus" from *Tannhäuser*, and excerpts from *La vestale, Der Freischütz,* and the "Sanctus" from Gounod's popular *Messe solennelle.* Other Atlanta churches began to develop more active musical concert lives as well. Central Presbyterian Church presented Dudley Buck's celebrated *Te Deum* in E flat—by now a reigning sacred-music standard—to its morning worshippers in January 1886, along with selections from Handel's *Messiah.* First Methodist's Dime Club presented an entire concert the next month on Tuesday evening 14 February that drew together most of the eminent musicians of the city: Barili, Professor Dencke (piano), Professor Schultze (violin), and Mrs. Katzenberger (voice).[35]

In the spring of 1888 Atlanta had another musical first when Patrick Gilmore (1829-92) brought his celebrated band to town for a three-day jubilee. Born in Ireland, Gilmore had emigrated through Canada before assuming the directorship of the Boston Brigade Band in 1859. By 1862 his outstanding command of the twenty-fourth Massachusetts Regimental Band had earned him the appointment as director of bands for all of occupied Louisiana the next year. After the war he returned north and assumed leadership of the Twenty-Second Regimental Band of the New York Militia in 1873. Gilmore brought the level of band performance to new heights in this country during the following years. In 1878 he took his sixty-six players on tour of this country, Canada, and then Europe.[36]

By the time he arrived in Atlanta, Gilmore had become America's preeminent band director. The frenzy over his visit to Atlanta resembled that of modern-day rock concerts where the patrons camp-out the night before near the box office. The repertoire was designed to appeal to everyone, which it did. The marches, operatic excerpts, and fantasies on popular airs delighted Atlantans for three days, beginning Thursday evening 19 April. A mass chorus of 412 conducted by Sumner Salter joined Gilmore's group when needed. The opening night program was typical of their concerts. [37]

Overture, *Tannhäuser*	Wagner
Quartet for French Horns	
"Come Where My Love Lies Dreaming"	Foster
Scene and Aria, *Rigoletto*, "Caro nome"	Verdi
"Gloria", Twelfth Mass, Chorus and Band	Mozart
Song, "The Palm Branches"	Faure
Morceux de Salon, *Valse caprice*	Rubinstein
Song "My Queen"	Blumenthal
Cornet solo, "Remembrance of Switzerland"	Liberati
Overture, *William Tell*	Rossini
"Hail, Bright Abode," *Tannhäuser*	Wagner
Chorus and Band	
Grand Popular Selection	Baetens
Quartet, *Rigoletto*	Verdi
Grand Scene, *Il Trovatore*	Verdi

    Chorus and Gilmore's Band with Anvil and Artillery Accompaniment

* * * * * * *

By this time, Barili's reputation as a conductor and teacher had grown considerably since the Music Festival in 1883. The *Constitution*, some years after the event reminded its readers, "It was he who was mainly instrumental in making the first Atlanta music festival the great success that it was . . . an unqualified artistic triumph . . . ." He was easily the outstanding musician in the city, if not the entire region. Notwithstanding his prestige, however, when an Atlanta musical association was being formed in 1885, a "squabble" arose "over the selection of a director." Apparently, artistic jealousy reared its ugly head among some of Barili's musical colleagues. Of course everyone involved vehemently denied this. The problem supposedly centered around Barili's refusal to allow "the riff-raff to take part in the festival chorus." It seems that in order to avoid Barili's election, which would have resulted from an open vote of the entire group, the appointment was to be made by the Board of Directors, a majority of which opposed his election. The *Constitution* predicted that the association was about to ruin itself by choosing someone else to be director. The *Evening Capitol* reported what a "certain few" would rather do "than to thrive and not be controlled by their narrow ideas." The *Journal* pointed out that "his directorship would prove eminently beneficial to the association, and his appointment would meet with favor from the general public." The Board elected their candidate anyway, claiming that this was forced upon them "more by the divided opinion of the people than by the lack of fitness on the part of several of our musicians." Sumner Salter, a recent arrival in town and organist at the First Methodist Church, accepted the position as director. He seems to have been a competent director from the reports of his first two concerts with the Association on 11 March and 6 May 1886. For the second concert he led the group through the challenging *Stabat Mater* of Rossini.[38]

The Board's choice must have pained Barili, perhaps deeply. Because he was a very private person, we will probably never know. Barili brought to Atlanta the finest musical professionalism; he had worked tirelessly, and had been given a singular accolade from America's most important musician in front of the city's leading citizens. He had also seen to it that all the bills from the Festival were paid. To make things worse, the papers were clamoring for his appointment during the whole mortifying episode. What else could the association board want? Here was one of the most outstanding conductors anywhere, right in their midst, and they chose an organist for Atlanta's first important music appointment.

Barili's reaction reveals a great deal about him. His graciousness of spirit carried him above any signs of pettiness, and he refused to let the decision sour him. No bitter or mean words from him have *ever* surfaced. Nor did he petutantly retreat inside himself. His self-confidence was so thorough, so second nature, so effortless, that something like this, though disconcerting, failed to defeat him. He had made the decision to move to Atlanta after having lived in many of the major cities in the West; now he reaffirmed that decision. He would remain in Atlanta in spite of all this brouhaha, knowing full well what that entailed, and, simply put, do the best with what he found there. Rather than further fueling this dismaying division in Atlanta's small musical community, he decided to get to work and show the city exactly what he could do. If one group felt they could go forward without his leadership, he would offer his talents to others and move ahead with them. The result was that before 1886 ended he would make the most significant professional changes since moving to Atlanta.

Barili moved his family to larger quarters on Edgewood Avenue and continued teaching at the Female Institute. In addition, he continued to perform throughout Atlanta. He accompanied a group of the Atlanta Amateurs to Covington in November 1885 as part of a concert where he played his *Cradle Song,* which had become his most well-known piece; he also played regularly for Atlanta functions like the Art Club. Throughout all of his musical activities, on whatever scale, Barili shunned any blatant self-promotion. His life-long commitment was to music and beyond that he said and did little. His demeanor had earned him warm praise from many quarters. When the Young Men's Christian Organization wanted to form a sister musical organization in early 1886, they asked Barili to do it, which he did. The news community applauded him and unstintingly recognized him for his steadfast service to the musical community: "Like all of his work, it has been carried on steadily and efficiently without being thrust before the public." Or the *Sunday Telegram*: "Quietly and without display he has labored in this community, content to be recognized as a musician solely on whatever merit he possessed." The Polymnia Club gave its debut concert on Thursday evening 20 May 1886 at the Female Institute with thirty-three women in the chorus. Of course, Barili would have been anxious for this concert to shine. And apparently it did. His keen sense of musical programming and selection of performers carried the evening with flying colors. He had Emily accompany the chorus, whose selections were chosen to appeal to the audience. He also enlisted the help of Atlanta's three most prominent singers: Mrs. Katzenberger, soprano, Mr. Samuel Snow, baritone, and Mr. Goldsmith, tenor. To balance the lighter style of the choral works, he accompanied his finest student, Carrie Matthews, in the exhilarating opening movement of Beethoven's first piano concerto.[39]

The newspapers rushed to point out the justice of his success. The *Constitution*, in a rare moment of honest insight, admitted that their glowing report was, "by no means, fulsome praise." It went on to confess that concert life in Atlanta had had a rather hard time of it. The city, "as is well known, has not given that attention to musical matters the art deserves." The writer offered this concert as a call-to-arms to take notice of what musical treasure the city possessed. The Constitution had much support; at least six different reviews have been recovered regarding the Polymnia Club's premiere. The *Constitution* continued, "his work last night places him foremost among American's artists." The Beethoven concerto "was faultlessly rendered by Mr. Barili and Miss Matthews," whose "fame as a pianist is well known to the people of Atlanta, but last night she fairly eclipsed all her former efforts." The *Sunday Telegram* (23 May 1886) went even further; it claimed that the concert was one of the most polished programs ever given in the South, that "Mr. Barili is one of the strongest directors as well as finished musicians in the country" who "has worked quietly and diligently without politicking." One reviewer declined to comment on the performance for fear of undermining its dignity by "meaningless adjectives and phrases." The club's second concert the following December brought similarly positive reports.[40]

The Polymnia Club concert echoed the success which Barili had enjoyed three months earlier when he conducted a Grand Concert of Sacred Music at First Baptist Church on Friday evening, 5 March, to benefit the organ fund. He programmed two top-of-the-chart favorites of Victorian sacred music, Mendelssohn's *Hear My Prayer* and *The Prodigal Son* by Arthur Sullivan. The chorus and soloists sang well, demonstrating "excellent training," but even more impressively, "musical intelligence." In other words, Barili not only trained them *how* to sing the music, but he had led them to understand *what* they were singing. When one realizes that he was dealing with amateurs having modest musical backgrounds, at best, his achievement assumes an even more striking stature.[41]

The year was not yet half over and Barili's successes kept coming. Whatever distress he had felt a year earlier seems to have driven him inside himself, where he drew on his own inner resources. For the 9 June closing exercises at the Female Institute he again demonstrated his exceptional pianistic talent by performing Beethoven's Op. 27/2 (Moonlight) sonata, which not surprisingly became "the feature of the evening." He repeated the *Sonata pathétique* for the opening exercises the following September.[42] On the 28th of that month, the *Evening Capital* announced Barili's retirement from the Female Institute in order to form his own school of music. The paper rightly recognized it as "an epoch in our musical annals." Now, "we may look for Atlanta to become the musical center of the South . . . ." The *Sunday Telegram* seconded the move, asserting that a community can have no better influence than "high class music," and certainly no one was better qualified to direct it than Alfredo Barili.

The new school at 22 Church Street had as faculty Alfredo Barili, Emily Barili, and Carrie Matthews, teaching "Piano-forte," with "voice culture" taught by Alfredo and Mrs. Anna Werner; organ was taught by Mrs. J. P. Donnelly. Italian language and music theory were offered as well, and an orchestra was soon formed. The fees showed that Barili was serious about his new school:

20 vocal lessons	$30.00
20 piano lessons (A. Barili)	$30.00
(Emily Barili)	$20.00
(Carrie Matthews)	$15.00

Organ, per term $30.00
Music Theory
    Harmony, Counterpoint, Composition
    and Chorus, per term $ 2.50

There was no extra charge to regular students for history and theory class. Lessons missed because of student absences were not made up. Finally, the policy statement leaves little doubt as to where Barili stood musically: "The Director does not desire to retain in his School, pupils who are careless or indifferent. The term bill does not compensate for the annoyance of imperfect lessons." Clear here is the Barili family perfectionism. While it may have put some off, it made for musical excellence, in which Barili was unyielding. For Atlanta in 1886, this surely was an artistically (and financially) courageous position.[43]

About this same time Barili formed a piano club, not unlike a performance lab or seminar today in a music school. The girls—no male names have appeared in student listings in the surviving records—played for one another every other week, alternating with lectures by the young ladies on various composers. This enabled them to play for one another and to receive immediate feedback from Barili and others. In June 1887 the club presented its final recital of the season. A number of the young women appear to have achieved a serious level of ability given the ambitious pieces they attempted. Blakely Sharpe performed the challenging *Rondo Capriccioso* by Mendelssohn; Carrie Mathews played Moszkowski's *Fantasie Impromptu*; and Catherine Vertrees showed impressive musical courage with the daunting Ballade in G Minor by Chopin.[44]

Barili made one final move at this time when he assumed the position of musical instructor at the Washington Seminary. This was in addition to running his own music school. By the second year he already had a music class of seventy-five students. The students included some talented young women, such as Catherine Vertrees and Carrie Mathews. Their final concert in June 1888 at DeGive's drew an impressively large crowd, with the ground-floor orchestra filled and several hundred in the balcony. Barili cleverly programmed four of the young women in an eight-hand piece by Schubert. There must have been some quality playing that evening, even discounting for the *Constitution's* huffing and puffing. Given Barili's thoroughness and high standards, he would not have allowed them to program works he did not think they could perform well, which apparently they did. [45]

The next June (1889) the *Constitution* reviewed the closing recital of

Barili's School of Music at the Washington Seminary. Not surprisingly, everyone received favorable reviews. One young lady must have had a healthy amount of talent and technique to have handled Thalberg's difficult *Fantasy on L'elisire d'amore*, while the Schubert Impromptu demanded skill and poise.[46]

By this time, Alfredo Barili was increasingly being noticed for his teaching, something that would eventually eclipse everything else he did, including his playing and compositions. His reputation as a teacher lingers even today (1995), not just among those few students who survive, but also among those to whom they have talked. One can safely predict that remnants of his reputation will echo into the next century. Barili possessed those qualities that make a master teacher. The noted French teacher, Nadia Boulanger, made the same impact on her American students during the 1920's. These students subsequently revolutionized music in the United States when they returned home. Boulanger's location in Paris quickly brought her into an international field and gave her teaching worldwide recognition. Barili's net was cast much closer to home, restricting his influence mainly on students drawn from a region around Atlanta. Nevertheless, reports from students, colleagues, family, newspapers, and periodicals report the same kinds of musical enchantment with both Barili as with Nadia Boulanger.

Like Boulanger, Barili began his career as a pianist and composer. In both areas, he had superb training at one of the finest musical institutions of the day. This professional dualism provided him a two-fold insight into the music. As a pianist (and conductor), he had been forced to wrestle with the demands of performance. Only someone who has been thrust onto a stage and tackled a Beethoven sonata or Chopin etude knows what it takes to make music happen, how daunting it can be to cope with the notes racing by, the problems of chord voicing, the subtle gradations of tempo, the pedaling, and the shaping of the phrases all the while one tries to remember what comes next. No one can ever really explain everything involved in this mysterious activity. Words go only so far in describing it; beyond that they make little headway. The music becomes the language, the explanation itself. Instead of talking endlessly, Barili, like other master teachers, would calmly sit and play the passage, repeating it until the student could do it. Through this type of teaching, learning becomes a journey shared by teacher and student, not a dialectical lecture from on high.

Barili's other life as a composer endowed him with an entirely different type of musical knowledge. The task now changed from how to execute a completed piece to the *a priori* challenge of how to reassemble it, a vastly different issue. Having wrestled with the dismaying prospect of a blank piece of manuscript paper, Barili well understood what it took to imagine sounds, then put them into a notational shape so they could become living music. By then reversing this imaginative process—by studying the finished score—he could lead the student to understand how the sounds were put together, the different levels of construction, why the work made logical sense, and how to bring the music to life faithfully. All great teachers have some compositional-type insights. Even though they may never have put the first note to paper, they *know* what is going on in the score. This fact is evident throughout their own playing and their students' performances. This element is what the newspapers accounts are describing when they report that Barili's choral groups and students performed intelligently. He had helped them to understand what they were doing.

Great teachers possess another quality, a more personal one, something that allows them to connect on multiple levels with those they teach. Without the first, a musician may be a great performer, but be unable to impart this to someone else; without the second, the teacher becomes a therapist who can offer the student personal support, but not much musical insight. This does not mean that the teacher and student necessarily become fast friends. Rather, an exceptional teacher develops an intuitive awareness of the unique needs of each person. This sense enables the teacher to focus on the exceptional qualities of the student while working to remove the musical or technical blocks. This is why over a professional lifetime, a superior teacher can motivate students with widely varied backgrounds, skills, and problems. Simply put, teachers like Barili consistently brought out the best in a sucession of students, whether they were talented professionals or would always remain committed amateurs.

When he opened his own music school, people already knew of Barili's excellent and justly deserved reputation. One reviewer well understood his dual musical capacity: "He is happily possessed of two points of accomplishment in the musical art: he is an eminent pianist . . . besides being a scholarly musician in the ethics and perfection of the art." The *Evening Capitol:* "He is capable of the highest possible work. He has turned out some of the brightest pupils in the country, who typify his high school of teaching and illustrate his rare methods." His work with Carrie Matthews showed through the reports of her playing, as well as the excellent literature he guided her to: Bach, Schumann, Mendelssohn, Chopin, and Beethoven. Newspaper reports about performances at the piano club uncharacteristically avoided boosterism and calmly told what happened. Barili has teaching skills "that no other teacher has, and he is remarkably successful in imparting them to his pupils." The paper realized that his musical and personal abilities were "an unusual combination to find with uncommon power of performance and thorough capacity for communicating it." One pupil had recently returned from studying with a Mr. Mills in New York, who reportedly praised Barili by observing that "The lady had nothing to undo, and says that Mr. Barili is as a good a teacher as there is on the continent." He supposedly told the young lady that she could have saved herself a trip, "You did not need to come to me."[47]

Barili taught voice as well as piano, something that should surprise no one given the family into which he was born. Apparently his voice teaching prospered sometime after he started working in Atlanta. But when he finally presented a student the reports gleamed. One Miss Woods apparently sang very well for her debut, so much so, that the audience gave Barili an ovation on the spot. As with his piano and choral concerts, Barili's astute sense of programming did much to add to the evening's success. He guided his young charges to those composers who instinctively understood the voice and wrote well for it: Handel, Scarlatti, Rossini, Saint-Saëns, and the American songwriter Gilchrist. Looking at the program, one sees that Barili never missed a step. Again, the paper's report catches his masterful understanding of how the music was constructed and how to communicate that structure: "Her phrasing throughout was beautiful, and her introduction, development, and climax were always true and artistic." Another singer, Miss Bessie Rathbun, sang one of Barili's songs, with "a quiet repose and confidence in her work." Once more, Barili gave her the foundation essential to any successful singer: "She accomplishes vocal difficulties with the greatest apparent ease. Her fine breathing and phrasing were especially noticeable." After moving to Chicago she later wrote about his teaching, "Mr. Barili is so enthusiastic himself and inspires his pupils with such love for the great art of singing that he develops the greatest good in them and keeps them always on the highest plane. He seems to have the gift of awakening enthusiasm and a desire to work hard; and he is so thorough and painstaking and so careful not to overtax the delicate vocal organs that the merest drudgery becomes interesting and helpful." What finer praise could any teacher ever hear?[48]

There was some kind of magic in Barili's teaching; he did not just instruct, he inspired. Reports from all sides — newspapers, journals, programs, students, and family — all fumble trying to describe something indescribable: how this magic worked. After scanning these accounts one comes away with a faint sense of a magic that he somehow imparted to those that worked with him, a radiance that lingers to this day. The *Journal* left no doubt what it thought of his work, "But it is as a teacher, however, that he has won his principal success. He has turned out more good pianists than any other teacher in the south." The *Constitution,* for once, pointed to more reliable evidence of his work: "That he is an eminent teacher of the piano the long list of successful local pianists who have acquired both profit and honor from his instruction bear unmistakable testimony." Barili claimed that his greatest pleasure came from teaching. While he always thrilled at performing on the piano, he found deep satisfaction when sharing with a student the excitement of discovery, of finally seeing that "*yes* this is how the music happens, this is how I can bring it to life." Barili took great delight in this common experience of together producing something fine, something great, and something excellent.[49]

Accounts of lessons describe some of what made Barili the superb teacher he was. One former pupil remembered lessons during which "he was never anything but completely gracious and enthusiastic." Always dressed in a dark, pin-striped suit with a stiffly starched linen handkerchief in the pocket, he would listen patiently as the student played the work completely through before commenting. Then he would sit down on the bench and play the work, demonstrating how it should be done. His commitment to the music above everything else came first. "He was meticulous. He demanded that you do it right. He didn't care really how long it took, but you had to do it right, whatever his version of right was," another former student recounted. Lessons would last about fifty minutes if everything went well, "which it never did." He was gracious and generous if he thought the student was serious. "If he had something he wanted you to understand, which you obviously weren't getting, he would spend whatever time he thought was necessary." He never pushed unduly, nor became sarcastic or abusive. If the student failed to grasp the point, could not play the passage as he wanted, he simply resigned himself to it and went on. Neither did he insist on memorizing. It was much more important to play the music well then to memorize it mechanically.[50]

In 1888 the *Musical Courier* in New York noted the work he was doing. "As a pianist Mr. Barili possesses a brilliant technique and thoroughly musical touch, while his interpretations are always forcible and thoughtful." Of late, however, "he has devoted his attention to teaching and composing. He resides at present in Atlanta, Ga., where he has been since 1880, and where he has done no little work in elevating the standard of music, also being eminently successful in teaching both piano and voice."[51]

By the end of the century his reputation would spread beyond the South. W. S. B. Mathews's *Music*, a Chicago monthly, ran an extended article (1897) on his work, which "owing to his extreme modesty and dislike of publicity" was comparatively little known, "but his gifts as a composer, pianist, and teacher entitle him to a place in the first rank of the musicians of to-day; not only in America, but also in Europe." The writer recounts his history up to the founding of the school of music, "which is the only school of its kind in the South," a remarkable statement. As accounts attest, his teaching "is so thorough and conscientious that he always inspires and brings out the very best there is in a pupil. They all adore him, and no one who has ever studied with the 'little master,' as he is affectionately called by those who know him best, has anything but praise for him." The writer argues that "In the South he has done more than anyone else to promote the best interests of music."[52] Details aside, what impresses the reader are the consistent threads running through all the reports about Barili's teaching: his kindness, gentleness, support, combined with an unrelenting commitment to the music, thoroughness, and inspiration.

Family matters changed during the middle years of the decade. Barili's father Ettore died on 19 November 1885 at the age of fifty seven in Philadelphia, where he had lived for twenty years, teaching voice and conducting the choir at St. John's Church. His life was widely praised in numerous journals, including notices in New York, Philadelphia, Atlanta, Brussels, and Paris. As the *Constitution* poignantly pointed out, he was "the Rigoletto of twenty-five years ago." He would also be remembered as the instructor of Adelina Patti. Alfredo traveled to Philadelphia for the funeral, where he played the Funeral March from Chopin's Sonata in B Minor. Ettore was survived by his wife and three sons. Enrico, the oldest, was connected with the Philadelphia conservatory, and Armando was still a voice student. At some point after this, Antoinetta Barili apparently moved to Atlanta and lived with Alfredo and his family as she is buried in Westview Cemetery.[53]

Two years later, on 31 July 1887, Barili's only son, Alfredo Barili, Jr. was born. Young Barili inherited talent, but from his mother's side, which included artistic gifts, as evidenced by her two brothers, Charles and Frederic. After studying fine arts for two years at Columbia University, Barili, Jr. returned to Atlanta and became an architect and member of the American Institute of Architecture. In 1937 he opened his own architectural firm of Barili and Humphreys, which would design important Atlanta structures such as the new Post Office, Haygood Memorial Methodist Church, and the Federal Reserve Bank. He married Mary Hudgins and they had three children, Alfredo Barili, III, Mary Barili [Goldsmith], and Ann Emily Barili [Carmichael]. He died on 23 March 1957.

* * * * * * *

By the end of the 1880's Barili had become the most prominent musician in the Southeast. His work in Atlanta began bringing him national attention as well. An article in the 21 March 1888 issue of the New York *Musical Courier*, one of the leading contemporary music journals, commented on his work. After a brief biographical summary, the writer concisely summarized the ingredients of Barili's professional success: "As a pianist, Mr. Barili possesses a brilliant technic [sic] and a thoroughly musical touch, while his interpretations are always forcible and thoughtful. His repertory is large, although of late years he has devoted his attention to teaching and composing." Also noticed is his work with the Polymnia Club, which after "his unremitting labor and gentlemanly bearing has accomplished great results."

These comments, which only serve to typify the many that would come his way for the next two decades, reveal the impressive way in which Barili handled the disappointment following the absurd outcome of the Choral Union directorship. Instead of letting it set him back, as it well could have, he paused only briefly, then recommitted himself to the musical task at hand and moved towards a new plane of professional activity. As a pianist he had demonstrated his incomparable skill. He not only played on a level rarely heard in the city, he also introduced Atlanta to major works from the keyboard repertoire, most importantly Beethoven sonatas. As a conductor, nothing could eclipse his experience with Thomas. Even so, concerts with the Polymnia Club continued to elicit enthusiastic receptions. His music school continued to prosper, attracting the most talented students from the area. Finally, he enjoyed increasing recognition as a composer.

Barili had studied composition in Cologne, and after returning to Philadelphia began work in earnest as a composer (for a list of his compositions see Appendix C). His father had been a model for him here as in so many other musical endeavors. Ettore had composed *The Carlotta Waltz* in 1869 (G. Andre & Co., Philadelphia) for his famous sister. After Alfredo returned from Europe, he followed in his father's steps and took up his pen in 1876, writing the first extant work we have, the song "Pass'd Away" Op. 4 (A. H. Rosewig, Philadelphia). Shortly after his move to Atlanta he produced his most famous piece, the *Cradle Song* Op. 18 (1881, Atlanta, Phillips & Crew), which would go through twenty-six editions and reportedly sell more than a quarter million copies. Had he written nothing more, this single piece, which does not strike the listener as more exceptional than some of his other works, would have ensured his prominence for decades. But somehow the timing was just right, as happens almost capriciously with certain works, and it became popular.

The *Cradle Song* typifies Barili's overall musical output, which consists of parlor songs and piano pieces in that tradition of sentimental expression and genteel emotionalism that proved so popular among Victorian Americans. Such pieces fed the growing appetite for music in the United States. By mid-century all but the meanest homes could afford a piano. Increased output continued to lower the prices on new instruments to as low as $300, often available on convenient installment plans. American piano builders such as Alpheus Babcock, Jonas Chickering, and Henry Steinway were among the manufacturers, producing more than 20,000 pianos a year by the time of Civil War, for a population of 31,000,000. Moreover, piano music had been central to American music publishing, rivaled in quantity only by songs, which nearly always had piano accompaniment.[54]

After the Civil War, piano music by composers in the United States reflected the European "cultivated tradition" that they had acquired during their study abroad. Virtually every serious American musician, Barili among them, had migrated to Europe (mostly to Germany) where they had been immersed in the music of early German Romanticism, principally that of Beethoven, Schubert, Mendelssohn, and Schumann. When they returned, composers such as Barili, John Knowles Paine, Dudley Buck, George W. Chadwick, Horatio Parker, and Arthur Foote confidently and *successfully* transplanted to these shores the styles and forms of the music with which they were comfortable. Even after becoming established, they made little attempt to find a national identity in their music. Many scholars in the twentieth century later came to criticize them for it, belittling their music as a "academic" and "Victorian" in the worst way. Their music was glibly dismissed as effete and overly sentimental, lacking innovation and substance. These Victorian composers were not alone in being rejected, however. The same fate befell the American visual artists of the period. The New York artists and critics of the post-World War I era smugly "relegated the Bostonians to the winds . . . . They were ridiculed for their cult of beauty and condemned for the knowledgeable workmanship which a rising generation of art students was being taught to despise as academic. Sneered at as the Genteel School by a new group of art writers . . . the Boston painters were shoved into temporary oblivion."[55]

Upon reflection, it should not surprise us that composers such as Barili looked to European models for their musical styles. "The fact that the composers of Paine's generation and those immediately following him did not discover typically American paths is no cause for wonderment," observed composer

Howard Hanson. "Their inspiration, their musical sustenance, was drawn almost entirely from Europe. The United States of that period had little to offer them from the musical standpoint in the ways of encouragement or assistance. The path of the pioneer . . . is a difficult one . . . ." These composers were working in a vacuum with no artistic guides to follow. Moreover, American audiences had few artistic reference points from which to appreciate any music except the simplest ballads and psalm tunes. "Aesthetic appreciation—that is, the quality that permits an artistic experience to be received and enjoyed as such— was almost entirely lacking," as Gilbert Chase points out. As Atlanta in the 1880's more resembled a rough frontier town than the settled cities of the northeast, audiences here would simply not have understood music more complicated or avant garde.[56]

Barili's keyboard compositions enjoyed broad appeal because they resided firmly in the mainstream of the "cultivated tradition." The abstract titles like "Danse Caprice," "Gavotte," "Moment Musical," and "Mazurka" show his indebtedness to German models with their emotional restraint and close adherence to formal structures. As John Knowles Paine argued in his inaugural lecture for the Music Department at Boston University in 1872, "What is lost in subjective expression is compensated for by architectural beauty of form. The highest aim of art is to avoid extremes; to unite the individual and the general . . . ." Throughout his works, Barili exercised moderation in an effort to keep his music within the "proper" bounds that his listeners expected. He scrupulously avoided dissonance except for melodic coloring. Out of fifty-seven measures in the *Cradle Song*, only twelve contain any chromatic notes at all; only one of those is a tertian-related chromatic chord, and the others are used as secondary dominants. The elegantly rising melodic phrases in four-measure periods above gently rocking figures in the left hand reinforce the overall feeling of calm repose in a child's sleep. The simple technical demands put the piece within the ability of all but the most elementary of pianists.[57]

Barili, like most of his fellow composers, found these German romantic musical styles eminently suitable for their music. Audiences of the day did not find the styles of Beethoven, Schubert, Mendelssohn, and Schumann exhausted. On the contrary, they contained a vitality for the American works modeled on them. For nineteenth-century listeners these inherited techniques, as used in the *Cradle Song* for example, were still new and fresh. These factors made the music immediately accessible to Barili's audiences, who found comfort and artistic merit in the music's gentle naivete. While today many musicians discount any art-music with a familiar mood as derivative and imitative, the Victorians found it fundamental to their enjoyment of a piece. Conformity and respectability were the finest compliments one could bestow on a work. Understanding all of this does much to explain the popularity of Barili's music, which the *Constitution* claimed was played from "Maine to California."

Barili's works evoked enthusiastic responses from other quarters as well. The *Christian Index* (Baptist) reviewed the *Cradle Song*, noting its power to move the listener, as its theme "so rich in tender associations, so potent in its power to stir the heart with subtle influence of hope and love and peace, is developed with the success which can only come alone by the conscientious observance of classic art rules, so frequently violated now-a-days by the glaring and flashy trumpery of musical quacks." The writer assured those readers who "abominate the sensational" and who possess pure taste in music will be delighted with the piece. Moreover, any "who feel that a dew drop distilled from the very heart of melody is worth an ocean of ranting, unmusical phrases, and of rhapsodic, meaningless sound," will also be moved.[58]

Charles Wilkinson in his *Well-Known Piano Solos and How to Play Them* (1924) took three pages to discuss the work. He calls the *Cradle Song* a genuine lullaby. "And it is music to the core, music of the kind of Italian type in which melody everywhere predominates. Technically not beyond the fourth grade, it nevertheless calls for genuine musicianship for its proper interpretation." He concludes the long essay by declaring that "If much space has been given this unpretentious morceau, it is because in it there is much meat for the nourishment of a refined taste for music of the best type."[59]

The *Cradle Song* appeared in a format other than print. Years after the invention of the phonograph it still sounded rough and crude. Thus the most reliable method of reproducing music was the player piano—a sophisticated device that expressively repeated performances of famous pianists through a system of piano roles. The Aeolian Company, which owned the Duo-Art reproducing system, hired pianist Hugh Hodgson (head of the University of Georgia music department for many years) to record the *Cradle Song*, much increasing its appeal.[60]

The *Musical Courier* lauded Barili's *Gavotte* as an excellent piece for a young pianist, easily fitting the reach of small hands, but without sacrificing musical integrity, "There is no sense of want of connection, or scrappiness, or childishness, or that aggravating monotony resulting from a constant succession of short phrases of the same length that make the music of quadrilles and some comic operas so extremely tiresome . . . ." The writer correctly recognized that

Barili's music succeeded on the level that he aimed for, and succeeded well.[61]

Barili's seven songs enjoyed some success, though not on the level of his piano works. Like his piano music, they are firmly in the European tradition that also forged the "serious" songs of Dudley Buck, John Knowles Paine, John Hill Hewitt, George Chadwick, Horatio Parker, Arthur Foote, and many others who wrote American art songs in the last quarter of the nineteenth century. Together with these works, Barili's maintained a middle ground between art music and popular song, in both the sentiments of their texts and as their musical styles.[62]

Barili's songs were part of the popularity that the parlor song enjoyed in the years following the Civil War. Improvements in printing technology and lithography had lowered prices to within the reach of most Americans. Before the advent of recorded sound or the freedom brought by the automobile, music was American's favorite pastime—at home, church, picnics, civic meetings, funerals, and weddings. Americans from all walks of life sang, almost everywhere. Virtually every home had a musical instrument, if not a piano. Americans who traveled assumed the parlor of their hotels would have a piano which could be used to entertain the guests after dinner. Moreover, in genteel society it became the mark of good breeding to join in the singing. To encourage this, journals printed advice for their readers to help them choose "favorite" and "fashionable" songs. The *Boston Euterpeiad* assured its readers that skill in music was "an indispensable requisite," especially for young women. Young men, likewise, could show their cultivated manners with a fine singing voice.[63]

These songs may strike us today as artificial or contrived, but for years they comprised the mainstream of American popular music. Indeed, if we feel them to be shamelessly sentimental and emotionally saccharine, they are. But these are the very factors that accounted for their success. Had their imagery been more subtle and less sentimental, it would not have worked. In an era where public display of emotion was discouraged, these songs played a vital role in allowing the listener, moved by the song, to give vent to his inner feelings in a socially approved manner. "They allowed the soul to breathe." The moving words and touching melody often moved people to tears, an accepted sign of release, providing a needed outlet for the powerful suppressed emotions. The generally melancholy and nostalgic texts encouraged weeping, reminding the listener of former, happier times surrounded by loved ones. The artistic release also confirmed the idea that suffering does have a purpose, that it ennobles the sufferer. If one will only endure with his head held high, he will become stronger in the face of adversity and emerge more able to face life with new strength, hope, and serenity.[64]

Given the harshness of nineteenth-century life, it is not surprising to find the theme of these songs to be that of loss, expressed through subjects such as sentimental love, home, parting, nostalgic yearning, lost childhoods, or even death. Placed in contrast with loss was the image of a distant past earnestly believed to have been blissfully happy. The tension created by these dually juxtaposed images produces the bittersweet nostalgia pervasive throughout the songs. A marvelously poignant example comes from lyrics by H. Avery in his song "Ah! Sing Again":[65]

> Sing of the past,
> When all the joyous dreams of youth now gone
> Their brightest pictures cast
> Around our hearts while bidding us speed on;
> Yet though these scenes have fled, love,
> And those bright days are now forever flown,
> Still by thy sweet song led,
> Again those happy years seem all my own.

The words for Barili's "There Little Girl Don't Cry" Op. 29/1 (Phillips & Crew, 1897), penned by James Whitcomb Riley (1849-1916), point in both directions: backwards to a remembered past of happy childhood times, and forward to a future where heartaches will be assuaged by heaven's bliss. Along the way, Riley manages to evoke nearly every sweetly- painful image typical of the Victorian parlor song, finally assuring the desolate young girl that all her cherished hopes, now vanished, would be restored in heaven:

> There little girl don't cry! They have broken your doll I know;
> And your tea set blue, And your play house too,
> Are things of the long ago,
> But childish troubles will soon pass by.
> There little girl don't cry.

> There little girl don't cry, They have broken your slate, I know
> And the glad wild ways of your school girl days
> Are things of the long ago,
> But life and love will soon come by,

There little girl don't cry.

There little girl don't cry, They have broken your heart I know;
And the rainbow gleams of your youthful dreams
Are things of the long ago,
But heav'n holds all for which you sigh,
There little girl don't cry.

Musically, the song fits the expected styles of the day. Set in a duple
meter, the melodic phrases, cast into eight-measure units so as to comfortably
fit the poetic structure, are harmonized by primary chords. The vocal line moves
in a lyrical contour, avoiding difficult melodic intervals. Uncomplicated
rhythmic patterns reinforce the metric stress of the text, while the piano supports
the voice with repeated chords.

* * * * * * *

As Barili's music found a growing audience, it brought increased respect
for him in national musical circles. James Huneker, an important music critic
and essayist, as well as boyhood friend of Barili, wrote for the *Etude* in the
1880's. His reputation spread largely through his work as a columnist ("The
Raconteur") for the *Musical Courier* (1889-1902). After serving successively
as music critic, drama critic, art critic, and general critic for the *New York Sun*
(1900-17), he was music critic for the *Philadelphia Press* (1917-18), the *New
York Times* (1918-19), and the *New York World* (from 1919). In 1886 he
corresponded with Barili, "I would be proud if you dedicated the Polonaise to
me [Barili did dedicate his *Danse Caprice*, Op. 23, to Huneker]. Please tell
Phillips & Crew to send The Etude all of your compositions and the gavotte
and valse you wrote a year ago. I will review that whole of them in a separate
article." The next year he reminded his friend, "Now Alfred whatever you can
send me I will review but I particularly want that Polonaise! Have you published
it? I will give it a good notice." As the century wore on, other leading publications
such as the *Musical Courier* and the *Saturday Review* also took notice of Barili.[66]

Barili's choral conducting with the Polymnia Club only added to his
growing reputation. In January 1887 the touring Mendelssohn Quintette Club
of Boston joined the group for a concert on Friday evening, 21 January at
DeGive's Opera House. The Quintette performed two chamber works, possibly
for their first time in Atlanta: the Mendelssohn Quintette in B flat, Op. 87, and

Beethoven's Quartet in C Minor, Op. 18, No. 4 (Andantino). The thirty-nine Polymnia women sang contemporary choral works that had proved so popular the year before:

Twilight	Abt
Fly Fourth My Song	Abt
The Sea Fairies	Gilchrist
Distant Bells	Mackenzie
Briar Rose	Vierling
Approach of Spring	Gade

The orchestra section was filled, "every seat being taken by a cultured and highly intelligent audience." The *Constitution* claimed "The Polymnia is the only ladies' club in the south," not considering Baltimore. While one might question that claim, Barili's group undoubtedly had few southern musical peers, as it demonstrated later that spring on its 17 May concert. To the new repertoire sung by the club, Barili and Carrie Matthews added Thalberg's glittering *Norma* fantasy for two pianos and Schumann's Fantasy for Clarinet and Piano with clarinetist Fred Wedemeyer. The *Constitution* articulated clearly for Atlanta the split in musical entertainment now prevalent in American concert life. Art music now aimed at a higher class of society, a select audience whose refined tastes allowed them to fully value it, for "All persons cannot appreciate classical music, for the ear must be drilled and the taste cultivated before they can understand compositions of purely classic form." The good news, however, was here at the door of the century's final decade, Atlanta now possessed a vibrant, if modest, concert life in addition to an excellent music school, all thanks to Alfredo Barili.[67]

The Quintette Club must have thought well of the experience with Barili and the ladies as they returned at the beginning of the two subsequent years, in February and January 1888 and 1889 respectively. The paper claimed that "the Mendelssohn Quintette club of Boston only consented to return to Atlanta with the assurance that they would be assisted by the Polymnia . . . ." The structure of the programs and the repertoire were much the same, with Barili drawing most of the choral music from contemporary American composers, and the Quintette Club inserting instrumental solos and chamber works such as the Quintette in a minor, Opus 82 by Joseph Rheinberger. The newspapers routinely praised Barili's hard work and well-deserved success. One review of the 24 January 1889 concert, however, marked a hitherto unseen level of journalistic honesty, something that held out a faint hope that maybe the media were finally coming of age in the Gate City. The writer pointed out that the news media "are not disposed to be critical in the extreme, but the program would have been improved considerably by leaving out the numbers sung by Miss Ryan." The worst musical miscreant was the Scene and "Jewel Song" from *Faust*, a daunting challenge for even the finest singer. The reporter, avoiding any moralistic editorializing, stated calmly, "We will simply say that it was badly sung." Even worse: "Miss Ryan has no conception of what singing in tune means." Suffice it to editorialize *here*: If a singer wants to demonstrate *really bad* singing, there is no more efficient route than to launch into the "Jewel Song" from *Faust*. With its opening trills, succeeded by high, exposed, pianissimo lines, followed by a series of vocal fireworks, it has derailed many an able soprano. With an *unable* soprano, such as Miss Ryan appeared to be, the entire train quickly jumps the track and plunges down the artistic gorge. Indeed, the performance might have been even worse than reported. One suspects the writer was restraining himself.[68]

Barili's finest hour came on 22 May 1888 when the Polymnia Club, joined by a forty-voice male chorus, presented the first complete Atlanta performance of Gounod's *Messe solenelle,* "St. Cecilia," accompanied by Wurm's thirteen-piece orchestra. The Polymnia Club also sang two other selections alone. The Gounod *Messe*, however, was probably the first extensive choral work rehearsed, conducted with orchestra, and entirely performed by local talent. Of course the paper achieved previously unseen billows of puffery about the concert. But the closing paragraph of the *Constitution's* 23 May review was not puffing when it described exactly what made Barili "a superb conductor." "The singers and instrumentalists are kept in complete control, and they never lag or hurry." Anyone who has ever sung under or observed a great conductor such as Robert Shaw knows how critical it is to keep a hundred performers exactly together, why unvarying rhythmic control is so essential. Personal experiences as a conductor and accompanist lead me to suggest, as I read account after account from these years under discussion, that the newspapers were not exaggerating Barili's excellence. Virtually all of them, if they comment in enough detail, point to the same precision, careful intonation, and *thoughtful* singing by the choruses, going back to the Festival Chorus of 1883. The reviewer for the New York *Musical Courier*, who had reportedly "heard the same music presented in Europe over and over again," described those things that constitute a first-rate choral experience. He found Barili's work "really remarkable." The performance was "finished and artistic, while the volume, quality and shading of the chorus would be hard to improve." The club showed Barili's "master hand" and "most careful, conscientious and painstaking rehearsing." Everything about the man, his dress, handwriting, teaching, suggests care, thorough attention to detail, and a disciplined tenacity, all of which added up to keeping at the music until it was right. To Barili, as to any fine conductor, there is simply no other way. What endeared Barili to so many, from that time to this, is how he produced this unqualified excellence with patience and graciousness. Not one mention of petulant pouting, barbed sarcasms, baton throwing, or stomping off the stage exists. He was, as the accounts said, a gentleman.

In this light, the *Constitution's* opening paragraph might be taken a little more literally: "If to conduct the best concert ever given in Atlanta [by local musicians] is something to make a man feel proud, then Mr. Barili's pride is pardonable." Much of DeGive's was filled, and by musicians who "turned out en mass to show their appreciation of Mr. Barili's efforts to elevate the standard of music in Atlanta." "The Polymnia Club never sang so well." Barili himself thought so, as he told the *Saturday Review* later. When asked which concert was the most successful that he ever gave, he responded "The one given in Atlanta, on May 23rd [sic, 22nd], 1888, by the Polymnia Club when several part songs, solos and the Messe Solenelle—"St. Cecilia"—were given." After the concert ended, the audience poured onto the stage "and almost consumed him. He was modest as usual, and timidly thanked them . . . ." Observant people in Atlanta knew what they had.[69]

By the end of the decade Barili's work as a teacher and conductor further enhanced his professional standing. For the closing of the school years in 1888 and 1889 he directed the musical programs to great success. A "brilliantly dressed audience . . . composed of the elite of Atlanta's population" nearly filled DeGive's for the 6 June 1888 concert presented by some seventy-five young ladies. Barili was still glowing from the success of the Gounod *Messe solenelle* in May, of which the *Constitution* took due notice: "Nothing that we can say at this time can express the great obligations that our people are placed under to Mr. Barili, for the second superb musical treat given in a little over two weeks."[70]

4 BARILI AND MUSIC IN THE NEW SOUTH

As the final decade of the nineteenth century opened, Atlanta pulled ahead of the rest of the South in economic and population growth. With 65,000 inhabitants, it outpaced most other southern cities and by 1900 would be the most populous town in the South. The end of the century would see a dramatic change as the heart of urban growth in the South migrated from the seacoast to the interior. This transformation resulted from the collapse of the plantation system, the growth of cotton agriculture, and the spread of the southern railroad network. New opportunities attracted entrepreneurs from many regions, who grew wealthy as the city itself prospered. In addition, it drew artists such as Barili who would offer needed cultural leadership. "Atlanta is beginning to see her destiny clearly," the editor for the *Atlanta Journal* wrote in 1890. "She is to be the metropolis of the most magnificent section of the United States, the . . . southeast."[1]

The most outstanding feature of the Gate City was its economic growth, which helped pull the region along with it. As one writer for the *Philadelphia Times* observed, "Such a city in the heart of the South is a perennial stream of progress." By 1890, Atlanta's commerce had nearly tripled its 1880 volume and the value of the city's wholesale trade had risen to an estimated $80 million dollars, much of it due to the growth of the railroads. This economic and industrial expansion enjoyed the support of an increasing number of banking institutions. The eighteen private or joint stock banks in 1890 had a combined capital stock worth more than $2.5 million with net deposits during the year of about $60 million. This did not include the city's twenty-one building and loan associations, with more than $4 million in capital and loans in excess of $1.25 million.[2]

Impressive as these statistics may be, Atlanta was only beginning to build the infrastructure of a modern city. The corporate limits extended just one and a half miles in a circle from the passenger terminal. There were few paved streets, and utilities such as gas, water, sewage, and electricity had just started to develop. The new Georgia School of Technology, which opened its doors in the fall of 1888 with five faculty, was on the northwestern edge of town, almost in the country. "The surrounding streets were almost devoid of paving, and the nearest car line was on Marietta Street," William Emerson, the first professor of chemistry, later wrote. "In winter, North Avenue, Cherry and Luckie streets were deep with mud, and roundabout trips were often necessary to secure passage. Grant Field was almost an impassable, swampy wilderness, thick with briars and underbrush. One of the main sewers of the city discharged at the upper end and flowed through it."[3]

City leaders, proud of their progressive urban capitol, raised boosterism to new heights in promoting Atlanta. As the Chamber of Commerce, the Manufacturer's Association, and other civic groups organized, they worked together to promote the city with a fervor seen in few other American towns. Atlantans had pulled themselves up by the bootstraps from the ashes, built a "brave, new city," and were proud of it. As wealthy lumber merchant Frank P. Rice pointed out in 1889, "Atlantans . . . have built up the city themselves, and they are always ready to put their money into any local enterprise that promises good for the community at large." With all of this pride in the city and its achievement, it is not surprising that Barili's leadership came to be prized so much. It was only fitting that the leading city of the South should indeed have the most outstanding musician in the region.

* * * * * * *

"Atlanta is a great musical center," the *Constitution* trumpeted at the start of the decade of 1890. While it may not be obvious to everyone, "nevertheless, it is a fact." What exactly constitutes greatness, the paper did not explain. And whether Atlanta had it in February 1890 is difficult to say. Nevertheless, standing on the threshold of a new century, the city could confidently point to gratifying progress in its musical life. As the population grew, the city was able to support more musical performances of all kinds. Established as well as new musicians expanded Atlanta's concert life. Pianists such as Constantine Sternberg performed abroad as well as in Atlanta, adding to the city's reputation. Mr. J. P. O'Donnelly left in 1883 to study organ in

Europe for five years before returning to the Gate City. Other local musicians, such as conductor Charles Wurm and pianists William Rehm and Emma Hahr, also continued to perform.[4]

The number of traveling artists increased slightly during the decade. Adelina Patti returned for a visit in January 1894, succeeded the next year by her African-American counterpart, the Black Patti. The Mendelssohn Quintette Club made another appearance, as did Gilmore's Band, under the direction of Victor Herbert. John Philip Sousa brought his players for a first visit as well. The number of opera companies visiting the city fell, as groups like the Grau Opera Company returned for an entire week of opera, which was becoming the norm. In 1895 Walter Damrosch brought his company from New York and introduced complete Wagner operas to Atlanta with *Lohengrin* and *Siegfried*.

Local developments encouraged the city's musical life, such as the Freyer & Bradley Music Company. The company opened its new music hall on Peachtree Street in September 1894. The Atlanta Opera Club and the Atlanta Music Study Club both moved forward, attracting more members and increasing their visibility in the process. Musical instruction likewise increased, with the number of teachers growing every year. As the city expanded, music programs multiplied. Typical evenings consisted of an orchestral concert by Charles Wurm's twenty-piece orchestra, or William C. Rehm's pupils' recitals, Barili's Polymnia Club, an organ recital by J. P. O'Donnelly, a Gilbert and Sullivan operetta produced by the Atlanta Opera Club, or a musicale at the home of Atlanta society doyenne Mrs. W. L. Peel.

Barili remained the outstanding musician of the city, "a real patrician in music." He had moved his family and the music school to their new residence at 22 Church Street in 1889 and continued teaching at Washington Seminary. While he had limited his own playing, Barili still elicited praise when he performed, which he did for the musical soiree held at Mrs. Steele's early in 1890. True to form, he played two Beethoven sonatas for the guests.[5]

In June 1890, Barili left to visit Patti at her Craig-y-Nos Castle in Wales. She had only recently returned following another ragingly successful tour of the United States, beginning in December 1889, to Mexico City for January, and then back to the States from February to April. The castle had recently been enlarged, with two wings and a clock tower added by 1888, at a cost of more than half a million dollars. Barili, who arrived by the second week of July, remained Patti's favorite relative, as her effusive letters to Emily indicate, ". . . we enjoy him being here with us *thoroughly*—and again dearie you will be pleased to hear that we all love him with all our hearts. As you say how can one help doing so after one has learned to know him." Her last sentence echoes the affection that seemed to mark the feelings of many who knew Barili.[6]

Guests at the castle enjoyed the most luxurious treatment. Patti, who was one of the richest private citizens in the world, could afford to pamper them, and she did. Like other visitors, Barili had a valet assigned to him for his stay. Twenty-four hour breakfast was available, served in the room upon demand. After eating, the guests could entertain themselves with shooting, fishing, riding, walking, or just relaxing until they gathered for an elaborate lunch at 12:30 in the glass pavilion, when the Queen of Song made her first appearance of the day. Dinner could often be an elaborate affair, especially if there was an occasion such as a new arrival, birthday, or imminent departure. The sumptuous cuisine was outshone only by Patti, resplendent in her jewels and reflected in the elegance of titled aristocracy, talented artists, and wealthy business leaders from around the world.[7]

Patti's letter hints at another, darker cloud that would soon disrupt the Barili family. "I offered him to give up Atlanta and find something for him to do over here . . . . and besides he has great affection for Atlanta." "I'm quite *determined* to have him come over here, someday—and remain near us *for good.*" Some of this concern results from her own growing desire to have her family near her, as well as an interest in seeing his professional life placed in a more cosmopolitan setting. Subsequent events, however, suggest that the paragraph referred to other, deeper problems that bothered Alfredo at the time and which he surely discussed with Patti. In fact, given their close relationship, it would be surprising had he not. Seen in this light, her letters in the months after his return to Atlanta in August could be seen as almost too cheerful, too interested in keeping things happy.

We will never be able to prove incontestably what issue was troubling Alfredo so much during this period. The following conclusions arise from months of research and from discussions with Barili's former student, Cherry Emerson, and family members. The Barili penchant for family secrecy has made it impossible to determine events incontrovertibly, especially at the distance of a century. The written evidence remains limited to a few reports in the *Constitution* and isolated letters to Louise and Emily. Aside from this, nothing else appears in the Barili archives in Atlanta, nor in available family papers. As the family appeared to recover eventually from Alfredo's personal crisis, it seems that he confronted his distress and worked through it, just as he did with the affair over the association directorship. Whatever was troubling him, however, must have been severe, because he seriously considered moving from Atlanta permanently, and indeed did leave for a period.

Barili seems to have put these concerns behind him temporarily as he returned to Atlanta in the fall of 1890 after his visit to Craig-y-Nos. The family and the school seemed to be prospering, as Patti wrote him in October, "I am *so pleased* to hear such good news about your school." She dramatically repeats her thoughts about him and the family, "As for sitting out on the veranda I would give *anything* to be able to be there and sit with you all—how nice and jolly it must be!" Unfortunately, only the letters from Patti to the family in Atlanta survive, along with their correspondence home when they visited her. In a communication from John Frederick Cone (22 August 1994), the author of the fine Patti biography, he stated that he had not found any letters from the Barilis to Patti. He was told that much material was destroyed after her death in 1919 and even more lost during World War II. In light of Patti's statement (22 October 1890) that "Alfredo writes me regularly every Thursday" a great many letters must be missing, from him as well as Emily and Louise, who were prolific correspondents.

The New Year brought another performance with the Polymnia Club. The Club repeated its presentation of Gounod's "St. Cecilia" Mass on 21 April 1891. Joined by more than thirty male voices, the eighty-voice chorus, this time accompanied by organ, enjoyed as much success as it had three years earlier. In fact, the *Constitution* claimed that "it was the largest and most fashionable audience that has attended the opera house at any concert during the past two years."[8] Barili also presented a private piano recital, where he played Beethoven, Schumann, Chopin, Mendelssohn, and others.

A more disturbing newspaper item lies on the same page of the family scrapbook as the above review, apparently from a paper in Kansas City. The item praises Barili's concert therein, and also announces that "Mr. Barili will locate in Kansas City and last evening was his debut." The announcement is strange because there is no previous material on the issue, nor any follow up—it just appears abruptly, then disappears, raising serious questions. The article is not dated, but it is in the scrapbook along with other materials dated for the first half of 1891. Nothing seems to have come of this interest in moving, but the incident does point to some somber issue active in Barili's life. More puzzling is the next item: his residence for the year is listed in the 1891 City Directory as Juniper Street, between sixth and seventh streets. Emily is no longer mentioned, as she had been regularly since their move to the city in 1880.

The issue bothering Barili seems also to have affected his health. Patti had written him from Nice, France on 15 March 1891 "You say your health is not what it should be—I do wish it were time for you to come to us, for I know the air of our lovely Welsh mountains would put you straight again in no time." Asthma/respiratory problems would also help to explain why he was considering Kansas City. It was a large enough town to support his teaching, but it would not have developed the industrial pollution that had seemingly made his breathing so difficult in the northeast. It is clear, however, that he was trying desperately to escape from something.

No further information appears until 6 June 1891 when the *Atlanta Journal* reported Emily as preparing to leave "in a day or two for New York. She will spend the summer at some watering place in New England." She probably was going to stay with her brother Charles Vezin in New York. At the same time, Alfredo had departed for Wales, in a very distraught state, as the *Constitution* reported from a letter which Barili wrote to his friend Major T. M. Barnes at the end of July: "He left Atlanta much broken down in health, but is rapidly improving." He was gone most of the summer and left for America on August 20, which put him back in Atlanta by the second week of September.[9]

Shortly after his return to Atlanta things worsened. Within a month Barili was preparing to leave town, for good it seemed, and alone. The 24 October *Constitution* reported that "Mr. Alfredo Barili will leave Atlanta tomorrow for a sanitarium in Washington City. He goes by the imperative order of his physician, who tells him it will be as much as his life is worth to continue his arduous labors in teaching his large class of pupils. He expects to remain in the sanitarium till a complete cure is affected." Mr. Rehm taught Barili's pupils during his absence.

Health does not explain everything, however. In fact it only further obscures the actual issue. The paragraph above the one describing his imminent departure reads "that Mr. A. M. Burbank . . . has been elected to succeed Mr. Alfredo Barili [with the Polymnia Club]. It seems that Mr. Barili found it necessary to relinquish his position on account of nervous prostration." Of course nervous illness for Victorian society could mean almost any human ailment except gunshot wounds and broken legs. The family would have much preferred the socially accepted explanation of nerves in place of revealing more dismaying problems. Moreover, were Barili undergoing some personal crisis, in addition to a history of asthma/respiratory illness, then one could set off the other, which in turn would worsen the whole problem, until he found himself with a rather threatening situation, as the doctor indicated.

Barili's departure turned what had been a distressing family problem into a public uproar. On 12 November 1891 the *Constitution* ran an extensive article headed by the statement, in large-point type (much larger than any of Barili's performances ever received): "WHY BARILI WENT." In the best yellow-journalistic fashion, three other headlines in descending point size catch the eye before the article begins: "Various Reasons Given for His Departure from Atlanta. HE AND HIS WIFE ARE ESTRANGED. Mrs. Barili Talks About It—The Friends of Both Parties Have Their Say—Did Patti Cause it?" In an era that prized proper appearances and respectability, this must have been mortifying to all involved. And to both Emily and Alfredo, gentle, rather private souls, it must have seemed almost unendurable. One other fact emerges also: the length of the account, as well the type-size, shows how significant and visible Barili had become in the city. Only someone so well known would merit such extensive coverage. The writer begins:

> Why did Professor Alfredo Barili quit Atlanta? This question has been asked hundreds of times since the distinguished musician took his departure a few weeks ago. In fact, Barili's going away has produced a decided sensation in the musical and society circles of Atlanta. Sundry rumors have been set afloat, and these have afforded gossiping tongues plenty of exercise. Mr. Barili is now in Philadelphia. Mrs. Barili and her three children are still in Atlanta. It has transpired that Mr. and Mrs. Barili are estranged, and it is currently reported that a libel for divorce will soon be filed by Mrs. Barili. This has excited much comment, and musical Atlanta is agitated as never before. There never was a more popular musician in Atlanta than Alfredo Barili, and his most estimable wife shares that popularity.

The writer briefly summarizes Barili's eleven years' work in Atlanta. "Soon his classes were too large for him to manage, and his wife took a considerable number of pupils off his hands." It goes on to describe other successes: his outstanding performances, the Music Festival of 1883, and his compositions. In addition, Emily is credited with rendering "invaluable assistance" in all these enterprises, especially her business acumen. Then the prose falters and poisonous speculation sets in. Until recently the Barilis had a model home but "there is now a broken home and desolate hearts." In search of an explanation, the *Constitution* reporter interviewed "a very intimate friend of Mr. Barili" who launched forth with ruinously moralizing gossip, purporting to explain the whole thing. According to the so-called "friend," Barili bolted to join Patti in England and live the high life, abandoning his family in Atlanta. He said that Barili "intimated to me something of the kind." The informant, rapturous at being consulted for the article, betrayed himself by using the two alluring and damning words that supposedly absolve any gossip from accountability: "*I hear*." Given the political jealousy which had denied Barili the directorship of the music association almost a decade earlier, followed by his subsequent string of professional successes, Atlanta doubtlessly had a number of people delighted to rejoice *and speculate* on Barili's difficulties. That this reporter should have interviewed this "friend" proved unfortunate indeed. A true friend would simply have declined comment on the whole thing, as B. B. Crew seems to have done. The source that came forth, however, and the venal way in which he surmised the problem, could not have done Barili more harm.

One can easily visualize the scene: the informer moves up close to the reporter, puffing himself up virtuously, and explains, **in italics**, "*I hear*," he whispers, "that Patti has made certain offers to Barili; that she has proposed to him to become an attache of her court . . . ." As it turned out, Patti was shortly arriving in New York to begin another tour of the United States in 1892. "He himself told me he expected to join her soon after she reaches New York." Should Barili move to England, "unencumbered by a wife and children she would assure him a life of ease and luxury." Almost nothing would have horrified proper Victorian Atlantans more than Barili abandoning his family in return for an unearned life of indolence. The "friend" quickly admitted that other "hypotheses are broached" explaining Barili's puzzling behavior, "but the one I mention is the right one I am sure."

Next it was Emily's turn. The paper admitted that it had not found anyone "able to give facts." (Of course, this did not stop it from printing the entire venomous interview with Barili's "friend"). In pursuit of a satisfactory explanation, a reporter called on Emily, now living at the Washington Seminary. Emily acknowledged hearing "some vague rumors" but preferred "not to speak about this matter at all." She agreed that she did not think that Alfredo would return, but that he had been providing for the children. He was indeed in Philadelphia, where he probably went to stay with his brother. She offered one explanation: "He was anxious to remove to a larger city where he could get a good opening, and he may not stay there if he can find some more desirable place. He had an idea of going to some western city." She quickly absolved Patti from any mean compliance in this. The celebrated soprano had enormous affection for the entire family and probably was as heart-sick as anyone over the whole affair. Emily finished by revealing her love and respect for Alfredo's pain: "please do not say anything that could injure Mr. Barili."

One last interview, with "one of Mr. Barili's closest friends" (quite likely W. Woods White, financial advisor and future president of Barili's School of Music), suggests one issue that indeed plagued Barili for much of his life in Atlanta. "Barili chafes under the limitations enforced on him in so small a place as Atlanta," the friend pointed out. "He craves a wide field where he can mingle with the master musicians of the world." Either the friend was not aware of another problem, or kindly refused to bring it up. He did show distress at the whole dismaying episode, though. "I am pained that he has acted in such a weak manner, but I attribute it to sickness."

Nothing in the Barili archives sheds light on this whole distressing incident. There is a thundering silence about anything in the family chronicle for these two years. Why the ominous silence in the record? There are no newspaper accounts or journal articles, and — most peculiar of all—no letters from Patti until they resume in October 1894. The lack of material either in the archives or the family documents pertaining to these years — in contrast with how the family saved almost every other sentence written about Alfredo, Emily, their extended families, and anyone else who ever talked to them, or wrote about them, or studied with them, and much, much, much more — cries out urgently. But about what? And what happened to Patti's letters? One could argue that they were simply missing. This seems odd, though, as there is a continual stream from 1890, which then is interupted in 1891, before resuming in 1894 to continue until her death in the fall of 1919. As the family was fastidious in keeping all their archival materials in mint condition, that they should lose two years of correspondence from one of the most famous artists in the world, seems unlikely. Perhaps she did not write ; but this is not convincing either. With Alfredo and the family suffering the most acute crisis of their lives, which would have distressed her deeply, she would have likely increased her correspondence. Patti was not only concerned for nearly every aspect of their lives, but her letters often inquire after the most mundane things, such as how the dog is doing, or one of Louise's girl friends. With Alfredo back in town by 1892 and things not entirely settled for some time, she would have written often with anxious questions and advice, questions that could have later revealed a dark family secret to others.

This two-year silence is so thorough that it produces just the opposite effect than that intended by the family: it points to something not only hidden, but horrific. All families have secrets, and Victorian families, constrained by enormous social pressure, would frantically attempt to keep their skeletons closeted from the world, most immediately by destroying any documentary materials relating to any of these distressing events. In this case events conspired against the Barilis. The very intensity of their efforts at secrecy points to the existence of something, unseen though it may be.

For some time—maybe for all time—this secret stubbornly resisted all efforts at disclosure. After much additional research, there were only conjectural explanations, none of which really explained the intensity and depth of the crisis. After a while, it appeared that no further documentary material was going to surface. All the circumstantial evidence suggested something of the most dreadful magnitude, something outrageous enough to cause Barili to consider leaving his family, expose himself to appalling publicity in the newspaper, and put the city to gossiping. Something exceptional by Victorian standards lay underneath this tempest.

Finally, after every possible interpretation remained unconvincing, Cherry Emerson shared a conversation more than sixty years old. This conversation seems to offer a credible explanation, though it must be stressed that considerable efforts at verification have proven futile. Emerson studied with Barili from 1931 until Barili's death in 1935. During that period he and the respected musician developed a fast friendship, one which still evokes fond affection from Emerson to this day. Emerson's mother, Sina White Emerson, was the daughter of W. Woods White, a well-known banker and president of Barili's School of Music. The Whites had become close friends with the Barilis since the Barilis moved near them in College Park sometime before 1893. As neighbors, the two young daughters, Sina White and Louise Barili became friends, Sina being about ten years younger than Louise. Cherry Emerson heard from his mother that the Barili secret concerned the intimate involvement of Emily with Carl Wolfsohn, who had been the teacher of Alfredo Barili until he left Philadelphia for Cologne. Wolfsohn had left Philadelphia in 1873 for Chicago shortly after Alfredo departed for Cologne in 1872. In subsequent years he apparently maintained contact with Barili and his family in Atlanta. It seems that during the summer of 1890 Wolfsohn had visited Atlanta, and formed his relationship with Emily. Their reported affair probably occurred at the time, as the family troubles appear shortly after Alfredo returned in the fall of 1890 to Atlanta, and came to a head the next year when he and Emily spent the summer of 1891 apart, before Alfredo left again in November.

It is impossible to prove this with complete certainty, but this affair comes closest to explaining why the Barili family nearly disintegrated. Only a transgression of this magnitude would account for all the hysteria. For one thing, the two-year break in the family record indicated that something appalling had taken place. For another, the frenzy in the press followed by Barili's departure pointed to something alarming in the extreme. Finally, that Alfredo and Emily had even considered a divorce, in an era when it forever tainted the family, cloaked something of the darkest consequence.

If one accepts the explanation offered by Emerson's mother—which, though speculative, does seem to account for all the known facts— Alfredo's behavior is placed in an understandable light. Just when he learned of the affair is unclear. Given his virtual nervous breakdown in the fall of 1891, which is part of the record, he must have discovered the affair sometime in the previous months. With his sensitive nature and high moral standards, it came close to destroying him. He had to leave to survive. Barili probably did go to see Patti in New York. Outside of his family, she was his closest confidant as well as relative. Whom else could he turn to with his crisis? Knowing Patti's own colorful past as well as her love of Alfredo, Emily, and the children, she quite likely counseled him to return to Atlanta. She knew that a divorce would permanently scar Emily and probably wound Alfredo so that he might never heal. Moreover, with the wisdom which Patti had acquired by this time, she probably thought (and rightly so as it turned out) that should Alfredo find the inner strength to forgive Emily, and return to Atlanta, the family would recover and eventually go forward.

She was right. Once again, as in the affair over the association director, Barili discovered the inner strength to begin healing. Whatever transpired between the fall of 1891 and the ensuing year, Barili did return to Atlanta and his family, for the rest of his life. He appears in the 1892 city directory at the same Juniper Street address as in 1891. Exactly when he and Emily reconciled is not clear. The three Barili children attended school for sometime at Mrs. Ballard's, where they lived, which suggests that Emily and Alfredo were separated for a year or more. The directory in 1893 lists his residence on Manchester Street, but fails to mention Emily again. She does not reappear until 1900, but they must have reconciled before their move to College Park by 1893. They continued teaching at the school, which moved to the YMCA building that same year. She had run the school in his absence, with the help of William Rehm and Carrie Matthews.

After some rest and inner healing, Barili found his way back—back to himself first, then back to Atlanta, to Emily, the family, and finally back to his musical life. His listings in the city directory do not skip a year. Aside from this, however, the conspicuous documentary silence—he had been continually in the press from his arrival in Atlanta until this time—suggests he returned to work slowly, gradually regaining his strength and resuming his musical activities. Notice of his work does not increase until 1895, though the directory locates his music school at the YMCA from 1893 along with his residence on Manchester Street. No record survives of Barili mentioning the affair.[10]

* * * * * * *

While Barili was returning to his professional work in the years after 1891, Atlanta was enjoying her first serious musical growth. As more musicians moved into the area, they expanded the number and variety of local concerts, as well as the opportunities for musical instruction. Additional performing spaces also increased the frequency and accessibility to concerts. New musical organizations arose, such as the Atlanta Opera Club and the Atlanta Music Club, both of which would add much to the city's cultural life. The overall number of touring artists, companies, orchestras, and bands visiting the city changed little during the century's final decade. The type of musical concerts they offered changed, though. Operatic music, whether in staged or concert versions, declined somewhat, supplanted by more solo performers and professional bands. Orchestral performances remained uncommon and would remain infrequent well into the next century. Finally, organ and church music, which would lead much of Atlanta's local musical activity during this century, began assuming a life of their own.

Leading the way in concert space was the Grand Theater, the new opera house which Laurent DeGive finished in February 1893. Lit by electric lights— probably a first for a city theater—the Grand was dedicated formally Friday evening, 10 February to a house packed from pit to dome. The *Constitution* writer likened the evening to a gala night in Paris. "Everybody seemed entirely happy over the occasion. How much everybody enjoyed the fresh scenery, furnishings, boxes, and above all the handsome new drop curtain," as well as the three large balconies. Reportedly, the young people were so enthralled that they kept quiet for once, and the tired old "blase men opened their eyes wider than they had since their first love affair . . . ." Mayor John. B. Goodwin led the audience in applauding Mr. DeGive, whose generosity made the new house a reality. In spite of a request that he appear, the retiring Belgian had disappeared, at which point the curtain dropped, the orchestra played briefly, and the curtain rose again on Belasco and De Mille's play *Men and Women*.[11] Two additional concert halls were constructed as part of new music stores. Phillips & Crew's new building on Peachtree included one when it opened in 1891. The hall in the new building for the Freyer & Bradley Music Company had an organ that was played for the dedication on 11 September 1894. The Young Men's Christian Association Hall, Edgewood Avenue Theater, and Concordia Hall continued to be popular performing spaces as well.[12]

New musical organizations added much to Atlanta's musical life. By 1892 the Atlanta Opera Club was staging its own productions of *The Pirates of Penzance* (February) and *The Chimes of Normandy* (December). The 12 December 1892 *Constitution* praised the performance of the latter work, but decried the lack of support for these local endeavors. The paper pointed out that up North, such a local performance "could play for a week and draw crowded houses every night . . . ." Unfortunately, Atlanta still "cannot appreciate her own artists (for such they are) enough to support them in a permanent organization." By 1893, the Atlanta Music Club was "fully organized, but up to date no time has been arranged for a meeting. Most of the members are teachers, and morning or afternoon hours seem to conflict with the lessons of each." The club excluded male members. One wonders when they finally agreed to hold their first regular meeting. The Orpheus Glee Club presented cooperative concerts, such as the one led by Professor Carlisle in April 1893, when the Glee Club performed with the Banjo Sextette in a "splendid entertainment." The next year the club staged two concerts in April, one at DeGive's and one at First Baptist Church. For the first one, the group joined Dr. J. W. Bischoff and His Celebrated Quartet from Washington, D. C. for an evening of piano selections, contemporary solo songs, and a number of operatic excerpts, including the quartet from Rigoletto. To open the performance at First Baptist, Dr. Bischoff led off with the overture to *William Tell* for organ, possibly in the transcription by Dudley Buck, the most popular version of the period. Also on the program, and noticed here for the first time, is a prelude and fugue for organ by Bach. Music of the Leipzig master was by this time gaining some currency in this country, but he remained rare on Atlanta programs.[13]

Instrumental concerts continued to draw impressive crowds. The Boston Mendelssohn Quintette Club returned in February 1890, two years later in 1892, and in January 1893, when they filled the hall "to its limit." The concert was so successful that the audience demanded it be repeated the next afternoon. In May that same year Atlanta had its second music festival in the new Grand Opera House. The central attraction this time was Walter Damrosch and his orchestra of nearly seventy players. According to the *Constitution*, Atlanta had not heard a serious symphonic orchestra in ten years, since 1883, when Barili and Carl Sentz had staged the first music festival, followed two weeks later by Thomas's orchestra. At age twenty-two Damrosch had succeeded his father Leopold as conductor of the New York Symphony and Oratorio Societies upon the latter's death in 1884. Since then Damrosch had led both groups to even greater acclaim. For this tour in 1893 he brought along vocalists Sofia Scalchi, the Italian contralto, and the young American soprano Lillian Blauvelt. The Atlanta sponsors must have been optimistic indeed, because they had 10,000 programs printed for the festival. In spite of its vaunted reputation, though, the repertoire for the two-concert festival harks back to an earlier period in American musical life. The programs that Barili and Sentz had presented aimed considerably higher in their literature and the performance of entire works. The Damrosch concerts included no complete symphonic works. The evening concert on Thursday 10 May leaned heavily on lighter and often operatic fare:[14]

Carmen Suite No. 1,	
"March of the Toreadors" and	
"Danse Bohème"	Bizet
"Reverie," solo violin	Vieuxtemps
"La Ronde des Lutins," solo violin	Bazzini
Symphonic Poem "Spinning Wheel of Omphale"	Saint-Saëns
"Figlio mio," *Le Prophète*	Meyerbeer
"March," *Tannhäuser*	Wagner
Allegretto, Symphony VII	Beethoven
"Brindisi," *Lucrezia Borgia*	Donizetti
"Spanish Dance," solo violin	Sarasate
Gavotte, string orchestra	Bach
Adagio Cantabile, string orchestra	Tchaikovsky
Rakoczy March, *Damnation de Faust*	Berlioz

Locally, Charles Wurm's twenty-piece orchestra presented a typical concert at the Kimball House to a large crowd in May 1891. Operatic excerpts dominated the evening, including the overture to Flotow's *Stradella,* selections from *Les Huguenots* and *Il trovatore,* Wagner's *Tannhäuser* and various waltzes.[15] In May 1894 the leading vocalists of the city presented an evening of favorite Victorian choral and solo music at the YMCA Hall. Appropriately, the concert opened with Dudley Buck's *Festival Te Deum,* one of the most enduring sacred favorites of the period. A selection from *Messiah* as well as an

Ave Maria, arranged from Mascagni's *Cavaleria Rusticana*, were also sung. Gounod's seductive Sanctus (*St. Cecilia* Mass) concluded the evening. Opera once again filled the evening later in the year when a large concert was given in October to build a children's wing for Grady Hospital. Many of Atlanta's musical luminaries participated, including the reigning tenor Signor Enrico Campobello, organist J. P. O'Donnelly, the McPherson Army Post Regimental Band, and the Atlanta Schubert Sextette. In addition to the expected selections from Verdi, Gounod, and Donizetti, whose *Lucia* sextet was fittingly rendered by Atlanta's sextet, the evening concluded with "Dixie" sung "tutti." [16]

The level of repertoire and piano recitals had risen appreciably since Barili's premiere a decade earlier. Visiting artist William Sherwood played Bach's "Bouree" from his second English Suite in the first month of 1891. The remainder of the program reflects the serious conservatory training he undoubtedly had received. Along with some opera transcriptions, he performed Beethoven's Moonlight sonata, Schumann's *Fashingschwank aus Wien*, one of the *Songs Without Words* by Mendelssohn, Chopin, Gottschalk, as well as Liszt's demanding arrangement of Paganini's *La Campanella*. By this time in Atlanta, Beethoven had taken his revered place on better keyboard programs, like the one played by Nealy Stevens in February 1893. Along with a work by Beethoven, she presented music by Saint-Saëns, Mozskowski, and Chopin. For her encore she played Barili's *Cradle Song* (one wonders if he were present that evening). That same year Henry Howell began a series of recitals, that, according to the *Constitution* "will be principally educational, and will be particularly interesting to those who are devotees of classical piano compositions." The first two consisted of works by Bach, Beethoven, Haydn, Mozart, and Gluck with the second pair being devoted to "modern German and Hungarian composers." One evening was devoted to music of Chopin and Paderewski. Student recitals also had improved in quality. In May 1891 William Rehm's pupils played variously a Grand Fantasie on Mozart's *Don Giovanni*, Chopin, Mendelssohn's challenging *Rondo Capriccioso*, Chopin's B-Flat Minor Scherzo, in addition to Beethoven's *Pathétique* sonata arranged for two pianos. In any form, the work proved a fitting conclusion to an evening of piano.[17]

Opera production in Atlanta continued to change during this final decade. Appearances of the operatic heavy-weights so popular twenty years earlier became rare, displaced largely by operettas. Gilbert and Sullivan maintained their hold on the Atlanta stage, for example, when a traveling forty-five member troupe presented *The Gondoliers* in October 1890. Auber's *Fra Diavolo* reappeared in June 1893, presented by the McCaully Opera Company at the

Edgewood Theater for a number of performances. To encourage attendance, "at every performance that soul-stirring sextet from *Lucia* will be introduced." The next year the Grau Opera Company returned once more, but with a rather altered bill of fare. The only familiar work they brought this time was Flotow's *Martha*. New to Atlanta were their three lighter works, *Dorothy, Ship Ahoy,* and *Paul Jones*. May 1895 saw them again (this would be their twelfth visit) playing Atlanta, this time offering, among other works, *Boccacio* and *Fra Diavolo* at the Lyceum Theater.[18]

These productions in May began a pattern of summer opera that would endure for almost a century in Atlanta. By the second decade of this century the weeks in late April/early May came to be known as "Opera Week" for the annual visit of the Metropolitan Opera. The *Constitution* points out how popular summer opera had become. "With baseball and summer opera, it ought to be possible for the good people of Atlanta to spend some pleasant hours this summer. It looks now as if both branches of amusement would be winners." The year before, the Edgewood Theater presented the singer Adelaide Randall supported by a cast of thirty-five. In May 1895 the Campobello company produced three standards: *Lucia, Il trovatore,* and *Faust*. They had been in town just the month before where they presented a run of four tried and true works: *Carmen, Faust, Martha,* and *Il trovatore*. As evidenced by their quick return, they must have drawn good houses.[19]

Adelina Patti's second visit on 11 January 1894 was more anticipated than ever. The paper had publicized her return a year earlier; as the time approached, it ran an extensive interview with her as well. When she arrived, "Patti came, saw and conquered," the paper dryly observed. "That is the whole story summed up in a sentence; and that she conquered—won every heart—is not putting it too strongly." Not only was the Grand full by five o-clock, but the paper estimated that 1,000 people were turned away. She was supported by a group of four vocal stars and large orchestra conducted by Luigi Arditi (1822-1903), who it seemed, had conducted for nearly everybody and would go on almost until he died. Patti was apparently the only touring opera star able to draw large houses during this time. The financial crisis in the United States was so severe that few attractions made money. But she did. There is little need to reprint here, one more time, the effusive and exalted adulations heaped upon her by the *Constitution*. One point does stand out, again, and that was Patti's skill at connecting with her listeners. She did not just perform, she *shared*. "No artist ever knew better how to keep thoroughly en rapport with her audiences, and from the first moment of her appearance there seems to be a bond of good fellowship between her and each person before her." Persons did not go to a concert in a theater; they went to Patti's home, where she welcomed them personally and sang exclusively for *them*. Her magic was heightened by the timing of her entrance. She did not appear until the sixth selection on the program, with a performance of Rosina's glittering "Una voce poca fa" from *Il barbiere di Siviglia*. Following this the audience would not let her leave the stage until she had added "Home, Sweet Home," "Down on the Suwanee River," and "Coming Thro' the Rye." After intermission the company presented the second act of *Martha,* during which "she sang 'The Last Rose of Summer' over and over again."[20]

The next January (1895) another captivating soprano sang in Atlanta, Sissieretta Jones, or "The Black Patti." The *Constitution* claimed that she bore "the distinction of having sung to more people in one week than any other singer, and her record of 75,000 who flocked to hear her at the Madison Square Garden in New York stands unequaled in the history of singing." Her rich, powerful voice with its wide range and sparkling upper register had gained her a well-deserved reputation. She claimed that she was the first black singer to be engaged by the Metropolitan Opera Company to sing *Aida*. Unfortunately, the production was cancelled after the house burned down. Her traveling opera company, Black Patti's Troubadors, performed opera scenes and arias until her retirement from the stage in 1915.[21]

As opera slowly assumed a smaller profile on the Atlanta stage during the last two decades of the century, band concerts became ever more popular, as discussed in chapter three. Band music formed the central performance events of the Cotton States and International Exposition in 1895. The Exposition, situated in Piedmont Park, cost almost three million dollars, had 6,000 exhibits viewed by 800,000 visitors over a three month period, "started a new era of progress for Atlanta and raised the city from a provincial capital to a lusty young metropolis which grew at a tremendous pace in population, trade, industry and finance . . . ." President Cleveland opened the Exposition on 18 September 1895 from his library at Gray Gables by touching an electric key, which turned on the machinery in Atlanta in front of twenty-five thousand eager people. Celebrations included the largest and longest military parade every seen in the city attended by representatives of over half the states in the union as well as many foreign countries. A new piece "Salute to Atlanta" was performed by Gilmore's Twenty-Second Regiment Band under the direction of Victor Herbert, conductor since the former's death in 1892. The group performed another concert on 22 September at the Grand to an audience of 1,200, concluding with Herbert's *Grand American Fantasy* on such tunes as "Hail Columbia," "Suwanee River," "Dixie," " Red, White and Blue," and "The Star Spangled Banner." Throughout the next weeks the band played frequently for the Exposition. Later in October on the Exposition grounds Herbert programmed a Wagner evening, or at least half a Wagner evening, for the first part of the concert, playing the overture to *Rienzi*, scenes from *The Flying Dutchman*, selections from *Lohengrin* and *Die Walküre,* and the prelude to *Die Meistersinger.*[22]

Probably the biggest event for the Exposition came in November when John Philip Sousa brought his famous band of fifty players to the Exposition. At age twenty-five the young Sousa had taken over the U. S. Marine Band in 1880, which he then reshaped into the most celebrated band in the country. It was as a composer, however, that he achieved his enduring reputation. By the first decades of this century his marches such as *Semper Fidelis, Washington Post,* and *Stars and Stripes Forever* had made him undoubtedly the most popular American composer. As a conductor he earned praise from such eminent musicians as Theodore Thomas and Walter Damrosch, who held him in high esteem. After he had formed his own band in 1892 he played with Thomas for the dedication of the Chicago World's Fair that same year. In 1893 he joined with Damrosch for a concert at New York's Carnegie Hall.[23]

The group had been on tour for the entire year before they arrived in Atlanta. Sousa had earlier contracted to come to Atlanta and had composed *King Cotton*, which later became the official march of the Exposition. His visit was almost cancelled when the Exposition's expenses began exceeding income and the committee wired Sousa, cancelling his contract. He indignantly came on anyway and persuaded the directors to honor the arrangements. His performances at the Exposition drew more than enough audiences to pay for his visit. He ended the week by giving a concert on Sunday at the Grand.[24]

Sousa brought his band back to Atlanta two years later in January 1897. His music as well as his charisma seem to have won him many friends in the city. After a triumphal tour of Europe, he embarked on a six-month tour of this country, giving nearly 300 concerts in every principal city in the United States and Canada.[25]

Barili reissued his *Gate City Guard March* for the Exposition and retitled it *The Atlanta March* (Phillips & Crew,), which he dedicated to the Citizens of Atlanta. By this time things in his life had apparently settled down, allowing him to resume a normal schedule. Patti wrote him in January 1895 "I trust you are now feeling much better." Once again she cautioned, "You must be careful and not overwork yourself too much . . . ." His students' June (1895) recital at the YMCA hall received glowing reviews by both the *Journal* and the *Constitution*. The papers seem heartened by his professional reappearance; the writers reminded their readers of Barili's position as Atlanta's preeminent musician. He had to step down earlier for a while, "owing to wrecked health," but now he was back, had reorganized the Polymnia Club (which had briefly ceased performing) and was enjoying more successes than ever. His teaching continued to produce Atlanta's finest music students, and his compositions "are played from Maine to California." While his manner may still be modest and retiring, it should not obscure the contribution he made to the city's cultural life. When he arrived, Atlanta's musical life was in "a nebulous condition." Nevertheless, he set himself "to the task of bringing order out of chaos." Finally, "It is not unreasonable to declare that Atlanta owes more to Alfredo Barili than to any other musician . . . ."[26]

By 1893 the family had taken a house in College Park. Barili would ride the streetcar downtown to the YMCA Building, where the music school was located. He had incorporated it into "The Barili School of Music Company" and wisely chose two others to administer it: his good friend, Woods White as President, and W. L. Carraway, as the Secretary-Treasurer. This arrangement allowed Barili to concentrate on his teaching. His insistence on excellence and commitment had not flagged since he first opened the doors. The school aimed to attract talented students, acknowledging "the growing demand for more thorough and complete preparation for the work of the artist and teacher. Studious habits, prompt attention, and a comprehensive knowledge of the whole field of music, will be required of all advanced pupils." He had virtually ceased solo performing, devoting his time to teaching and conducting. In February 1898 the Polymnia Club honored him by reorganizing themselves as the Barili Musical Club. They subsequently broadened their focus from just choral performance to various types of music. Often he accompanied students, such as playing the orchestral part for the Grieg Violin Concerto with a Miss Hunt in a concert for the Woman's Club. Sometime during this period Emily described their life to a friend: "Came to Atlanta in 1880. He has done real missionary work here. We lead a quite [sic] life as he is far from strong, but he is considered the South's most prominent teacher. He has pupils from many towns. He gives his best, and is most progressive. Being an idealist and working for results only, I have to be the business head of the family. I also have a very large class of beginners."[27]

The summer of that year Barili took Louise with him for her first trip to visit Patti at her Craig-y-Nos in Wales. Earlier in the year Patti had lost her husband, the tenor Ernest Nicolini, and was looking forward to seeing her family. Patti grew most fond of Louise, writing her more often than other family members, and supposedly broached the idea to Alfredo of adopting her. As Louise grew and became increasingly observant, her correspondence to Atlanta from Wales during her visits there provides some insights into life there otherwise unavailable. On this side of the Atlantic, she wrote Patti weekly on Sundays.[28]

In December, after Alfredo and Louise had returned home, Patti had a surprise for them. "And now, my dear Alfredo, I know you will be pleased to hear that I am engaged to be married to a very charming man, Baron Rolf Cederström, you met him here, and I believe you liked him very much." Indeed, Barili and Cederström seemed to have hit it off well, and would remain friends even following Patti's death in 1919. Whether Barili was surprised to hear this we do not know. He might have raised an eyebrow because of the Baron's age, however. Rolf, who was from an established Swedish noble family, would be twenty-eight to Patti's fifty-six shortly after their marriage 25 January 1899. Nevertheless, he would prove to be a devoted husband and warm family member to the Barilis as well.[29]

* * * * * *

By the end of the decade Atlanta's first enduring musical organizations had been established. The three leading groups, the Atlanta Concert Association, the Atlanta Woman's Club, and the Atlanta Musical Club, patronized local concerts and backed visiting musical performers. Well into the next century these would be the groups that supported much of the serious musical activity in Atlanta. Later, other music clubs arose and would supplant them, such as the Atlanta Music Festival Association, which sponsored the first visit by the Metropolitan Opera Company from New York in 1910. By the turn of the century, operatic performances had become limited to a few extended yearly visits by touring companies. The Metropolitan would crowd out nearly every other group until the early 1980's, when it ceased touring, an event that had a positive result for the city, as it forced Atlanta to turn to its own considerable resources, which it did. About the same time, the city became serious about opera and organized the Atlanta Opera under the direction of William Fred Scott. Even without its own theater, on a modest budget, and in difficult economic times, Atlanta Opera has served the city well, and continues to enjoy outstanding seasons.

But all of this lay in the future. The final years of the nineteenth century saw a crystallization of Atlanta's musical life into established series, performed by visiting professional artists, and various other local musical presentations. Eighteen-ninety six saw the most stellar musical series of the decade, led off by the appearance of Ignace Paderewski. The noted Polish pianist and composer had already earned an international reputation when he visited Atlanta. "Paderewski's triumph was complete," the *Constitution* wrote of his concert Wednesday evening, 22 January. "I have written of overwhelming ovations, but I have seen nothing like that manifested over the last three or four numbers of the Paderewski programme," the reporter confessed. The audience simply would not let him stop. The city had rarely heard such piano playing since Barili's recitals more than fifteen years earlier. And like Barili, Paderewski built his concert around the pillars of romantic piano music: Beethoven (Sonata in D Minor, op. 31/2), Liszt (Concert Etude No. 2; Rhapsody No. 12), and Chopin (Nocturne in G, Op. 27/2; Four etudes from Op. 25), with the Variations and Fugue on a Theme by Handel of Brahms included as a contemporary work.[30]

In April the *Constitution* announced what appears to be the first extensive music series for the city. There had been numerous single visits by performers since Thalberg had inaugurated Atlanta's serious concert music in 1858, but the five-concert series beginning in November 1896 became the model that would shape the city's musical life for much of this century. It is not clear who sponsored this first series, titled in large caps: "THE GREAT METROPOLITAN CONCERTS", nor why it did not continue the next year, though financial problems probably accounted for that. Interestingly enough, all five concerts still involved mixed genres of performers and works. Beginning in November 1896 Mme. Lillian Nordica, "First Soprano of the Metropolitan Opera house, and the greatest Wagner singer of the present time" and contralto Mme. Rose Linde presented an operatic concert, supported by tenor William Rieger and bass J. C. Dempsey. In December pianist Moritz Rosenthal played, joined by a soprano and violinist. The next month violinist Camilla Urso performed along with a contralto, tenor, and bass (one wonders if she *played* the soprano parts to the operatic quartets). Rafael Joseffy appeared in February assisted by soprano Marguerite Lemon, and cellist Hans Kronold, though he did not accompany them; they had as their pianist one Julie Levy, who had also accompanied the supporting cast from December when Rosenthal played. Finally, in March the series concluded with a vocal quartet and pianist, all supporting violinist Maude Powell.[31]

Operatic music continued to be popular, though Atlanta saw a relatively limited number of complete operatic productions during the closing years of the century. The Marie Tavary Grand Opera Company produced *Il trovatore* on 21 February 1897, while *Carmen* and *The Queen's Lace Handkerchief* appeared at the Lyceum in October. Operatic music in concert form likewise offered traditionally popular works, such as when Mme. Salchi and her company performed one act each of *Faust* and *Il trovatore* at the Grand in November, along with "several other of her favorite celebrated pieces," like Arthur Sullivan's inescapable "The Lost Chord."[32]

In October 1898 the Atlanta Concert Organization presented the first program of their inaugural series, a recital by contralto Gertrude May Stein and baritone Merrill Hopkinson. The Organization had been formed expressly to bring "to the city the best musical artists in the country." The Saturday night concert proved to be very popular, as "nearly every seat in the house was taken shortly after the ticket office was opened . . . ." The founders of the organization realized that unless they brought in professional performers, Atlanta's concert life would remain poor, limited to "perhaps only one or two good concerts during the year . . . . " This series enabled the city to participate in the rich musical culture on tour at the time. The 22 October program consisted of an intriguing blend of standard art songs such as Robert Franz, Franz Schubert, and Robert Schumann, along with English and American composers who have largely vanished from current programs, e. g., Sullivan, MacDowell, Clayton Johns, and Gilchrist. By the last season of the decade, the Association was giving seven concerts for the series, all of them vocalists and all of them forgotten today. Interestingly, the final recital of the season on 19 April 1900 returned almost entirely to operatic excerpts, opening and closing with Wagner's *Lohengrin* and *Die Meistersinger* respectively.[33]

The Atlanta Woman's Club, in contrast, mostly sponsored local musicians. Barili accompanied Walter Harrison in November 1898, when he sang Handel's "Where'er You Walk," Schubert's "Am Meer," and Chadwick's "The Miller's Daughter," while he and Miss Hunt played the F-Major Sonata for Violin and Piano by Schumann. At another recital that month Henry Howell played Chopin Etudes (E major and C-sharp minor) as well as Preludes (G Major and A Major). The next month, for the fourth of the "Woman's Club Recitals", Barili played one part for Bach's Concerto in D minor for two keyboards, in addition to the Andante, Op. 46 for two pianos by Schumann.[34]

The Atlanta Musical Club served more as a lecture-educational organization for music, hosting soirees studying genres such as solo songs by Mendelssohn or the life of a major composer such as Liszt. The Club began in 1898 as a smaller group within the Woman's Club, with which it maintained close ties throughout its history. The club was part of a growing movement to encourage learning about music in the city. In December 1897 the Atlanta Lecture Association brought the noted music scholar Louis C. Elson from the New England Conservatory of Music in Boston to talk on "Seven Centuries of English Song," a somewhat obscure subject for such an occasion. In support of this educational effort, the librarian of the Young Men's Library assembled probably the first circulating music collection in the city and prepared a bibliography of the volumes available. As expected in a century passionately curious about personalities, most of the works were biographical in nature (see Appendix B).[35]

Choral music in Atlanta still experienced ups and downs as the new century drew closer. An Atlanta Choral Club was organized in January 1898, but like so many local endeavors, prospered only briefly. Specific occasions could call forth a concerted effort and even an impressive performance, but few groups developed the financial and personnel resources to sustain themselves for any length of time. A choral-vocal concert under Professor McClain used invited soloists to present selections from Handel's *Judas Maccabeus* and Wagner's *Lohengrin* in December 1897. The next April the Woman's Exchange sponsored an evening of music and dance under Professor Samuel Burbank, who conducted a mixed chorus of ninety people in Buck's *Don Munio* (1874), taken from *The Spanish Papers* of Washington Irving. By this time Buck was arguably the most well-known American composer and his works consistently appeared on choral programs throughout the country. Few vocal recitals in Atlanta neglected to include at least one of his songs. By 1890 the *New York Herald* could write that "few will deny Dudley Buck's claim as foremost writer of Protestant American Church Music." In the *Musical Courier*, which regularly published lists of compositions popular on church programs, Buck's music consistently comprised at least one quarter of the works mentioned. Only Mendelssohn and the British composer Joseph Barnby were more popular.[36]

Church music in Atlanta started coming of age during this last decade. This development paralleled the artistic growth begun in sophisticated northeastern urban churches after mid-century. Serious organ and choral music had first taken hold in the Protestant Episcopal Church, primarily in upper northeastern cities. After the Civil War, prosperous urban churches of other denominations began to follow suit in other parts of the country, especially in larger towns along the eastern seaboard, the South and the mid-West. As class-conscious churches attracted increasingly affluent members, they began to demand better music to reflect their improved social status. Gospel hymns and choruses might be acceptable for country churches or small towns, but since they reminded downtown congregations of their humble roots, congregations gladly replaced this common music with more elegant fare. As churches grew they could also afford large pipe organs to replace the old reed instruments or pianos, and hire a trained organist to play and lead the surpliced quartet choir of trained, paid vocalists. By the last years of the century Atlanta's downtown churches were able to present serious music programs of high quality.

The city's first professional organist was quite likely J. P. O'Donnelly, who had left the city in 1883 to study for five years in Europe. He followed the example of nearly every serious American organ student of the day, who went abroad to study, inevitably in Germany. John Knowles Paine and Dudley Buck had been the first two important organists to do so in the 1860's. After them, nearly every serious organ student did the same. O'Donnelly journeyed to Stuttgart for three years of work at the Royal Conservatory before moving on to Munich for a year. After that he studied for a year in Paris under the renowned French organist Alexandre Guilmant. By May 1891 he was back in Atlanta, playing the organ at the First Baptist Church, where he instituted a yearly series of organ recitals. Organ concerts in the United States were one of the most popular classical venues before symphony orchestras supplanted them during the first decades of this century.

In Atlanta, which did not develop a serious symphonic institution until the second half of this century, organ music was widely popular. O'Donnelly's recital in June 1891 reveals a lot about the state of programming in Atlanta at the time. The concert more resembled a musical pastiche than a serious recital. O'Donnelly played the *Fuga Chromatica* from a sonata by Joseph Rheinberger, the "Chorus of Angels" (Clark), the Gavotte from *Mignon* (Thomas) and ended with Dudley Buck's variations on "Home, Sweet Home." The remaining selections were orchestral works performed by Wurm's orchestra and vocal solos. O'Donnelly continued presenting the organ series for a number of years. Accounts of his playing rarely fail to mention the factor that impressed American listeners most: pedal technique. Since O'Donnelly studied with the finest European organists, he learned the great organ literature that demanded facile pedal skill, which invariably astonished his audiences.[37]

By the middle of the decade other large downtown churches could point to extensive music programs as well. Second Baptist, Central Congregational, Church of the Immaculate Conception, the Cathedral of St. Philip, St. Luke's, All Saints', Trinity, First Presbyterian, First Methodist, and Grace Church all boasted fine choirs and talented singers led by able organists. The choral repertory in Atlanta choirs reflected that sung in other fashionable American churches during the years before World War I. Popular composers of the day included Dudley Buck, Joseph Barnby, Charles Gounod, Harry Rowe Shelley, and George Chadwick. With their elegant melodic lines, suave harmonies, uncomplicated rhythms, unforced musical styles, and uplifting biblical texts, these composers won a long-lived affection, and remained in the repertory, even in a diminished role, well into the middle of this century.[38]

With the close of the nineteenth century, both Barili and Atlanta had settled on artistic plateaus, he with his steady round of teaching, and the city with its yearly series of concerts beginning every fall and continuing into the late spring. Along the way local musicians and their students would perform mainly piano, organ, and vocal recitals, intermixed with choral groups singing popular works of the choral repertory. Opera productions continued at a modest level, depending on which touring groups happened along, until the Metropolitan Opera Company began making regular visits in the second decade of the twentieth century. This level of cultural activity provided the city with a comfortable, though not very challenging, concert life.

5 THE NEW CENTURY

1 January 1900 was a cold a day in Atlanta. The thermometer barely made it to 26 and skaters enjoyed the frozen lakes at Ponce de Leon and Grant Park. It was the first new century the young city had seen. With a population just 128 citizens shy of 90,000, Atlanta continued the prosperous growth that had marked the closing years of the old century. Appropriately, the city greeted the new century with an activity that would become one of its major industries, convention business. The Southern Journalists' Association opened its first annual convention at the Kimball House. Other important events that year would include visits by notables such as Ignace Jan Paderewski, William Jennings Bryan, and General Joseph Wheeler. Something perhaps more critical for the city's future happened that spring when City Clerk W. D. Greene issued a business license to a brand new enterprise, the Atlanta Coca-Cola Bottling Company at 125 Edgewood Avenue (the current Baptist Student Union for Georgia State University). Coca-Cola had been available in the city since May 1886 but only as a fountain drink. The new enterprise meant that it could now be bottled and sold in other places.[1]

* * * * * * *

The Barili family, which included Alfredo, Emily, twenty-year old Louise, eighteen-year old Viola, and thirteen-year old Alfredo, Jr., would see their lives change shortly after the New Year. By 1901 they had moved back into town from College Park with a house on 83 W. Fifth Street. Alfredo moved the music school as well to the Lowndes Building in downtown Atlanta. By this time the family had developed a daily and invariable routine. Meals occurred punctually every day. Like many Victorians, Alfredo and Emily came down to breakfast fully dressed, he in a tie with his smoking jacket. Lunch was at noon and dinner at the same time every evening. Getting reliable housekeeping help remained a problem for Emily, as letters from Adelina suggest. The household seems to have had at least two dogs because they form a constant thread throughout the correspondence.

What differentiated the Barili household from most of their Atlanta neighbors was its European flavor. The quiet reserve that marked European lifestyles was evident to family and visitors alike. Intellectually, Alfredo and Emily reflected their continental ancestry. They both spoke and read a number of languages, including Italian, German, French, and possibly Spanish. Their library collection impressed Mary Barili Goldsmith as a young child, and undoubtedly included a wide-range of authors and subjects. Unlike many Americans, they kept up with foreign events. After all, much of their family still lived there or had returned to Europe. Through correspondence and reading available periodicals, they maintained ties to relatives in New York and abroad, especially Patti, whose letters become a steady stream about this time. Emily remained proud of her aristocratic heritage, even signing letters "Emily Barili, nee Vezin."

This intellectual and artistic heritage worked to keep Alfredo and Emily somewhat detached from mainstream Atlanta society. They developed close friends, especially Alfredo whose personal warmth attracted many people. Both were gracious supporters of the city and its cultural efforts, but their names rarely appear in the record as being active workers in organizations like the Atlanta Concert Organization or the Atlanta Woman's Club. They were not snobs; they probably just decried the intense social focus of much of the city's artistic activity, and preferred to work in those few arenas where the music remained the primary focus. Alfredo seems to have joined few organizations. When some wealthy Atlanta gentlemen had earlier begun organizing the Piedmont Driving Club, they reportedly invited Alfredo to join them, which he declined, as he did the Atlanta chapter of the Italian-American organization. The family joined the North Avenue Presbyterian Church about this time and remained active there.

By the beginning of the twentieth century Alfredo's reputation had spread throughout the South and the east coast. It had never completely vanished in New York and Philadelphia, where influential critics like James Huneker and W. S. B. Matthews routinely wrote about him. Notices of Alfredo's work appeared in journals like the *Musical Courier* and the *Saturday Review* throughout the early years of the century. Informed musicians knew of his work. When the celebrated American composer Edward MacDowell planned a southern tour during the 1902-03 season, he wrote to Alfredo about the possibility of arranging a concert in Atlanta. Alfredo's reputation apparently earned him a Steinway piano on permanent loan from the noted piano firm. Having him teach on it exclusively would serve as good marketing material in the South. One of his most memorable pictures shows him seated at the instrument about this time. Sadly, a fire destroyed the fine piano in 1993 at the home of Randy Barili Harris in Atlanta.[2]

Alfredo's asthma seems to have settled down for a while. He took trips every summer to the north Georgia mountains. He liked the air because it made it easy for him to breathe. It also gave him much-needed rest from his heavy teaching schedule. In fact, his strength must have encouraged him to consider moving again. While he appears to have adapted well to life in Atlanta, it was clear in 1900 that the cultural situation was not going to change drastically any time soon. He had broached the subject again to Patti, but she could offer little help: "With regard to what you say about moving to New York, it is quite *impossible* for me to advise you on such a serious matter. I do not know enough about New York, or the possibilities of making money there by teaching music to be able to express any opinion of the subject." She offered to do what she could and recommend him to those she still knew there, but aside from that she could not assist him much. More uncomfortably, one senses a subtle additional message in the letter as well, one of distress over opening up another painful episode like the one a decade earlier. She cautioned him, "I think it is a serious step, which requires much consideration—therefore my dear Alfredo, I trust you will decide nothing hastily, but make full inquiries before giving up your present home." The issue seems to have caused him considerable anxiety as he complained of digestive problems, which likely stemmed from the stress surrounding the issue. Perhaps in hope of making life in Atlanta more pleasant Patti had begun sending the family 100 British pounds at Christmas times, a sizeable amount for the day, as it equalled almost six month's income for the average American.[3]

The family got to visit in person with their celebrated relative in February 1904 when she made an Atlanta visit on her final American tour. Robert Grau (younger brother to impresario Maurice Grau) with some difficulty talked Patti into one last tour of the United States. She had considerable reservations, as she was sixty years old and had essentially retired from the active concert and operatic stage. She finally agreed, supposedly to give her young husband (Rolf

Cederström) an opportunity to see America and because of the extraordinary financial arrangements. Moreover, Grau required her to sing only one aria and one encore in each program's two sections. Reporters thronged her upon her arrival in New York on 31 October 1903, where she insisted that this was the only authorized farewell tour that she had ever made. Indeed, it was the final one. Her opening concert on 2 November predictably filled Carnegie Hall. The assisting vocalists opened the evening, but when Patti appeared the audience erupted with delight. She was uncharacteristically nervous as she began with one of her old reliables "O luce di quest'anima" from *Linda di Chamounix* and later "Il bacio." For her first encore she offered "The Last Rose of Summer" and, after repeated curtain calls, "Home, Sweet Home," followed by a song written for her, "The Last Farewell." While the applause was gratifying, it lacked the frenetic intensity of years past.[4]

The reviews the following day proved disappointing. They pointed out the effects of a half century of singing: shrillness, strain on the highest notes, occasional intonation problems, and shortness of breath at times. Her voice improved for the two following New York programs. Concerts in Philadelphia, Boston, and Baltimore drew well also. She then embarked on a transcontinental tour, riding in a seventy-two-foot long Pullman car named *Craig-y-Nos*. The car had been refurbished for her and contained a dining/drawing room, separate bedrooms for her and Rolf, and a music room, with a specially built Steinway piano, that opened onto a glass observation car. The average box office for the tour earned $7000.

On 7 February her special train arrived in Atlanta where she was greeted by almost three hundred people, hoping for a glimpse of the celebrated diva. She hurried to the Piedmont Hotel where her troupe occupied a suite of seven rooms. As she would turn sixty-one in two weeks, the talk of the town had been what the famed soprano would sound like after all these years. "These fears faded rapidly, though as soon as the still great diva made her appearance, and they were quite gone after her first few phrases of song," the reviewer for the *Constitution* wrote. While she was dressed magnificently and adorned with jewels, "it was the exquisite preservation of the woman's physical charm as well as of her voice that was marvelous." Her careful performances of "Voi che sapete" and the "Jewel Song" also won her high praise. It was her "dainty coquetry" in "Robin Adair," "Home Sweet Home," and "Comin' Thro' the Rye," though, that threw the audience into wild enthusiasm. Only when the assisting artists finally walked onto stage for their selections did the listeners allow her to retire.[5]

Soon the hard work for the tour began to wear and, by the time she arrived in Louisville, she had decided to cancel the stops remaining after a concert at Hot Springs, Arkansas on 8 March. She wrote the news to Alfredo and Louise who apparently journeyed to New York to see her before she sailed home on 12 March on the *Lucania,* richer by $200,000.[6]

Back in Wales she grew concerned over Alfredo's health. He and Louise had visited Wales that spring, from April through June 1904. By that fall, the distressing issue of leaving Atlanta again emerges in her letters, where Patti began encouraging him to move to England. Her own growing desire for having the family close to her probably played an increasingly important role in the situation, as her letters take on a new urgency. With the children now older, the family could join her in England without too much discomfort. And as before, Alfredo seems caught by the dilemma, unable to come to a decision about his future. "I do not yet give up all hope," she wrote him in November 1904, "to get you over to Europe. Your place ought be on this side of the water, where you teach your great wonderful method—America is indeed no place for you." The whole affair distressed her considerably. She had been busy seeing how he could set up a studio in England, as she explained to Louise, "I wrote your dear papa a few days ago a very long letter with all details about the affair of coming over and giving lessons." Patti hoped it might be imminent, "You know how much I should love to settle the matter at once—and how I *dread* letting things hang on. I am almost frantic with it all, for I should *so* much like to have your papa placed here in Europe . . . . I am going to do *all* in my power to get him over some day."[7]

The letters during the next months suggest that the real impetus for Barili moving to Europe shifted from Alfredo's hopes to Patti wanting the family near her. Perhaps another factor had been her visit to Atlanta, which, she perceived, had not grown a great deal culturally. Sensing that Atlanta remained very young artistically, she might have become more interested in seeing Alfredo leave. By the next summer her pleas were taking on a new urgency. She wrote to him from Carlsbad, where Patti went every summer to take the waters, driving right to the heart of the matter, "My only ambition now in life is to have you come over to Europe and live and to give up living in Atlanta—Georgia! *Great Scott, what can anybody* have done to deserve ending one's life in *Atlanta Georgia?*" Not to be put off, she raised the issue again in January 1906, insisting that "Something *must* be done to get you *all* over here. I *cannot* stand" it without you any more, she pleaded. Alfredo was feeling better as well, which relieved her from worrying about his health.[8]

Now that Patti had curtailed much of her singing and was growing older, family became increasingly important, especially Alfredo, Emily, and Louise, who meant the most to her of all her relatives. During her American tour she had visited with Louise, who had now grown into a young adult (and incidentally much resembled her aunt physically as well as temperamentally). Patti and she had become very close, more like dear friends than niece and aunt. "I miss you *terribly*," Patti lamented to her. "Yes, I have many friends, and am sure they love me. But my Louise is more like myself—and we both understand each best." She was delighted that Louise was going to accompany her father on his visit to Wales in April, for "nothing can make up for one's own relations—I sometimes feel quite lonesome for something belonging to me!" She loved her husband Rolf dearly, "but that is *not* the same thing—but what the Italians call "*I legami di sangue*" [bonds of blood] is *quite* a different thing, & I feel that owing to my mother's side, if ever so little, there must be something of that kind between you & me!" In January she was still "counting the days for April to arrive." She was eager to see Alfredo's new compositions as well.[9]

Alfredo and Louise sailed on the Cunard ship *Campania,* arriving in Liverpool on 7 April 1906, tired as they did not do well at sea. They took the noon train and arrived at Craig-y-Nos late that afternoon to discover "Old Glory" waving in the breeze, as it was the custom at the castle to fly the flag of the arriving guests. Louise found Patti quite worked up, "Truly she is the most excitable creature I ever knew, and you know I am not much better." Dinner, as always, was the highlight of the day, where "Aunt Adelina's guests assembled in the boudoir next to the dining room. Here the guests awaited their hostess who invariably made a dramatic entrance amid admiring 'oohs' and 'aahs' seeing the diva arrayed in a brilliant gown and dazzling jewels." Patti launched right into discussions on the issue of the family's possible relocation to London, where Alfredo could teach, and they would be "near one another & never part until our Father above calls us." "Aunt Adelina does nothing but talk of getting us over here," she wrote to her mother. As it was difficult to disagree with Patti (who could be quite imperious), "Papa and I let her talk," Louise demurely pointed out. Continued discussions did little more than heighten the impasse and make everyone anxious, as she told her mother, "I am sorry to tell you there is nothing definite as to the London proposition and must say both Uncle Rolf and Aunt Adelina act like a couple of infants in regard to this question." From the tone of Louise's letters, Emily too must have been encouraging Alfredo to move, which meant that the family had split into two sides over the issue, with Alfredo—interestingly enough—joining Louise, and now Viola, in wishing to stay in Atlanta. Louise confided in her younger sister later in April, "I do hope Mama is not too disappointed because nothing is settled about our coming to England to live. When we are able to tell her all the details, she will understand, I am sure."[10]

Alfredo became overwrought over the possibility of breaking the bad news to Emily should he decide not to move, fearing she would be disappointed. Louise assured him that Emily only wanted him to be content remaining in Atlanta, with its modest cultural activity. Louise quickly assured her mother, "He seemed so relieved when I told him that you could make yourself contented anywhere provided he was satisfied."[11] Patti must have pressed the issue until Alfredo relented and agreed at least to visit London and see for himself before coming to a firm conclusion. To test the waters, in early June the group, made up of Louise, Alfredo, Rolf and perhaps Patti, made the 200-mile trip to London in Rolf's new motorcar, taking two days. Alfredo's worst fears were realized and he became very uncomfortable in the sprawling, frenetic, and overwhelming imperial capitol. With the wide-spread industrialization and coal dust covering the entire city, it took little time for the pollution to aggravate his asthma. Louise knew immediately that it would not work, that her father's health and the strain from such a drastic move would be too much for everyone, something she had suspected from the start, as she had told Viola, "I am sure that when we get home and can explain things better you will all understand the impossibility of our living in London."[12]

Fortunately for posterity, during their visit Alfredo agreed to accompany his aunt in two recording sessions. Cone provides a fascinating account of the Queen of Song's introduction to the new technology. For years various talking machine companies had tried to convince Patti to record, but she had steadfastly resisted all entreaties. Many leading singers of the day, including Caruso, Calvé, and Melba had already cut cylinders, but Patti held out. While she was in London in November 1905 for a concert at the Albert Hall the Gramophone Company's English manager, Sydney Dixon, persuaded her to listen to some recordings. She began to waver and he finally convinced her to sign a contract. She stipulated that the recordings would have to be made at Craig-y-Nos and at her convenience.[13]

In early December Fred Gaisberg and his brother Will set out with some intrepidation from London for Wales to record Patti. Their fears were soon alleviated when they discovered that she had graciously set up two large bedrooms for their work. "Here we assembled our recording machine. We had a curtain over one of the doors, and through a hole projected the recording-horn. The piano was placed on wooden boxes and when Madame Patti entered the room she was terribly intrigued as to what was behind that long horn. She had the curiosity of a girl, and peeped under the curtain to see what was on the other side . . . ." It took her two full days to get accustomed to the idea, and she finally agreed to record the next morning. Her accompanist for this first session was young Ronald Landon, whose memoirs provide a delightful account of the whole process. Nervously, she began with Mozart's famous "Voi che sapete" from *Le nozze di Figaro.* As soon as they finished she begged to hear it, which would destroy the cylinder owing to the primitive technology, but she promised to record it again. He then recounts what must have been an incredible scene, when one of the outstanding singers of all time, who had been singing for half a century, heard a recording of her own voice for the first time:

> I shall never forget the scene. She had never heard her own voice, and when the little trumpet gave forth the beautiful tones, she went into ecstasies! She threw kisses into the trumpet and kept on saying, *"Ah, mon dieu! maintenant je comprends pourquoi je suis Patti. Oh, oui! Quelle voix! Quelle artiste! Je comprends tout!* [Ah! my Lord! now I understand why I am Patti! Oh, yes! What a voice! What an artist! I understand all!]"

For four successive days they recorded from eleven to twelve in the morning, producing some twenty sides. Patti included some of her most popular warhorses like "The Last Rose of Summer," "Comin' Through the Rye," "Kathleen Mavourneen," and "Home Sweet Home" as well as opera arias "Voi che sapete", "Batti, batti" *(Don Giovanni)*, and the "Jewel Song" *(Faust)*. Ronald Landon made a telling observation during the days at the castle, "I have always instinctively felt that Patti was the only real diva I have ever met—the only singer who had no flaws for which to apologize."

She loved the whole thing, as she wrote Alfredo (8 December 1905), "You will be pleased to hear that I have been singing in a Gramophone and that it all has turned out satisfactorily—my voice and phrasing come easy & simply perfect out of the instrument and I think the company will make a fortune. . . . I have received a splendid deposit." Indeed, the fourteen discs chosen for sale included the "Patti label" pink, her favorite color, and sold for the high price of twenty-one shillings. They were so popular that the company planned another recording session in June 1906 during the visit of Alfredo and Louise.

Fred Gaisberg returned with an assistant for the second session. This time Patti and Alfredo made nine records, repeating some selections she had recorded earlier. New pieces included the song "La calesera" and the arias "Casta diva" *(Norma)*, "Connaise-tu le pays?" *(Mignon)*, and "Ah, non credea mirarti" *(La sonnambula)*. This time Alfredo was nervous along with Patti, as Louise later recounted:

> The facilities for making the records were crude compared to those used now. Aunt Adelina stood on a small movable platform which, for shading, was moved toward or away from the recording machine. As this was done while my aunt was singing, it made her very nervous. Father, too, was agitated because he had to play with the piano elevated, high up, on boxes. Papa was told not to do any shading, as it would not record, but he could never play mechanically.[14]

As one would expect from knowing about Alfredo Barili personally, his playing on these works (now available on Pearl GEMM CD9312) shows his exquisite musicianship—elegant, flawless, effortlessly controlled, and always musical. His phrasing captures the musical line exactly, and he shows that intuitive insight into the music just as writers and critics described.

Patti's voice, at age sixty-three shows some wear. Obviously, "much of the brilliance . . . was a thing of the past by the time she came to make recordings," Michael Scott wrote in *The Record of Singing to 1914*. One hears the scooping, too loud attacks in places, interrupted phrases, and some shrillness. "Still," he asserts, "her singing remains more affecting than anyone else's on records. In her recordings, we can hear so many of the ancient graces of singing." Even in the twilight of her career, "we have a recollection of all that was eloquent in the music of the salon."[15]

* * * * * * *

In July, Alfredo and Louise returned to Atlanta and settled into a comfortable routine, teaching at the School of Music with Emily, where Louise now also worked as a voice instructor, and Viola in elocution. Young Alfredo, Jr. had become a draftsman and was working at the Prudential Building for an architectural firm. Running through Patti's letters during the last three years of the decade is the constant concern over Alfredo's and now Viola's health. A letter of 20 April 1907 responded to an apparently urgent one from Atlanta, "I cannot possibly tell you how *miserably wretched* . . . I feel at the bad news of your poor dear father's illness," she wrote Louise, "and your letter saying that he is still in danger quite upset us." One senses the kind of danger that so alarmed the doctor back in the fall of 1891, when Alfredo left Atlanta for a while. With medical science still unable to do much for his asthma, a severe attack could indeed threaten his life.

The month of May seems to have brought Alfredo some relief. During that following summer, like a number of times previously, Alfredo, Louise and Emily travelled to Yonkers, New York to visit Emily's brother, Charles Vezin, who still managed the wholesale drygoods firm of Hinchman, Vezin & Co. In 1919 at age sixty-one he would retire and devote himself to landscape painting, earning a wide reputation and a membership in the Royal Academy of Art by the time of his death in 1942. They must have stayed at least a month because the correspondence covers that period and Patti addressed her letters to them there during July and August 1907.

That next year Viola seems to have developed an ailment similar to that of her father, or even more severe. Something, probably her breathing and nasal system, must have been causing her excruciating pain as she had to undergo an operation. The family's obsession with secrecy extended even to their beloved aunt, whom they kept in the dark as much as they have hidden from posterity the exact nature of Viola's (and Alfredo's) illness, for Patti indignantly insists that they tell her what is wrong with her young niece, "Why should she have to undergo an operation I would like to know! All this seems very strange." It was odd that they would feel such shame—and that seems to be the only word to describe it—about hiding their health problems. If anything, most Victorians seem to have enjoyed their poor health, and if their nervous conditions did not have clear biological origins they would seek other reasons for "taking to their bed." But the Barilis felt otherwise and scrupulously avoided admitting to anything more than they had to. Apparently Viola, sometime in the summer of 1908, underwent an operation in New York, which is understandable given the difference in medical facilities between the two cities. She also was treated by a female doctor, which riled Adelina, who still did not seem to know the nature of Viola's "complaint." She demanded an explanation from Emily, "why on earth do you give the child into the hands of a woman Doctor? You must *surely* have excellent Doctors in Atlanta? Of course you know best but if Viola were my child I should certainly place her into the hands of a *first rate man Doctor*."[16]

Viola's first operation was not entirely successful because by fall of the next year Patti is again concerned that Viola may have to endure another. Still, the family remained adamant in their secrecy as Patti is still asking for information, "What is the manner of the ailment she is suffering from?" By the end of November (1909) the Atlanta doctor seems to have decided that an additonal operation was necessary. This second operation seems to have been entirely successful.[17]

Alfredo continued to have dismaying bouts with his own health, which he described to Patti as nerves. In light of the family's obsessive secrecy on the issue, his "nerves" appear to have been caused by his respiratory illness, which is understandable given the panic which breathing difficulties can precipitate. Sorting things out is tenuous at best, given the paucity and one-sided view of the evidence. The most educated guess from this vantage is that Alfredo's breathing problems, compounded by his professional frustrations, all were lumped under the generic nineteenth-century complaint of nerves, which the family felt was a suitable explanation for public interest. Again and again, Patti assures Louise and Emily "how *awfully* sorry I was to learn by your last letter how ill your poor father has been again. He does not seem to improve in health at all!" Or, "What an awful family we have all been with those *terrible* complaints! but more especially the Barilis."[18]

The visits to New York seemed to much improve Alfredo's health. He had apparently written Patti in distress in June 1908, which upset her, "I do wish you were better and stronger so as to be able to look upon things in a brighter way!" After travelling to New York he felt better, as Patti confided to Emily the next month, who was with Louise in Franklin, North Carolina, "Yes, I have heard from Alfredo, Sr. He seems to write in better spirits this time." Her reply to Alfredo hints at the professional disappointment still bothering him in Atlanta—the quality of his students. While he was the most respected and honored musician in Atlanta, those students he taught who had serious musical talent and interest were few and far between. Rare was the student like Rosa Pringle who travelled from Athens to study with Barili for two years before moving on to become a concert pianist in New York. It is very easy to understand how Alfredo's spirit could be weighed down as the endless lessons with minimally motivated students dragged on. After having been refreshed by summers in North Carolina, New York, or even Wales, he would have felt happy and confident in September. But then, as the flow of students paraded through the studio week after week, with only a rare musical challenge or inspiration, he could easily have become despondent. "All those pupils must be, I know, a great strain on your poor nerves—If only one of them would become great and do you justice you would then have some satisfaction and something to look forward to," Patti wrote to him in early July 1908.[19]

In Franklin, Louise began her teaching career during the summer of 1908. This pleased Patti to no end, especially, "that you have already several pupils who want to attend—but just fancy having a school up in the mountains!" Emily and Alfredo joined her later that summer before returning to Atlanta. Louise gave private vocal instruction, as well as ensemble work. She also lectured on song writers such as Schumann, Schubert, Robert Franz, Amy Beach, George Chadwick, and Cyril Scott. By this time she had already developed into a vocalist of repute, as the *Musical Courier* noted in April 1904: "Miss Louise Barili, an Atlanta girl with a charming voice, recently gave a recital in the studio of her father, Alfredo Barili."[20]

Louise had been offered her first full-time job earlier that summer from a Madeline Keipp, who was connected with the School of Musical Art in Jacksonville, Florida. She apparently thought highly of Louise's abilities as she repeatedly pressed the offer throughout the summer and into the fall. She was prepared to guarantee Louise at least $100 a month, but felt sure it would soon grow to double that, as another teacher had made $200 easily in Jacksonville the winter before. Louise would teach the voice students at the school and conduct a church choir. Either Louise put Keipp off or had not answered her invitation in July because Keipp detoured without luck through Franklin to see her. Undaunted, Keippe wrote Louise later that month, saying that she regretted missing her because she wanted to talk with her in person and "try to convince you of the success of our Jacksonville plans. We have our hearts set on having you. Is there anything else we can do to *clinch* the matter with you?" Louise must have indeed impressed Keippe because she offered her a virtual blank check to come. "How much do you want guaranteed for the first year?" Louise apparently turned her down shortly thereafter. Once more Keipp pushed her point at the end of August, "Your letter was a great disappointment to me but nevertheless I am going to make one more effort to have Louise Barili with us this winter." Louise, like her father, knew her own mind, and when set, it remained set. She did not go.[21]

Of course, Louise sought the opinion of her renowned aunt, who was slightly aghast at the whole idea and even more astonished that Alfredo had agreed to it. While it appeared to be a flattering offer, Louise was probably right with her reservations; she thought Florida full of fevers. With the poor sanitary conditions, this indeed was a problem. Moreover, if Atlanta had proven to be limited artistically, one could only imagine how things were in Jacksonville during the early years of the century. This is probably what accounted for Madeline Keipp's strenuous efforts to lure Louise down there, as it must have been a difficult task at best to lure talented musicians to such rural places. Emily seems to have weighed in against it, which, added to Patti's discomfort, doomed the plans. Patti was delighted with Louise's decision to remain in Atlanta.[22]

* * * * * *

Broader musical life in Atlanta beyond the Barili family activities increased considerably during the first decade of the new century, setting the tone for years to come. The two ancestors of the social organizations that would drive this activity were in place, the Atlanta Concert and Festival Association and the Atlanta Woman's Club with its Music Study Club. They would sponsor nearly all of the artistically significant musical events for the next sixty years. Touring companies would continue to perform, organized on their own, but they became increasingly rare, while concerts by local musicians slowly increased. Finally, music in the churches became an even more important venue for the city's artistic life, most notably choral and organ performances.

Fittingly, a visit by the French Opera Company (from Paris) inaugurated Atlanta's twentieth-century musical life. The special train bringing the 100 members of the company arrived on 15 January from New Orleans where it had a successful run. That evening they presented the first of three operas, *Faust*. The reviewer, Louise Dooly, praised the production, but criticized some of the mismanaged technical aspects. She also found the four leads uneven in their roles. Mme. Clement as Marguerite got off to a slow start, but had settled in artistically by the time for the spinning-wheel scene; she sang the "Jewel Song"—that nemesis of so many sopranos—" with all the abandon and brilliancy" that it should have. Unfortunately, Mme. Frassart as Siebel was not up to the task, disturbing the audience with her "sharp and some parts rather gurgling" voice. The next night saw the company's production of *La juive* (Halévy), which was well received but not nearly as popular as *Faust*. They concluded their run with Gounod's *Roméo et Juliette*, which proved the most popular of the three.[23]

Opera in American life had become the most regal form of high art, the province of the rich and socially mobile classes. It was viewed as such by the majority of Americans, who sought out less elaborate musical entertainment, such as vaudeville. By the third decade of the century the motion picture industry would make major inroads into audiences for musical performances. One critical factor in opera's appeal to the higher classes was its performance in the original language, which only those people with the education and leisure time to study could most thoroughly appreciate. Early on, Atlanta became singularly occupied with the glittering social bustle surrounding opera performances, perhaps because the city had never really developed any other broad-based artistic institutions. With Reconstruction Atlanta frantically sought to make up for lost cultural time. Opera performances, limited to a few weeks a year, comfortably fit into the busy business schedule of the city. Moreover, the wives of the affluent business leaders could focus much of their activity around the opera season. When the opera troupes finally arrived everyone could dress up, endure the opera, enjoy the glittering parties, and thus discharge their "artistic" obligations for the rest of the year. Having done so, the city was spared the financial expense of constructing houses for operas, symphonies, and ballet companies, as well as the enormous costs involved with supporting them.

By the turn of the century this system was firmly in place in Atlanta. It comes as no surprise that the longest article in the *Constitution* covering the French Opera company concerned itself with social, not musical, descriptions of the event; moreover, it ran before the articles covering the music and the company (14 January 1900). "There is no occasion that admits of more elaborate dressing than the opera, and not only the ladies in the boxes, but those in the parquet, will appear in evening costume, and the gentlemen in their conventional evening attire," as the writer so aptly began. She—one assumes it is a she as it is not signed—continues about the current fashion of wearing brooches on the dresses, something new from Paris. Further, she makes it clear that it is "necessary to know thoroughly the plots of the operas . . . to be affected by the beauty of the opera's sentiments, as well as the music." She points to something else telling about Atlanta's operatic experience. Atlanta audiences have gained a reputation for "coldness and seeming indifference that is almost habitual," except for opera. During these brief periods the audiences felt that they could allow themselves to become involved in the artistic experience.

Fascinating, from a sociological point of view, was the appearance of the Wilbur-Kirwin Opera Company two months later at the beginning of March. Here were musical productions more reflective of stage music a half century earlier, where the entertainment was designed for everyone. The productions were done in English (the French Opera Company sang all three of their operas in French) at the Columbia Theater, the old DeGive's Opera House. The fare avoided the highbrow opera repertory, presenting traditional favorites instead, such as *Fra Diavolo, The Two Vagabonds, The Chimes of Normandy,* and *Cavaleria Rusticana.* Unconcerned about artistic purity or dramatic consistency, the troupe offered between the acts of these works *The Girl with the Auburn Locks,* a sacred tableau which could not have failed to delight the city's church-going, reverent citizenry. For a brief moment, the audience could ascend beyond this vale of tears as it watched a beautiful young girl gaze heaven-ward from a choir loft while she sang a number of sacred songs, most fittingly "Nearer My God to Thee," accompanied by a surpliced organist. Few scenes held more powerful symbols for Victorian Americans. The sweet innocence of the young girl, the familiar song, the religious setting, and the uplifting "propriety" of the whole scene would have drawn murmurs of approval from the whole house. The entire evening is more typical of a night at the opera sixty years before where the entr'act materials reflected the social issues of the day. No one was bothered by the incongruity of the whole affair. Finally, and perhaps most significantly, the Wilburn-Kirwin Opera Company, which presented more works than more prestigious companies, received scant notice in the *Constitution.* Not only was it relegated to an inner page, it barely lasts five paragraphs. The city had already celebrated its culture for the year and there was little time left to pay attention to competing events, especially lowbrow ones in the wrong house, in the wrong language, and with the wrong operas.[24]

Fall of 1901 saw the city's next Grand Opera Festival. Maurice Grau brought the company then resident at the Metropolitan Opera House in New York, calling it the Grau Grand Opera Company. It was the first visit of the Metropolitan's artists as a single group, even though it was not officially organized by the New York house as such. The renowned Metropolitan conductor Walter Damrosch, along with soprano Emma Eames and contralto Ernestine Schumann-Heink were part of the company as well. With this tour, which had been to Canada, Albany, Buffalo, Memphis, and Nashville, Grau did much to prepare the ground for the Metropolitan's yearly tours, which would begin before the end of the decade. The paper declared that the three-performance run "will be the most important event socially and musically announced for the winter. Later attractions of whatever prominence that may be secured can hardly equal in distinction the engagement of Grau's forces . . . ." Of course, "the social and business features promise success as certain as the artistic, because the sale of tickets has been so gratifyingly large." Opening on Monday evening, 28 October 1901, the company presented *Lohengrin* (in German, as the advertisement clearly states), *Roméo et Juliet* (in French), and *Il barbiere di Siviglia* (in Italian).[25]

Critic Louise Dooley applauded all three performances. Not surprisingly, the social aspect loomed as large as the music, "Every box in the theater will have its attractive box party, all the occupants appearing in evening dress, and in the body of the house, too, there will be seen quite as formal attire . . . and numerous supper parties afterwards will require elaborate toilets." Interestingly enough, the company split following its Atlanta performances, part going to Birmingham and others to New Orleans.[26]

Atlanta seems to have missed any regular opera weeks for the next three years, but on Christmas Day 1904 the *Constitution* announced the appearance of the English Grand Opera Company. Opera in a foreign language had become so expected that the writer mistakenly called the event "an epoch in the history of Atlanta" and assumed that it was "the first time that southern people have had an opportunity to hear the standard operas of the world in their mother tongue." The majority of opera touring companies during the decades of the 1850's into the 1870's presented their productions in English. In fact, it was so unusual then for a troupe to sing in Italian that groups who did so included in the title "Italian Opera Company." This English Grand Opera Company only repeats the title of numerous (and often undifferentiated) English Grand Opera Companies that performed in Atlanta in the twenty years following the Civil War. The *Constitution* writer presents this group as the hobby of one Mr. Savage, who had managed other groups under the name Savage Opera Company. During his nine-year work as an opera impresario, his companies sang eighty-one different operas in an incredible 4,000 performances, many of which, it was claimed, had never been sung before in English. *Lohengrin* opened the typical three-evening plus matinee run, on 16 January 1905. *Otello, Carmen,* and *Il trovatore* all followed suit, and all in English. While the series was well received, and had adequate coverage in the *Constitution,* there is a consciously lower level of journalistic fervor this time. Was it simply the way in which it was covered and attended this year, or was it that the operas were in English, which lowered them a little socially (obviously, the music did not change), thus diminishing their appeal? Also, being sung in English meant that Mr. Savage could not engage the most famous European opera singers, something that would have further lessened the glittering star attractions of the week.[27]

Church music in Atlanta continued building on the foundations established in the previous decade. The era of the professional quartet-choir persisted, consisting of a central core of four singers, a soprano, alto, tenor, and bass, directed by an organist/conductor. Music held the same place in the services as it does today, with the quartet providing anthems in addition to vocal solos, duets, or larger choral works such as oratorios or cantatas. For years to come, a majority of the city's well-trained music professionals would be organists, even though organ recitals did not take a regular place in the city's musical life until after 1910, when the Austin Organ installed in the new city auditorium began attracting more interest in the instrument. The city did host infrequent organists on tour, such as Clarence Eddy, perhaps the most famous organist of his day, who played in late April 1900. Eddy's program featured typical organ literature, which reflected the symphonic conception of the music. He was noted for being one of the country's finest Bach players, following his teacher, Dudley Buck. The review in the paper illustrates the state of organ music in the city; the writer does not identify the church or the name of the instrument, except to say that "the big organ was in excellent condition." Occasions such as the installation of the new instrument at St. Luke's Episcopal Church would produce a local organ recital, such as the one which J. Lewis Browne gave on Wednesday evening 18 December 1901. While Mr. Browne did play Bach's Prelude and Fugue in B-flat, the rest of the program consisted of extremely light works such as Rheinberger's "Vision," and Stern's "Soupir." The listings of music for church programs did not consistently specify the organ work played.[28]

During the first decade of the century church music still focused on the quartet choir and choral music. Typical was the program presented by J. W. Marshbank at First Presbyterian on Sunday 18 November 1900. The morning service offered two anthems, "The Lord is King," (Marston), and "Lead Kindly Light" (Buck), while the evening services offered five pieces, including Buck's "Rock of Ages," and Shelley's "Savior, When Night Involves the Skies." Major choral works were beginning to appear more frequently in Atlanta churches, such the First Presbyterian's presentation of Mendelssohn's oratorio *St. Paul* on Tuesday evening, 2 February 1909. Mr. Marshbank conducted the chorus and Wurm's orchestra for the performance.[29]

The leading churches of the city remained those that had been prominent earlier: Sacred Heart (Catholic), Immaculate Conception (Catholic), First Methodist, Trinity Methodist, St. Mark Methodist, St. Philip (Episcopal), First Baptist, Second Baptist, Grace Church (Methodist), and First Presbyterian. The dean of Atlanta's organists continued to be J. P. O'Donnelly at First Baptist, who directed a popular program of church music, including an entire evening service consisting of music by Wagner, including the "Pilgrim's Chorus" and March from *Tannhäuser,* and a solo and quartet from *Lohengrin* as an anthem!

New to Atlanta's organ benches were the number of young women assuming leadership roles. The profession of organist was finally becoming suitable and respectable for women. By 1901 a number of the city's leading churches had women organists, a trend that would grow.[30]

The early years of the new century likewise solidified the concert life of the city, which was largely directed by the Atlanta Concert Association. Throughout the first part of the decade, the organization typically presented five or six concerts during the season, which lasted from the fall into early spring. Musical artists under concert management now toured the United States regularly. Atlanta had become one of the major cities on these tours, able to support large audiences at the Grand Opera House. The first months of 1900 brought a number of outstanding musicians, including violinists Leonora Jackson and Alexandre Petschnikoff, pianists Ignace Paderewski and Mark Hamburg, and the fourth Atlanta appearance of Theodore Thomas with his recently established Chicago Orchestra. The concert by Paderewski on 22 February was his second in the city, and it proved no less successful than the first. The *Constitution* critic amusingly noted that while wild audience enthusiasm was standard from Paderewski's viewpoint, "it was very unusual for an Atlanta audience, and they seemed surprised themselves that they were so emphatically moved." The program presented by the famed pianist demonstrated why his listeners reacted the way they did. It included, among other pieces, Beethoven's *Appassionata Sonata*, Schumann's *Etudes symphoniques*, Chopin's Ballad in A-Flat and Nocturne in D-flat, Liszt's *Hungarian Rhapsody No. 6*, and Paderewski's own Minuet in A. Thomas's two programs revealed the keen programming skill that had served him so well for nearly a century. He mixed Beethoven's Fifth Symphony and excerpts from Wagner's *Tristan und Isolde* with, among other works, a Strauss waltz, Smetana overture, and Handel's indomitable "Largo". The audience was respectful during both performances, but not as enthusiastic as the year before at his concert. Not surprisingly, the Strauss waltz "was without doubt the most popular number. . . ."[31]

A first for the city occurred that year on 12-13 June when the Southern Music Teachers' Association held its inaugural convention in the auditorium of The Young Men's Christian Association. The idea had been suggested a year earlier by one of Atlanta's matriarchs, Mrs. William Peel, vice-president of the Concert Association. In addition to the lectures offered, a number of recitals were also presented. The convention concluded the second evening with a grand concert of piano and choral work, led by Barili.

A week before the convention opened the *Constitution* ran an extensive article on the upcoming conference. The article included a general assessment of Atlanta's current position musically. From the outset, the discussion raised the issue (once again) of an annual music festival for the city, like the one Cincinnati had enjoyed since the early 1870's. Oscar Pappenheimer, a prominent local musician, had attended the last fourteen of the Cincinnati festivals. He thought Atlanta could establish its own festival "if a chorus can be formed of sufficient proportions, and with the musical interest at heart." Other southern cities had managed to do it, even with orchestral accompaniment. Atlanta could engage an orchestra, such as that of Theodore Thomas, if the city could maintain an adequate chorus, which "would be the difficult thing—to arouse and keep the interest of 200 singers or more during the many months of earnest study." He had few doubts that Atlanta had shown progress in support of serious music, but "Whether this interest is as yet sufficient to make a grand festival chorus feasible can only be proved by experiment." Unfortunately, there was insufficient interest to support a chorus until Robert Shaw arrived in the city and established the Atlanta Symphony Orchestra Chorus in the early 1970's, which, incidentally, today numbers some 200 singers.[32]

Barili was interviewed at length, longer than anyone else (he also enjoyed the largest picture of anyone in the 13 June article). He diplomatically praised the city's enthusiasm for music, but decried the lack of musical education, "Our greatest need just now is musical lectures. The people of Atlanta love music and they wish to appreciate its highest forms; their concert attendance and attention show that, but they cannot understand it, because they have not been taught. Their musical education is at fault." He found the young people lacking in dedication, which he blamed on their teachers, who "all favor a showy course of instruction" in lieu of serious, thorough preparation. Students learned a few flashy pieces before their technique was solid or before they could manage the works musically, just to impress their friends and family. Until a student was ready, Barili forbade his charges from performing in public "until their education is such that they are no longer amateurs, but can enter the ranks and take a good stand among professional musicians." This attitude explains much of Barili's frustration with his Atlanta music teaching. Few teachers enjoy the luxury of a studio full of serious, potentially professional music students, especially in Atlanta at the turn of the century. Growing up in the family as he did, Barili inherited the hard-driving, single-minded musical commitment that characterized virtually every member of his family. With his enormous talent, he followed in their steps, all the way to one of the most outstanding places in the world of music at Cologne. When he arrived in Atlanta, it apparently took him a long time to adjust to the reality of the musical life there. He welcomed the Teacher's Association and its various recital programs because it would do a great deal for the young women studying music throughout the South to hear musicians perform at a professional level.

As for a festival, he thought "it a splendid idea and one that is popular and would be possible with the right kind of a chorus. The chorus for the convention which is rehearsing now under my direction is small for a festival, but I think it could be augmented when the time should come for its reorganization for a festival." One cannot help but wonder if Barili was speculating on what might have happened to the choral group nearly twenty years earlier had they chosen him as director. Could he have kept up the momentum? Would they still be singing? Certainly most of the city's musicians and journalists had thought so. Most musical institutions reflect the personality of the director, perhaps none more so than a choral group. Again, witness the ASO Chorus, which took firm root only under Robert Shaw. Could the city have had an outstanding chorus nearly a century earlier? Cincinnati, Boston, and New York had. Barili possessed as much personal magnetism as Shaw, according to every account, along with the necessary musical excellence and technical precision. Were nineteenth-century Atlantans so much less capable of a commitment than those in the 1970's? We will never know.

Another successful Atlanta music teacher, Mary Madden, seconded Barili, almost verbatim. "What we need in Atlanta and the South for its best musical development is earnest, patient, good teachers. When our young students are properly directed in their musical pursuits, they cannot fail to appreciate the highest there is in music and to demand it." She understood that young people could not appreciate performances like Paderewski's unless they had been well taught. She likewise decried the number of teachers—the majority—who are teaching only with "the idea of gaining a limitless number of pupils by showing off the ones they have." Until the students learned to love the music for itself, "outside the glory of applause," the musical situation would not improve. She likewise questioned whether Atlanta could sustain a large festival chorus over a number of months. Of course, "I believe Atlanta has not yet been tested as to whether its many good singers include a large enough number who would be willing to give several months study and time . . . ."

The organizers of the convention did possess enough musical wisdom to invite Barili to conduct the chorus for the closing concert at the Grand.

Before that the participants heard a number of lectures interspersed with recitals. The content of the lectures reveals an interest in redirecting arts toward a more scientific basis, which the biologically-oriented nineteenth century had engendered. Ferdinand Dunkley, an organist from Asheville, spoke on "The Application of Mental Laws to the Study, Performance and Teaching of Music," and Frank Thompson came from Richmond to offer some hints on "What It Means to Train A Voice." For pianists, one Mrs. Virgil discussed "Technic [sic] and Its Relations to Artistic Success; How It May be Acquired and Retained." President Joseph MacLean's opening address raised the critical issue of teacher certification, of "requiring them to reach a certain percent before they are given a license to teach . . . ." While it took some years to put this in place, it did more to raise the standards of music in the South than any other single factor. The level and repertoire of the recitals also showed respectable levels, especially the organ recital of Mr. Dunkley at First Methodist, where he played Bach's magnificent Fantasy and Fugue in G minor, quite possibly a first for the city. The concert on the final evening of the conference ended with Barili conducting the chorus and soloists in Cowen's "The Rose Maiden."

The concert season for 1900-01 showcased some new artists in addition to performers the city had already heard, such as Leonora Jackson. The Spiering Quartet played in December 1900, followed the next month by Miss Jackson who had proved enormously popular the year before. In November 1901 the Concert Association opened the season with cellist Jean Gerardy and bass Herbert Witherspoon. During the succeeding months they presented four more concerts, including famed soprano Lillian Nordica (who arrived in her own private railroad card named "Brünhilde"), pianist Harold Bauer, and contralto Ernestine Schumann-Heink. Membership in the Atlanta Concert and Festival Association for this season cost $7.50 (for two) for the best seats in the Grand and $5.00 for the remaining ones.[33]

That same fall, a number of Atlanta instrumentalists met to play more serious literature and consider forming an orchestra. During the week they played popular music in various theaters and wished for something more challenging musically. They clearly articulated their purpose to take the artistically high road by declaring that "Not a single number will appear on any programme of a light opera, dance form or secular character." To increase the attraction of their concerts, they also included some sacred songs, which would help entice Atlanta audiences to hear local instrumental music. They intended to program each of four concerts on successive Sunday afternoons with a "standard symphony, classic overture, a group of sacred songs and excerpts for orchestra from such composers as Brahms, Wagner, Beethoven, Jensen, Neven, et al." By January 1903 they were opening their fourth season at the Grand, where they played a concert including Haydn's "Military" Symphony, Handel's "Largo," the overture to Rossini's *Tancredi*, and concluded with Johann Strauss's *Vienna Woods* waltz. Later, the audience heard Schubert's Unfinished Symphony and music from *Tristan und Isolde*. The next year in April they added Beethoven's First Symphony to their programming, as well as Grieg's *Peer Gynt Suite*. After that the group unfortunately disappears from the record.[34]

The fall of 1902 saw musical offerings decline, as the heading for an article in the *Constitution* bemoans: "Musical Prospects Here Appear To Be Dreary" (23 November). Critic Louise Dooly, whose discerning eye and engaging style marked a refreshing improvement in arts' journalism for Atlanta, showed her dismay with the "People who are fond of 'a tune,' but haven't even a bowing acquaintance with one when it is elegantly dressed, have been glorying in the music that is mainly lingerie and inference. Those who prefer music in its noble and ennobling phases are becoming embittered or philosophical." By this time it had become a distressingly familiar litany, repeated at regular intervals since the city recovered from the Civil War (and would continue until the 1960's when the leading citizens became serious about supporting the arts). One wonders if Ms. Dooly could be thinking of Alfredo Barili with her next sentence: "The embittered rail at the fate that keeps them here, perhaps, but philosophy has the better of it, as is usual with the practical kind."

She asked a number of people, "What do you think of the musical prospect, or more properly speaking, the lack of it?" The "unanimous opinion" showed some anger and frustration: "Atlanta will have no music this winter, because her people do not wish it; they do not enjoy good music, and the fault lies with the teachers." Her respondents continued, angry that although the city could have had a "series of high-class concerts" at little cost, its citizens remained indifferent. The only thing the local artists asked from the public was to show some interest in the concerts. One can almost hear whomever it was that she was quoting (anonymously), his/her voice rising and becoming mad, hurt, and righteously indignant all at once, "The encouragement they received was not enough to secure one concert, and the plainest inference was that music was not wanted, and the matter was dropped." The music lovers of the city "long for good music. We would take the first train, if we could, for the busiest music center. We did what we could to bring the music here." It is interesting to speculate on what she did *not* quote.

All was not lost, however, as Ms. Dooly admitted, thereby putting a little better face on the whole discouraging state of Atlanta's concert life. The 1903-04 season promised to bring a better series of artists. Then, in the same article, the whole issue of a chorus comes up—once more. Everyone seems to agree that "A choral society is what we need more than anything, but it is the hardest thing in the world to accomplish." People like to sing, and there are a good many with fine voices, but "Atlanta singers are unwilling to admit it, apparently, or perhaps they do not need it. Then, too, it is hard to obtain the choral director" owing to the amount of work demanded and the salary issue. It is difficult to know exactly what kept derailing the choral efforts. It was probably a number of things. Barili, along with others, probably refused to assume the position until a board would guarantee him a salary and recruit the singers. No conductor of Barili's class was going to go about the city recruiting singers and doing all the organizational work, which is probably what kept defeating the efforts at establishing a choral society. Few people wanted to make an ongoing financial and administrative commitment to support the musical activity. Once again, interest in a standing choral group dissipated and nothing happened.

Sparse concert activity was not the only frustration to exasperate Atlanta's music lovers, as Ms. Dooly reveals in an extended article in the *Constitution* on 19 February 1905. Even when the musical organizations succeeded in drawing enough listeners to pay the bills, they had to endure the eternal rudeness of some of the audience. Not everyone displayed bad manners, thankfully; "the unappreciative attitude is to be found only in spots." Many of the men attending enjoy the social interaction afterwards, but not the concerts, which is understandable. But they could certainly at least show some respect for the performers. It would be much better for "people to stay away from a concert or go home at once if they consider the music too much for them, unless they can preserve at least the outward semblance of attention . . . ." If they can not even handle that, then do something engaging with their minds, and perhaps they would "lose the depressing and distressing expression of boredom that must influence their neighbors . . . ." And why must young couples, given tickets they did not seek, talk during the music? However, Ms. Dooly reserves her harshest words for those women, who afraid that they will miss the last street car home, put their hats on during the last movement or opera finale, ruining it for those behind them. "What if they do miss a car? Have there not been many opera finales and closing concert numbers in Atlanta that were worth more than a walk home? And it is not always the women from East Point and Decatur who so yearn to return to their headgear." She realizes her task is futile, but gets a jab in anyway, curtly dismissing "the women who are addicted to it are usually the women who haven't time to read the newspapers." Most humorous, though, was the following incident in 1901, from which she claims some still have not recovered (Dooley also demonstrates a wonderful gift for literary satire). Apparently Atlanta audiences could demand reprises in the most dramatically unsuitable places. The French Grand Opera must have been spectacular in the finale to *Faust* where Marguerite dies and is welcomed to heaven, because when the curtain dropped on the scene, the listeners would simply not quit demanding a repeat. "Especially hard it was on the poor soprano who had not only to rise again on the beautiful ascending strains of this masterpiece of Gounod's music to a dramatic height that weak Marguerite could have reached only once in a lifetime, but she had to die all over again."

The disappointing music season of 1902-1903 prompted new calls for a spring music festival. Interest in grand music celebrations had never completely vanished since Barili and others had presented the first one in 1883, though discussions waned and reappeared with varying regularity. Probably the grim concert offerings during this season did much to reawaken it.

Louise Dooly minced no words about Atlanta's concert life. Like an economic boom built on inflated money, she argued, perhaps the poor musical offering was not an aberration after all; maybe "the present condition is the normal one; that the few brief years of musical brilliancy was a matter of inflation—an unnatural state which collapsed." No one wanted to face the blunt truth that the city simply did not hold a broad, solid, and enduring support for the musical arts. Occasionally, fine musical activities obscured this unpleasant truth for many. But "talk is cheap, and hints that Atlanta's elevation of 1,100 feet must be nearer to the breezy level of the music best accompanied by the swish of lingerie than to that musical atmosphere rarefied by intelligence and soul." Pointedly, she complained. "This is not a happy suspicion, and must be kept a dead secret, until it can be proven untrue but the suspicion is a strong one." Finally, local musicians are doing their best. Even when they falter in stretching beyond their artistic reach and come in for criticism, it "probably won't hurt. Hitching your wagon to a star, though, is not nearly so hopeless of result as it sounds, and ideals are oftentimes realized." Atlanta was indeed fortunate to have such an insightful and articulate musical journalist.[35]

The city did manage to stage a festival in the spring of 1904. The following year saw the appearance of the Atlanta Music Festival Association, which would become the leading musical organization in the city, supplanting the efforts of the Concert and Festival Association. The critical difference this time, however, was that the group secured the decisive support of important business and civic leaders, such as Walter Rich, who was wisely appointed head of the Ways and Means Committee. Dooly states that plans had already been made for a local orchestra and chorus of 250 singers and that all the workers and plans were in place to bring about a glorious music festival. Fearful of traditional Atlanta indifference, however, she warns that "unless they are given the sympathy, cooperation and assistance of the Atlanta public their efforts will be useless." She also points out the need for an auditorium to house the concerts and entertainments, as well as the growing number of conventions the city is attracting.[36]

Others had been clamoring for an auditorium as well. Certain funds had already been raised for an exposition in Atlanta in 1910, but by 1906 those plans were abandoned, and it was decided to redirect the money toward an auditorium. On 7 February 1907, a delegation of twenty-five citizens proposed the idea to the city council, who approved the organization of the Atlanta Auditorium-Armory Company with a capital of $75,000. The Council authorized the group to buy the land, arrange financing, construct the building, and then sell it to the city. The site chosen ($60,000) was the corner of Courtland and Gilmer Street (the front part of the building was remodeled in the late 1980's and currently serves as administration offices for Georgia State University). Construction began that year and continued into early 1909 when the building was completed for approximately $190,000.[37]

The enthusiasm for the unfinished auditorium must have sparked increased support for the 1907 music festival because it proved a smashing success. The Festival opened on 29 May at the St. Nicholas Auditorium at Ponce de Leon, which held 3,800 people, and ran until 1 June. For the fifty-piece orchestra they brought in players from the Thomas Orchestra, Bauer's Symphony Orchestra, and the Cincinnati Symphony Orchestra in addition to local musicians. The chorus numbered 200, with a 400-member children's choir that sang at the Saturday matinee. Highlighting the programs were three of the leading stars from the Metropolitan Opera, Madame Ernestine Schumann-Heink, Giuseppe Campanari, and Bessie Abott. The climax of the three days came Friday night when the entire group performed Mendelssohn's popular *Hymn of Praise*; Bessie Abbot also sang the Mad Scene from *Lucia*, and Mr. Hugo Olk played Mendelssohn's Violin Concerto in E minor. Atlanta citizens seemed to have caught some artistic spirit, for attendance increased each night, culminating in record-breaking crowds for the Friday night climax.[38]

As completion of the auditorium neared, it was decided to celebrate the event by producing the city's grandest music festival yet in 1909. The festival was to consist of five concerts, opening Tuesday afternoon, 4 May and concluding Thursday evening, including two matinees. As the star attraction, the legendary tenor Enrico Caruso was engaged to sing at two of the concerts for the phenomenal sum of $10,000. Adding brilliance to the festival was a stellar constellation of additional opera stars, Geraldine Farrar, Olive Fremstad, Antonio Scotti, Riccardo Martin, and Giovanni Zenatello. They were not secured without effort. Miss Farrar was contracted to the Victor Talking Machine Company and able to sing here only after being given permission by the company; Giovanni Zenatello, another famous tenor, had never appeared in concert in America and agreed to do it only after frantic telegrams and phone calls across the country; Farrar and Scotti were supposedly already committed and could not be engaged. All of these activities only served to increase interest in the festival and whet the public's appetite. The Festival drew over 25,000 people, many from neighboring towns who came on special rail excursions at reduced rates. The box office earned more than $32,500 for the three days, of which the Music Festival Association cleared about $10,000.[39]

The festival presented a hearty serving of musical fare. One half of a single program included the complete New World Symphony of Dvorak, Liszt's E-Flat Major Piano Concerto, a soprano operatic aria, and a choral number with bass solo. The Festival Chorus was composed of 500 local singers, rehearsed and conducted by H. W. B. Barnes. Two of the artists from the Dresden Philharmonic both returned to Atlanta. Albert Spalding, twenty-one years old at the time, played the violin and continued to visit the city for a number of years. Mary Lansing later took a faculty position at the Atlanta Conservatory of Music.[40]

The astonishing attendance for the festival encouraged two immediate developments. The first was the installation of a large pipe organ in the auditorium, partly funded by money left over from the Festival. Built by the Austin Organ Company of Hartford, Connecticut, the instrument contained seventy-seven speaking stops and cost about $32,000. On 22 and 23 April 1910 the Music Festival Association brought in Dr. Percy Starnes from Albany, New York to inspect the completed organ. Dr. Starnes praised the instrument, declaring that it "exceeds in tone and majesty any organ I know of in this country."[41]

Atlanta had never seen or heard an organ like this. Seven thousand citizens attended the dedication recital on 31 May. The *Atlanta Journal* advertised the event on the front page that day with a cartoon showing the "Greatest Organ in America" with a slim, blond, lady "Atlanta" at the console. Edwin H. Lemare (1866-1934) played the opening recital. Noted for his vigorous rhythmic playing and superb performances of orchestral transcriptions, he had been popular in this country since his first American tour in 1900-01. The *Journal* lauded his program, excepting "one or two numbers which could not possibly be popular as music were 'lugged in by the ears' just to show the mechanical possibilities of the instrument." The reviewer was probably referring to the Prelude and Fugue in D by Bach, which he found "brilliant, bewildering, but cold as the Aurora Borealis." The following Boccherini Minuet found a more favorable reception. The climax of the recital, according to the reviewer, was the Mendelssohn Sonata No. 6, in which "he made the very soul of the organ speak." Unfortunately, the organ developed a cipher during the performance, as many new instruments do. It brought undignified responses from the audience, which offended Louise Dooly of the *Constitution*, "It was a pity that some of the audience seemed to find the humor of the situation stronger than the probable embarrassment of the musician."

Starnes, who had impressed the city's dignitaries during his visit, was soon engaged as Atlanta's first city organist. He began offering organ recitals every Thursday night and Sunday afternoon, which, by the second opera season, had been attended by an estimated 125,000. The next year, however, he reduced the weekly fare to one recital on Sunday afternoons. In January 1914 Edwin Arthur Kraft (1883?-1962) succeeded Dr. Starnes as city organist. After study with Horatio Parker at Yale, then Alexandre Guilmant and Charles Marie Widor in Paris, he had been organist at Trinity Cathedral in Cleveland before assuming the post in Atlanta. He would return to Cleveland after his tenure in Atlanta. In his twenty-two months as municipal organist, Kraft played seventy-six recitals at the auditorium-armory, which typically included opening works such as the overture to Wagner's *Tannhäuser*, with his "Ride of the Valkyries" to close the program.[42]

Following short tenures of two local organists, Charles A. Sheldon (1886?-1952) took the position as the third, and last, long-term city organist. He had been associated with the Austin auditorium organ since its inception, writing about it for the press and accompanying singers on it for other recitalists. When he assumed the position in October 1915 he was already organist at Trinity Methodist Church and head of the organ department at the Atlanta Conservatory of Music. He played at the Temple on Friday nights as well. Sheldon presented Sunday afternoon recitals weekly until about 1940, when he retired, holding the title of municipal organist until his death in 1952. In 1923 Oglethorpe University conferred upon him the doctor of music degree.[43]

The second outgrowth of the 1909 Music Festival was the first official visit of the Metropolitan Opera Company. The invitation to the Metropolitan was supposedly suggested by Geraldine Farrar during her time at the festival the year earlier. She was riding in the motor car with the secretary of the Music Festival Association, Victor Lamar Smith, and remarked to him that "You have no idea how stiff and constrained an opera singer feels on the concert stage—in evening dress-singing for example, the big aria from 'Madame Butterfly'—no scenery, no acting—no chance to portray the character. Why don't you people have the Opera—the Metropolitan Company?" Coming on the heels of the city's most successful Music Festival, her suggestion encouraged the directors of the Festival Association to consider Grand Opera for the 1910 Festival.[44]

The idea was a risky venture for a city of just 150,000 people with a very checkered history of supporting the arts, especially on an annual basis. The Metropolitan required a guarantee of $40,000, but it proved no problem—it was quickly subscribed by over 200 of the leading citizens and firms. The year-old auditorium underwent renovations to accomodate operatic productions. Then, to everyone's delight, not only did people attend in droves, they loved the music.[45]

The star attraction was Enrico Caruso, who had failed to appear the year before owing to an exhausting New York season. He created a sensation in his Atlanta debut as Radames in *Aida*, singing to 7,042 persons (not including the estimated 1,000 who did not get in), his largest audience to date. Other opera singers for the week included Olive Fremstad, Geraldine Farrar, Antonio Scotti, Riccardo Martin, Louise Homer, and Robert Blass. The newspapers had a field day with numerous pictures, feature stories, and extensive interviews.

The opera evenings were only part of the week's festivities. While in Atlanta, the company members made the round of breakfasts, luncheons, teas, dinners, suppers, balls, toilets, and picnics. The stars missed few chances for publicity shots, which took Farrar to the Federal Penitentiary to sing; Caruso, Gadski, and Farrar spun around the Hapeville speedway at 85 miles an hour; other members appeared at baseball games and eating establishments.

The week opened on Monday 2 May and went through Saturday 7 May and saw offered *Lohengrin, Tosca, Aida, Madame Butterfly, Hänsel und Gretel,* and *Pagliacci.* The five performances generated incredible enthusiasm and drew many visitors, some from as far away as New Orleans, Baltimore, and Havana.

By the time the company departed, 27,000 people had attended, producing gross receipts of $71,030.50. Atlanta had never seen anything like it. Neither had the manager of the Metropolitan, Hirsch, who declared that "never before had the Metropolitan Opera Company sung to so many people for such an amount of money in one week, despite the fact that six or more performances are given in a week in New York."[46]

* * * * * * *

By the end the first decade, the Barili's seemed to be prospering. They had built a new spacious, two-story home at 167 Myrtle Street in the growing residential area around the northern edge of the city. Alfredo moved the School of Music there by 1911, where he, Emily, and Louise continued teaching. Alfredo, Jr. was now a draftsman with the Wachendorf Architectural Firm and had married Mary MacCamy Hudgins. They would have their first child Alfredo Barili III in 1913.

Alfredo again visited Yonkers in June 1910 for a rest before returning to Atlanta that fall. He resumed his teaching, now acknowledged as Atlanta's foremost music instructor. There survives from this period a rare document by Barili giving advice to a student who was preparing Mendelssohn's *Variations sérieuses*. It summarizes his whole teaching philosophy and illustrates why he was so successful as a musician. His approach comes down to two main points: thoughtful study, infused with patient, careful preparation. "You must be sure that you start properly in trying to master such a large work," he begins, "that in the early stages it is absolutely *wrong* to try to play in the grand style that the composition finally demands." This practice accounts for much of his criticism of local teachers, who allowed their students to perform before they had sufficiently prepared the work. "In the first place study the thing with deep concentration. Be sure that everything fits well and that fingering is right. A finished pianist does not put vim and energy at first in learning a new composition. In other words, don't blunt your ear and wear yourself out before you know a thing well." "Concert players are careful not to let *things get stale*." He closes with the gentle confidence that so infused everything he did, "If you take my advice all will go well."[47]

The Barili's close relationship to Patti continued. She was increasingly occupied with family during these years. She also reached out more to her remaining sister, Amalia Strakosch, who lived in Paris, and to Amalia's son Robert Strakosch and to her husband's brother, Gustaf. It was to Alfredo and his family that she remained the closest, however, as she wrote Emily on 22 November 1910: "Nothing gives me greater pleasure than to hear about all his doings, and besides—he is *my* boy! and the only *real*, good boy I have in my family—also, his wife and children are, I can assure you, very dear to me, and my love, very great for them!" She continued worrying about him overworking himself: "*Do, darling* Alfredo, take things in, peacefully & quietly. I am *so* much older than you are, & have found out that this is the only way to get on well in this world." Alfredo had indeed been taking things more slowly, but it would still be some time before he finally learned to relax and take life in Atlanta at the gracious pace in which it moved.[48]

Louise likewise had grown close to her aunt, to whom she wrote regularly on Sunday afternoons (to Patti's consternation, as it proved difficult for her to keep up her end of the correspondence). When Patti finally had a chance to reply, she gushed: "I have tried to persuade you of my true and sincere devotion—I am quite sure, you believe me when I say, that I love my dear, sweet darling Louise '*avec toute la force de mon coeur*'. . . . *Oh*! how I wish you were mine! and how I would thank God for having given you to me!" Patti reportedly discussed the idea of adopting Louise with Alfredo and Emily. She envied the whole Barili family, who had parents and children (and dogs) intact, while she "besides my husband, only have numerous of strangers [sic], people about me, but *nothing* which I could call my own . . . . sometimes it is very sad . . . ."[49]

In 1911 Alfredo and Louise journeyed to see Patti at *Craig-y-Nos*. They embarked from New York on 22 April on the *SS Lavrentic* for his sixth and Louise's fourth visit. Patti was even more glad to see them than ever, if that were possible. Louise found her more emotionally dependent on the Baron and suffering from numerous ailments. Patti's nervous and excitable temperament also could make things difficult for everyone at the castle; as Louise wrote her mother, "Conditions are far from ideal in this place but I am trying so hard to make the best of it." The tense atmosphere also made Alfredo nervous, "I am sorry to tell you that Papa is far from well and he seems terribly restless." Once again, Louise tried to lay to rest any talk of moving, "I am afraid he could never begin in a new place!"[50]

During their visit Patti sang a benefit which proved memorable for a number of reasons. The benefit was for Patti's accompanist of many years, Wilhelm Ganz; it also marked the fiftieth anniversary of her London debut. She had written her nephew in Atlanta earlier about the affair, "So Rolf and I have decided that you should accompany my pieces at the concert. . . . Would you care to do so? I feel it would do you a *great* deal of good in your profession and I shall be *so* proud to show you off & make a fuss over my own darling boy." The concert on 1 June 1911 in Royal Albert Hall drew a prestigious crowd, including many royal listeners. Alfredo's excellent playing received notice in London and Atlanta, along with Patti's singing of Mozart's "Voi che sapete," and "La serenata" by Tosti. Alfredo and Louise left for the United States on 17 July aboard the *RMS Baltic*.[51]

Back home the other two Barili children seemed to be prospering. Viola was in New York studying at the American Academy of Dramatic Arts. In December 1911 Alfredo, Jr. became engaged to Mary Hudgins. Patti, as usual, was curious, "*Do* write and tell me about her—Her family. If she is pretty—if she is musical or not." Alfredo's brother Armando, whom he seems never to have mentioned, at least in the surviving records, died in Philadelphia on 7 September 1912 from tuberculosis. *Musical America* reported that as a young man he "gave promise of being one of the leading baritones" in the country. Some few varied sources suggest that he may have been the black sheep in the family, perhaps because of drinking. Whatever the real issue, Alfredo and his immediate kin left no record of the family ever being in touch with him.

Alfredo's health problems continued intermittently. He and Emily travelled to New York the next summer to visit her brother, Charles Vezin, but when they returned to Atlanta Alfredo was not feeling well. Patti wrote him in September, "I am so sorry to hear that you have been so ill—and I sincerely trust that ere this you have been completely recovered again." Again, Alfredo's problems seem more linked to frustration than any physical ailment, for in her letters in December Patti again mentioned Alfredo's stomach problems and hoped that "dear Alfredo is feeling less depressed."[52]

The New Year 1913 brought good news for the family. Alfredo seemed to be feeling better. The *Constitution* on 4 June that year ran a lengthy article on him that fairly assessed his work in Atlanta. It credited him with bringing high-level music to the city and the region virtually singlehandedly. "Alfredo Barili is the man who, for twenty years, has stood at the head of musical life in the south," it begins. Students and teachers have come to him from all over the area and "left to spread his fame." It summarizes his early years, then describes Atlanta when he arrived as "young in musical development, but well-grown in responsiveness and appreciation." Enthusiastically, he set out to bring the best music and artistic cultivation to the city. His six years conducting the Polymnia club produced the finest choral music the city had ever heard, and "to this day a sort of radiance seems to invest the very recollection of it." He was able to evoke performances that everyone thought "would have appeared impossible" in a small southern town, but came off "in a manner truly surprising and reflecting the greatest credit." Nor did the writer forget the first Music Festival in 1883, which, "due largely to Mr. Barili . . . was an unqualified success." Of late, he "has withdrawn more into the seclusion of his studio, where he meets his students."

As he was approaching his sixth decade, Barili still kept his trim, erect figure of about 5' 8". He seems not to have lost the first strand of hair. Pictures from the period show a full head, with his familiar beard. His schedule of students kept him busy, but he always made time to rest. His breathing seems to have been less troublesome. Advancements in medicine provided some relief, such as the development of the atomizer, which greatly helped him breathe. For exercise he walked, often miles through the midtown neighborhood. Cherry Emerson recounts how as a young man he would accompany Barili, and that Emerson had to step quickly to keep up with him, often walking considerable distances together before returning home.

Louise enjoyed a growing reputation as a singer, both in recital and at church. "I am very glad to her that your recitals are always such a great success," Patti wrote her in April. "and it does not astonish me a bit—it would though were it otherwise." In June Alfredo and perhaps Emily travelled to New York to visit her brother again. The family also had the joy of expecting the new baby, Alfredo III, who was born on 17 August. In May 1914 Alfredo and Louise made another—and final—trip to Wales. Their departure for the United States in July left Patti, who was now seventy-one, more despairing than ever, and she begged Louise not to leave. Shortly thereafter, Patti and the Baron took their usual summer trip to Carlsbad for the baths. Unfortunately, the sudden outbreak of the war caught them by surprise and made their return to England difficult.[53]

The European war affected life in Atlanta little at first, and Alfredo, Sr. and family saw things continue as usual with teaching. For Patti however, these years proved increasingly difficult. The staff at Craig-y-Nos dwindled considerably as most of the able-bodied men left for the war, which left the Baron to do much of the manual work. She became active in war relief efforts, jumping in with her usual *elan;* as she wrote to Louise in November 1915, her duties were "*so* numerous that days ought to be made double as long" if she were to get everything done. She and the Baron rarely entertained and only occasionally left the estate. The death of Amalia in 1915 affected her deeply. Her correspondence with Atlanta grew darker with her despair over the war and her declining health: "How full the world is of sadness. In every paper one takes up one reads of the death of people one knew." She found life so different that she and the baron lived in "*complete* darkness and misery." They discussed little besides the war, "no more music, no more laughing, nothing but war," and that she felt increasingly like she was "sinking and *terribly* tired out." On 25 January 1918, her nineteenth wedding anniversary, she wrote Louise: "We shall try and feel happy if possible which I doubt—as this war is *absolutely* finishing me slowly up."[54]

Later that spring she became depressed and nervous, suffering from poor digestion and a weak heart. In a letter to Louise in April she wondered if she could go on, that the war had made things so difficult. Rolf became increasingly more critical to her, as she wrote Emily: "All I can say is that my dear husband has behaved like an angel, and has done all in his power to make the remaining part of my existence as agreeable & peaceful as possible in this infernal time." Even with the end of the war in November her health did not improve. By the first of the year she continued to deteriorate. On 2 March 1919 she penned her last letter to Alfredo, in a somewhat more optimistic vein, "The papers must have written very serious things about my health, for everybody has been writing for news of me to Rolf! *Dieu Merci.* I feel much better but not yet completely well." Gradually, she grew weaker as her heart worsened, and on the morning of 27 September 1919, she lost consciousness, lingered for several hours, then died peacefully with Rolf holding her hand. He cabled the news to Alfredo that day.[55]

Her body was placed, as she requested, in Pere Lachaise cemetery in Paris. Her tomb contains no epitaph, just the single word which the world would remember, PATTI. After all, following more than half a century of accolades, what was there left to say? Nothing really. John Cone suggests scouring the past for a fitting epitaph, such as the one written by Henry Krehbiel:

> The Reign of Patti set a standard by which all aspirants for public favor were judged except those whose activities were in a widely divergent field . . .. Her talent was so many sided and so astonishing, no matter from which side it was viewed, that rhapsody seems to be the only language left one who attempts analysis or description of it.[56]

Patti left 4,000 pounds in her will to Alfredo, equal to $20,000 at the time—a large sum, easily ten times more than the average family income of the period. Barili requested the Bank of England keep the money and send him yearly checks from the principal. The bank claimed it did not keep deposits that way and finally sent him a check, which he subsequently returned to the London Branch of the American Guaranty Trust Company of New York.[57]

* * * * * * *

Concert life in Atlanta made considerable progress during the second decade of the century. The successful opera weeks energized efforts to build a symphonic ensemble. In 1913 the Atlanta Musical Association took as its immediate goal the establishment of a "permanent symphony orchestra, with all that means for Atlanta's educational and civic prestige." The group felt that the time had come to go forward with the project and that the city could support it. With three hundred members, annual income of $3,000, and people willing to guarantee $10,000 yearly to cover any deficit, the idea appeared to be on sound financial footing. The Association had engaged fifty musicians under the conductor Mortimer Wilson and Alexander Skribinsky as concert master. The writer, Mrs. Meek, claims that the group had presented four seasons and been well received. But soon the orchestra disappears from the record. Like so many earlier attempts in the city's history to establish a choral or orchestral organization, the proposal floundered and soon ceased to exist. The city would not become serious about another orchestral project until the 1940's.[58]

Soon, however, three other organizations which would endure were in place—finally. They would shape the city's musical life for half a century. The Metropolitan Opera Company had already inaugurated what would become a long-standing relationship with the city. In 1914 church music received a boost when the Georgia Chapter of the American Guild of Organists was established. Finally, in 1916 the Atlanta Music Study Club, which had been meeting for some years as a part of the Atlanta Woman's Club initiated what would become the All-Star Concert Series that served the city so well for many years. All together, these three groups supported the largest part of Atlanta's musical life well into the second half of the century.

Opera had already been set on a firm footing in 1910 with the Metropolitan's first opera week. And even though it had been remarkable in every way, the Metropolitan officials doubted "whether another season would prove financially successful." So did the directors of the Music Festival Association, "who are too tired to think about it now anyway." Both were wrong. The 1911 season broke the previous year's records, even without Caruso making an appearance. The four operas, *La gioconda* (Ponchielli), *Königskinder* (Humperdinck), *Il trovatore,* and *Otello* brought vocal stars such as Emmy Destinn, Louise Homer, Riccardo Martin, Leo Slezak, and Geraldine Farrar and averaged $15,411 per performance, ahead of the $14,206 the year before. Making his Atlanta debut was the young conductor Arturo Toscanini. Numerous social activities again surrounded the operatic evenings.[59]

The 1912 season proved just as successful, firmly establishing the annual Atlanta performances by the Metropolitan Opera Company. It also showed the directors of the Music Festival Association that the city indeed could support an artistic activity on an ongoing basis. People in other cities also took notice of the season's success, such as Otto Jahn, managing director and one of the financial backers of the Metropolitan:

> Grand opera for the South in Atlanta is an established institution now, and in the future anyone who wishes to hear grand opera as given by the Metropolitan Company in America must either go to New York or Atlanta for it. Our three seasons in Atlanta have been so successful that we are going to give opera in the future only in Atlanta and New York.

Caruso returned for the season, to triumphal acclaim; Alma Gluck made her only Atlanta appearance in *Rigoletto* and *Faust.* The singers once again were subjected to rounds of social activities, such as prizefights and baseball games. Fort McPherson honored Farrar with a dress parade. Unfortunately, Atlanta audiences still carried their social amenities into the opera performances, inducing an indignant press release from one irate association director: "If opera-goers would keep their conversations bottled up until the opera is over or the curtain drops on the acts, they would add greatly to the pleasure of their neighbors who go to hear high-priced singers and not cheap conversation. It might be worthwhile to mention, too, that if enthusiastic listeners would restrain their applause until the last note of the orchestra has died away after a thrilling aria the effect would not be lessened and the singers would appreciate their ovation just as heartily. I haven't heard the last note of a good number since the overture of the first night."[60]

The Metropolitan showed its appreciation the next year (1913) by bringing the complete cast of its newest production, Walter Damrosch's new opera in English, *Cyrano de Bergerac.* The work was not received well here (or in New York) and was dropped from the Met's repertoire after its Atlanta performance. Caruso appeared again, as did Emmy Destinn and Louise Homer, along with Toscanini as conductor. New to the city was the coloratura soprano Frieda Hempel. Atlanta again outdid itself and established a new weekly record in attendance and box office receipts, "Not even New York has ever turned in $91,000 in a single week for grand opera," declared one of the Met's accountants. Income exceeded that of 1912 by $10,000, and the audience averaged more than 5,000 per opera. The Atlanta Music Festival Association earned $18,000 in profit.[61]

The next season opened on 27 April to a historic production of Massenet's *Manon*. The production paired Caruso with Farrar and was conducted by Toscanini in front of an audience of nearly 6,000. Caruso discovered again the pitfalls of working with live animals on stage when the donkey pulling the cart for his entrance in *Pagliacci* refused to budge. There was little else to do but take the matters into human hands, so half a dozen members of the chorus, in exasperation, shoved the beast "out before the footlights, making his entrance sitting flat upon the floor and with his forefeet firmly planted before him." The week included two operas new to Atlanta, *Der Rosenkavalier* by Richard Strauss, and Verdi's *Un ballo in maschero*. Attendance again exceeded the year before. On Friday evening, when Farrar sang the role of Cio-Cio San in *Madama Butterfly*, every one of the 6,405 seats in the auditorium was sold. Apparently, the audience had learned better manners as the newspapers reported less talking.[62]

One telling event occurred during the season when a Macon man offered $10,000 towards the construction of a $500,000 Atlanta opera house, which would produce a resident twenty-week season in addition to the Met's yearly visits. His offer found no takers when he suggested it be matched by fifty prominent Atlanta businessmen. It is intriguing to speculate as to what the successful response to his offer would have done for artistic life in the capitol of the South. Suffice it to point out, sadly, the city remains without an opera house here at the turn of the next century, forcing Atlanta Opera to stage its excellent and well-attended productions wherever and whenever it can find available space.

The 1915 season brought some doubts to the directors of the Music Festival Association owing to a number of factors. The country was in the midst of a severe depression which caused the northern cities that had supported the Met for years to turn the company down. Perhaps more disturbing was the rise to $60,000 in the guaranteed amount the Metropolitan needed to produce the week. With Caruso unavailable, things looked bleak. Nevertheless, the week proved successful and the guarantors were not asked for any money. The highlight of the week, which included five new productions, was the new *Carmen* with Farrar in the title role. She had caused a sensation in New York and the excitement drew 5,800 to hear her in Atlanta.[63]

More people than ever heard the seven opera performances the next season, which opened on 24 April. Box-office receipts grew again as well. An estimated 15,000 visitors streamed into the city from as far away as New York and Dallas to see productions of *Samson et Dalila, Die Meistersinger, Aida, La bohème* and those mainstays from years before, *La sonnambula, Martha,* and *Lucia di Lammermoor.* The week's audience totaled nearly 37,000 and the box office earned almost $100,000.[64]

Two weeks before the opera season of 1917, the United States declared war on Germany, which gave Atlanta things to think about during the season other than opera. Virtually all of the performances were punctuated between acts with renditions of the "Star Spangled Banner" to the rousing excitement of the audience. But nothing matched the week's final performance, *Rigoletto,* when the cast (Caruso included), clad incongruously in medieval costume, waved American flags as they sang the national anthem. The company staged a production of *Siegfried,* seen only once before in 1895 when Walter Damrosch brought his opera company to the city. The most artistically significant work for the week was the production of Musorgsky's *Boris Goudounov.* The uncertainties of the war situation caused the directors of the Association to announce that "Atlanta will have opera next year if conditions justify." They didn't, and it was the spring of 1919 before the company returned a series that remained unbroken until 1929.[65]

Locally, the Atlanta Music Study Club, which had worked for sometime as a group within the Atlanta Woman's Club, formally organized its concert series in 1916. The group's concert series would become the All-Star Concert Series. By the next year, they were fully organized and opened the series on 3 November 1917 with a concert by pianist Percy Grainger (who was also serving in the U. S. Army). He was followed by lieder singer Julia Culp, returning pianist Harold Bauer, Dutch pianist Conrad Bos, and the Cincinnati Symphony Orchestra. Tickets were $45 for a box of four, $10, $5, $3, and $2.50. The next year saw Swedish singer Julia Claussen, Harold Bauer again, the Russian Symphony Orchestra, and the beloved Geraldine Farrar. With the opening of the 1918 season, the series had assumed the title "All-Star." The programmed artists certainly earned the title: a quartet from the Metropolitan Opera, Irish tenor John McCormack, pianist Joseph Hofman, violinist Jascha Heifetz, soprano Alma Gluck, and coloratura Amelita Galli-Curci. Prices had risen to $8, 6, and 4. Finally, the city had an established, ongoing concert series of outstanding quality.[66]

Church music likewise took an important step forward in 1914 when the Georgia Chapter of the American Guild of Organists was founded in the Fall of 1914. On 29 September the *Journal* announced that "Organists of Georgia will form Association." "A Meeting of the organists of the city will be held in the office of Dr. Edwin Arthur Kraft, city organist, at the Auditorium, Wednesday evening, September 30, for the purpose of the organization of a Georgia Chapter of the American Guild of Organists." As the article explained the Guild had been organized in New York "To advance the cause of worthy church music; to elevate the status of church organists; to increase their appreciation of their responsibilities, duties and opportunities as conductors of worship." There were only thirty chapters in the United States at the time. According to Ethel M. Beyer, the last original member of the chapter (died 1969), the preliminary meeting occurred on 29 September on the steps of the auditorium. A formal organizational meeting took place a week later on 6 October at Cable Hall. Dr. Kraft presided and was elected dean of the chapter. A series of monthly meetings was established, beginning in December and continuing through May, when Dr. Kraft's recital concluded the season, after which the group adjourned to the new Kuhn's Cafe for a banquet. The national organization issued the chapter's charter on 26 October, and by the end of the first year in May 1915, the Georgia Chapter had thirty-three members who paid annual dues of $3.[67]

The 1914-15 first recital series included performances by members Eda Bartholemew, Charles Sheldon, Walter Peck Stanley, and Kraft. Miss Bartholemew was long remembered as the finest performer of the local church musicians. After study at the Royal Conservatory in Leizpig, she went to Chicago and worked with William Middelschulte. She taught at several Georgia colleges before assuming a long-time position as organist at St. Mark Methodist Church. Bartholemew also taught in her own organ studio, as well as at Agnes Scott. Another important organist of the day was Joseph Ragan who played at North Avenue Presbyterian Church, where the Barili's attended. Mrs. W. H. L. Nelms at Second Baptist was also a popular organist, preferring simple melodic pieces to more complicated fare. At Trinity Methodist Church, Charles Sheldon offered a thirty-minute recital before each Sunday night service.[68]

During that first season, the programs show the firm position already occupied by J. S. Bach, represented by four major works. In 1917 Eda Batholemew devoted an entire Sunday evening recital to his music. This was a significant change from just a decade earlier, when works by Bach were rare on any recital programs. Orchestral transcriptions continued to dominate the recitals, which better suited the symphonically conceived instruments. These could be challenging to perform, such as Rossini's *William Tell Overture* and Wagner's *Ride of the Valkyries* and *Liebestod.* Also popular were elegiac organ miniatures holding direct lyrical appeal and uncomplicated textures such as "Berceuse" or "Dawn."[69]

Opportunities for music education likewise improved in the city by the end of the first decade. In 1909 the Atlanta Conservatory joined with the nine-year old Klindworth Conservatory. The Klindworth Conservatory had already established a solid reputation in teaching not only applied music but academic courses as well. By 1920 the Atlanta Conservatory was offering a broad range of training in piano, organ, voice, dance, English and dramatics, cello, violin, harp, wind and percussion, and public school music. Unfortunately, like so many other artistic endeavors in the city, it floundered and closed in 1938 after the Cable Piano Company burned, in whose building it resided.[70]

With the end of the war in 1918 and the ensuing economic prosperity, Atlanta would see a healthy growth in its artistic life, due much to the efforts of these organizations. The organizational, civic, and financial structures had been firmly established, and, perhaps more importantly, would endure throughout the next decade, providing the city with annual seasons of professional concerts, local recitals, choral programs, and a week of outstanding opera. For the first time in the city's history, it happily discovered an ability to support cultural activities on an impressive level. With its artistic life securely in place, Atlanta could now pride itself as a city that had finally come of age.

6 FINALE

The third decade of the century would prove to be a good one for Atlanta. The 1920 population of just over 200,000 would increase by nearly a third to 270,000 ten years later. Building permits grew, as did bank clearings and railroad activity. Artistically, the city began enjoying a new era of orchestral music at the grand movie houses being built throughout downtown. Across the country, a wave of magnificent film palaces arose, constructed on a scale never seen before and designed to lure movie-goers in by the lush opulence and awe-inspiring spaces. Atlanta's two most splendid theaters fittingly framed the decade, with the Howard Theater opening in 1920 and the Fox theater in 1929. In between, other important theaters were built as well, including the Rialto, the Atlanta, and the Metropolitan. During the silent film era, the largest of these movie palaces had their own orchestras to provide accompaniment.[1]

The Howard, billed as the "wonder theater of the South," was built in 1920 at a cost of a million dollars, contained 2,700 seats, marble columns, and majestic stairways reminiscent of the aristocratic palaces in Europe. To conduct its thirty-five instrumentalists, the management had engaged Enrico Leide, who began his tenure as conductor of the Howard Grand Concert Orchestra in December 1920. Born in Turin, Italy, Leide studied the cello and played there under Toscanini, Richard Strauss, and Hans Richter before moving to New York as a conductor at the Capitol Theater. The audiences received a terrific bargain for their ticket purchase. A typical week consisted of two programs. On Monday, Tuesday, and Wednesday, the evening opened with an overture, followed by the Howard News and Views, then the Paul Oscar Dancers (Direct from the Rialto Theater in New York) staging "Pierrot's Dream," a "A

Symphonic Scenic" ("The Most Beautiful Motion Picture Ever Filmed"), tenor George DuFrane singing "Vesti, La Giubba" from *I Pagliacci*, and finally the movie, *The Life of the Party* with Fatty Arbuckle.[2]

Within weeks people started talking about the Howard orchestra forming the core of an Atlanta Symphony Orchestra, "on the same mold as those of Cincinnati, Detroit, Minneapolis, St. Louis," and other cities. As critic Louise Dooly pointed out, the Atlanta Music Festival Association had successfully organized Atlanta's business community to support an ongoing opera season (albeit for one week a year). Why could not this method be used to securely establish an orchestra? In fact, it would only enhance the opera's attraction. And the orchestra would "be with us not just for one week in the year but all winter," and perhaps even for a pops series in the summer.[3]

Fall 1923 saw the realization of Miss Dooly's dreams. On 7 October, Leide conducted the premiere performance of the first organization to bear the title Atlanta Symphony Orchestra, with sixty players drawn from both the Howard and Metropolitan Theater orchestras. The ensuing twelve concerts on consecutive Sunday afternoons cost $10 total for two seats and included a membership in the symphony association. The Symphony Orchestra Association, organized in 1922, had taken a cue from the Festival Association and began a membership drive for a thousand supporters, which was soon oversubscribed. A full house greeted the symphony's first evening, with the stage "magnificently decorated" by the Dahl Floral Company. The program demonstrated that resident Atlanta orchestral performances had now moved completely to a serious (if thoroughly romantic) artistic level:[4]

Overture, *Oberon*	Weber
Suite from *The Nutcracker*	Tchaikovsky
Two Arabesques	Debussy
Symphony No. 8 in B Minor, "Unfinished"	Schubert
Overture, *Tannhäuser*	Wagner

The All-Star Concert Series brought an impressive roster of artists to the auditorium in 1920, beginning with the baritone Titta Ruffo, Amelita Galli-Curci on Thanksgiving Night, and violinist Efrem Zimbalist in January. Madame Schuman-Heink returned in January to sing her final American concert, followed by Rosa Ponselle and Josef Hofman in March. The Atlanta Music Study Club likewise welcomed the new decade with a stellar series beginning on 1 November 1920 that presented contralto Margaret Matzenaur, the Isadora

Duncan Dancers later that month, violinist Fritz Kreisler in January, the Cincinnati Symphony in January, and concluded with pianist Alfred Cortot in February. Season tickets cost as little as $3, up to $7 for box seats, and sold well.[5]

Fall 1921 began the fifth series of concerts sponsored by the Atlanta Music Club (the word "study" had been quietly dropped from the name). On 2 September the *Constitution* lauded the group in an editorial. "This course merits the patronage of every lover of cultural things in Atlanta," declared the writer. Unlike in distant years past, this group did not falter "when money was scarce and the outlook far from favorable." They launched every season with no financial guarantees and met all the expenses from the receipts. Perhaps most importantly, "they have afforded the great mass of the public the opportunity to hear the greatest artists and the most wonderful music at prices" that were below cost. By now, the pattern for the series was clearly set for the next fifty years, with Atlanta enjoying an outstanding procession of the world's finest musicians. The series generally included five to seven concerts a year featuring pianists, violinists, singers, and small chamber groups, with infrequent visits by touring orchestras.

* * * * * * *

The Barili School of Music continued to do well. The entire family, excepting Alfredo, Jr., taught together. Emily assisted Alfredo in piano teaching, taking the less advanced students. Louise taught voice and performed much throughout the area. Viola taught expression while Nana Tucker was instructor in music history. Alfredo was widely respected as the dean of Atlanta's music teachers. His health seems to have much improved, possibly due to advances in medicine that gave him some relief from the asthma and respiratory problems. Summers still took him to Franklin, North Carolina for rest, while Emily remained in Atlanta, something that continued to elicit comment from some quarters. The school reopened each September and ran into the spring when his students would present a recital.

Barili appears to have come to an accommodation with his life in Atlanta as any mention about depression and nerves vanishes completely from the record. Reports from late in the 1920's also describe him as cheerful, contented, and in perfect health. With the improvement of medical treatment for asthma his respiratory problems seem to have almost disappeared. The home life, from family reports, seems to have been warm and gracious as well, delighting the small grandchildren that came often to visit.

As the elder statesman of the city's musical community, Barili was widely respected. He also enjoyed a higher quality of students. As the city grew, an increasing number of talented and well prepared young pianists found their way to his studio. The *Journal* declared that he "has taught more outstanding artist students than any other master in this section . . . ." The substantial improvement in the caliber of his better pupils brought him much satisfaction. One Mrs. Herbert Taylor must have been an excellent pianist, judging from the program she performed in Barili's home. The program included Beethoven's Sonata *Pathétique,* three Chopin preludes, as well as his Polonaise, Op. 71, No. 2, and the challenging MacDowell Polonaise, Op. 46, No. 12. The critic thought Barili had "the satisfaction of seeing the Barili technique exemplified in marked degree." He had transmitted to her the elegant, quiet, and smooth keyboard manner that he had acquired in Cologne from Hiller. Displaying little apparent effort, she executed the most difficult passages with a convincing musical air. Frances Hatcher likewise played well, as Barili presented her in a program that included two Chopin Etudes (Op. 10, C and G), and the Sonata in C Minor by Grieg.[6]

One child prodigy was brought to him by her parents. Soon nine-year old Laura Schallenberger presented a solo recital, from memory, to a group of about seventy-five listeners at her parents' home in 1932. She performed works by Schumann, Schubert, Grieg, Barili, and others. She also accompanied her mother in two groups of French songs "in a manner that older heads and hands might emulate." Her talent must have been considerable, which Barili wisely guided through a gradual growth. The next year she appeared again. This time her program showed not only clear advance but her teacher's carefully planned instruction. She opened with Beethoven's "Variations on a Swiss Folk Song" with "the ease and poise which are the result of careful and intelligent training . . . ." She followed that with two works by two Bachs, first a "Solfegietto" by Carl Phillip Emmanuel, oldest son of the Leipzig composer, and then Johann Sebastian's deceptively difficult Two-Part Invention No. 8. Three works from Schumann's *Kinderscenen* surely delighted her audience, coming as it did from a young child. The second half opened with one of those gracious gestures for which Barili was often remembered. Ten-year old Laura announced and then played a waltz that Barili had composed for and dedicated to her. It proved the highlight of the afternoon.[7]

Barili's teaching of voice added even more lustre to his reputation. Typical was the program which Margaret Nelson performed in May 1926. Barili's astute and perfectly suited selection of repertoire shows how much ahead of this time he was in artistically, as the *Journal* pointed-out, once again, "The high standard of excellence which characterizes all Mr. Barili's work and is synonomous [sic] with his name was evidenced throughout the program." This program could be found today on any senior voice recital at the finest music schools in the country. Miss Nelson sang three songs by Schumann ("The Lotus Flower," "Moonlight," and "Dedication"), two songs by MacDowell, a Breton folk song arranged by Deems Taylor, a romance by Debussy; she ended with a group of songs by Cyril Scott.[8]

As some Atlanta citizens became increasingly interested in the city's heritage, more attention was paid to figures like Barili who had played seminal roles in its cultural history. On Saturday afternoon, 7 June 1924, the Atlanta Junior Music Club presented an entire program of his works at Cable Hall. Nana Tucker introduced the recital with a lecture on "The Work of Alfredo Barili in Atlanta." The following program included his best-known piano works such as *Gavotte, Minuet, Mazurka, Danse Caprice, Modern Minuet, The Butterfly*, and the *Cradle Song*, as well as four songs sung by Louise: "There, Little Girl, Don't Cry," "Your Tender Love is Best," "O, Say Not Love's a Rover," and "Maiden With Thy Mouth So Rosy."[9]

The Barilis had made friends with prominent musicians and artists over the years. A recent one was the composer Amy Marcy Cheney Beach. She was born in 1867 in Henniker, New Hampshire into a musical family. Precociously gifted, she debuted at the age of sixteen in Boston as a pianist. Within two years, she had been soloist with the Boston Symphony in Chopin's Piano Concerto in F Minor for piano and orchestra. She experienced something even more remarkable on 30 October 1896 when the Boston Symphony gave the first performance of her *Gaelic* Symphony—the first work in that genre composed by an American woman. Four years later she enjoyed another "first" when her piano concerto was performed by the same orchestra on 9 April 1900 with Beach as the soloist.[10]

Louise had sent Beach a selection of her poems, after having sung some of the composer's songs. Upon receiving Louise's poems, Beach responded by writing, thus beginning a decade-long friendship that culminated in the summer of 1922 when Louise and Emily journeyed to Hillsboro, New Hampshire to visit the illustrious composer. Beach then set one of Louise's poems to music, "The Artless Maid." She wrote Louise, "I have done all sorts of things and yesterday I made a sketch of your 'Artless Maid.' I hope it will please you when it is really done. It is such a rococo picture—this little bit from your pen—and I have tried to make a dainty, little minuet of it."[11]

Beach returned the visit in March 1928 when she came through Georgia on a southern concert tour. She paused two weeks in Atlanta, where she stayed at the Georgian Terrace Hotel and visited with the Barilis. On 21 March she played at Agnes Scott College before departing south for Bessie Tift College in Forsyth, Georgia for a concert on 28 March. Louise joined Beach for the Tift concert, singing six of her songs including her setting of Louise's poem "The Artless Maid." The Atlanta Music Club invited Beach back on the following 7 November for a concert, again assisted by Louise, at the Women's Club Peachtree Street Auditorium. Beach played, among other works, the Bach Prelude and Fugue in D Major, the "Cat Fugue" by Scarlatti, and Beethoven's *Moonlight* Sonata, in addition to works by Brahms, Chopin, Schubert, and her own compositions. Louise performed two songs by Schumann and three by Beach.[12]

Family life for the Barili's thrived during the late 1920's as Alfredo, Jr. and Mary now had three children. The oldest was Alfredo, III, whom the family affectionately nicknamed "Baci," followed by Mary (born 1919), and finally Anne Emily (born 1923). The Barili family had been close for generations, going back to the very beginning with Caterina and Ettore. Alfredo, Sr., whom the children called "Da," was beloved as a grandfather, as he had been as a father, teacher, colleague, and friend. His cheerful warmth and gentleness delighted the children every time they came to visit, which was regularly. Mary Barili Goldsmith recalls that the family would go over on Sundays for dinner and visit with Da and grandmother. She remembers how Alfredo would meet her at the door when she arrived and pull a quarter out of her ear. His endearing humor had not changed since the days he taught at Washington Seminary and showed off the electricity in his hair to his young students.

Louise grew more like her Aunt Adelina every day. Few reacted to her indifferently—either she charmed them immediately or put them off by her directness. But, she could captivate a young child, as Randy Barili Harris relates. Randy glows when she talks about her aunt, whom the children called "Dishie." Randy reports that just like Patti, Louise would fawn and make over the children, laughing with them, explaining everything to them, and of course, advising them on every matter under the sun. Families have distinct personalities, and Louise, like her grandmother Caterina, possessed an energetic magnetism and *passion* that had served all the Barili-Pattis so well on stage. Accounts of their music, whether sung or played, continually report the intense focus and vibrancy of their performances, at whatever age or stage. And like so many fine performers, the family members did not cease performing simply because they walked off stage. They were "on" most of their lives, to the delight (and sometimes fury) of their friends, admirers, and family members.

Alfredo, too, possessed this personal magnetism, but it was even more powerful, owing to his gentle, understated, and genuine manner. Unlike his grandmother, father, aunt, and daughter, he did not come directly at people. They came to him, drawn by his strong presence. People relate how they were captured by his charisma before they knew it. As they approached him, he engaged them without crowding them emotionally, which established a natural and comfortable personal connection. Throughout the record about him, whether written or verbal, runs a description of his inner joy, a serene confidence that captivated nearly everyone. With this he combined a very decided and clear-cut personality. Few people possessed more conviction, tenacity, and passion than Alfredo Barili, but it was a restrained, inner passion. This is what gave it such power. His unique gift lay in how he fused all the zeal and intensity so characteristic of his family with a calm and quiet demeanor.

* * * * * * *

By the end of the decade, Atlanta's musical life had finally been firmly established. Sadly, though, events soon undermined the musical world in the city. Almost as in a Greek tragedy, where a character is destined never to escape his fate, the crash on Wall Street in October 1929 brought these encouraging musical developments to a slow, grinding halt. It gave the *coup de grace* to the Atlanta Symphony Orchestra, which had been on shaky ground since the advent of motion pictures with sound. The Metropolitan Opera ceased its visits to the city after 1929. Other touring concert offerings to the city dropped dramatically as the nation fell ever deeper into financial difficulty. In 1938, as reported, the Atlanta Conservatory folded, unable to stay in the black.

The Barilis seemed to have coped with the Depression better than many families. It seems that Alfredo had been receiving about five percent a year ($1,000) from the bequest left him by Patti in 1919. This would have kept the family reasonably comfortable during the difficult years. The grim economic situation hit Alfredo, Jr. worse than the rest of the family. Building activity had all but ceased in Atlanta, which made things extremely difficult for architectural firms. By the early 1930's, the situation had become so bad for his firm that he,

Mary and the three children were forced to move in with Alfredo, Emily, and Louise at their home on Myrtle Street. Inevitably, tensions arose, especially between Alfredo III and Louise. He was in his late teen years, had a very lighthearted spirit, and enjoyed a good time. Louise probably took exception to many of his escapades, which he undoubtedly found irritating and controlling. She may have in turn resented the intrusion into the house, which could not have failed to be disruptive. Randy Barili Harris relates how her father never liked Louise, something that probably stemmed from these years of living together.

The School of Music seems to have weathered the bad times. Announcements such as that run in 1933 suggest they were getting along, in spite of the Depression: "Barili School of Music. For the Higher Art of Piano Playing and Singing and A Thorough Musical Development." It listed Alfredo, Emily, and Louise for the 4 September opening. The recitals at the School of Music, now located at Myrtle Street, move to a high level of excellence not seen before. Students like Marguerite Taylor, Laura Schallenberger, Nana Tucker, and Evelyn Wall presented splendid programs in the early 1930's. Evelyn Wall joined Mrs. W. C. Horne, a pupil of Louise, for a recital in May 1930. Miss Wall played MacDowell and Chopin etudes while Mrs. Horne sang Italian art songs and three American art songs, including one by her father.

One program from Marguerite Taylor's recital on 16 April 1932 is impressive for her selections, which included the Bach Chromatic Fantasy, the Sonata Op. 26 by Beethoven, and four Chopin pieces. What is even more remarkable is the handwritten notation next to her name, "age 12." If that is true—and there have been amazingly few inaccurate statements found anywhere in the entire record—then she must have been a remarkable young pianist. Whatever her age, her program reflects the best quality of piano instruction. Three years later, she played another program, opening with Scarlatti's Sonata in A Major (another repertoire selection that put Barili ahead of his time), the Mozart Fantasy in C Minor, Beethoven's Sonata, Op. 27 No. 2, Etudes by Liszt and Chopin, and two small pieces by Debussy and Moszkowski.[13]

Louise and Emily remained active in the city's musical life. On 18 March 1931 Emily lectured to the Atlanta Music Club on "The History of Song in Condensed Form from Haydn to Mendelssohn," while Louise sang some examples. Emily seems to have given a rather thorough lecture (after all, she was a European-trained Barili), probably with a level of detail rarely heard by her audience. She began with Haydn, then surveyed art song through Cornelius, Schubert, Beethoven, Schumann, (Robert) Franz and Mendelssohn. Her notes reveal a sophistication and insight unusual for the period in American musical criticism. For example, in comparing German and English art song, she insightfully pointed out that "The German type of ballad here meant, embracing poems of narrative character, rather than the English ballad of the present time, which is often purely lyric." She ended on a personal note, reminding her listeners that she and Alfredo had been *there* during the final days of German Romanticism, that they had studied with those who had been students when it was in full bloom; they heard personal recounts of what it was like working with Mendelssohn, Schumann, Moscheles, Ries, and others; they had met and played for Liszt and Brahms. Now they were valuable links to a colorful past quickly vanishing in the 1930's. She concluded, "But I wish to speak of Dr. Ferdinand Hiller, a warm friend of Mendelssohn, who had been Director of the Cologne Conservatory, celebrating his twenty-fifth anniversary then, when Mr. B. and I studied with him." Would that she and Alfredo had left more written accounts of those luminous years.

Alfredo enjoyed increasing respect and accolades throughout the city during this time. Helen Knox Spain, critic for the *Sunday American*, presented him as the first in her series "Georgia Composers," which began on 18 September 1932. She closed her article by honoring him for "building substantially for the perfection of the high ideals of music." On Sunday afternoon 30 October 1932 the Fine Arts Department of the Atlanta Woman's Club presented a program as a "tribute of love and esteem to Mr. Barili who, in the course of his long and notable career, has had great influence in shaping the musical life not only of Atlanta but of the entire south." Mr. William Cole Jones, editorial writer for the *Atlanta Journal* , gave the opening address on "Work and Influence of Alfredo Barili in Atlanta." Inviting Mr. Cole to speak was a brilliant choice. His position as editor of a prestigious regional paper—itself the mouthpiece of the city—enabled him to speak as the voice of Atlanta in recognizing Barili's contribution to the city's cultural life. Mrs. Dowman and Miss Battle, both students of Alfredo, performed five of his most popular piano works and four of his songs. Much of Atlanta's musical elite were in the audience, as well as many former students. One very interesting thing appears in the list of attendees: a number of male names. This is one of the few instances in the record where any of his male students are mentioned.[14]

Alfredo also enjoyed the continuing affection and friendship of many persons as he approached his eighth decade. Three of his students interviewed for this book had warm memories of him during this time, especially Cherry Emerson. Barili used to ride with Emerson to the mountains on Saturdays, during which they developed the kind of dear friendship that comfortably crosses generational boundaries. They were occasionally accompanied by Edwin (Ned) Hanley, a friend of Cherry Emerson, who later became one of the leading authorities on the music of Alessandro Scarlatti. Emerson studied piano with Barili during the time he was enrolled in the chemistry department at Emory University. His accounts of the time spent together glow with delight and fondness. Also clear are his memories of piano lessons discussed earlier, where Barili's insistence on excellence pervaded the entire experience. During their walks together Barili still stood absolutely erect. Emerson describes him as always vigorous, articulate, and immaculately dressed. Barili for his part must have much enjoyed the company of a bright, energetic young man just discovering a world of music that Barili had seen form and grow, and to which he and his family had contributed so much.

* * * * * * *

On Sunday evening 17 November 1935 during one of Barili's walks, an inter-city bus struck him as he stepped off the corner of Myrtle Street at Ponce de Leon. Exactly what happened remains unclear. It was almost dark, and he was probably wearing a dark suit. Ponce de Leon rises slightly at that point, making visibility somewhat difficult. He possibly looked to the left, did not see the bus, looked right, and stepped just as the bus accelerated. If the driver noticed him, he likely assumed Barili saw the bus and would wait. When Barili stepped off the curve, the impetus made it impossible to step back up or jump out of the way as the bus approached. Then it was too late to stop. Barili died immediately.

All Atlanta mourned him it seems. The funeral was held on Tuesday, 19 November, at the Spring Hill Funeral Home. It overflowed with friends, family, students, and many others. Dr. Richard Orme Flinn conducted the service, after which Barili was buried in the family plot at West View Cemetery near his mother.

The obituaries celebrated Alfredo Barili's enormous contribution to the growth of Atlanta's cultural life. The writer for the *Journal* (perhaps Mr. Jones?) remembered a different aspect, however—a more personal one. He had known the artist *and* the man, and he praised both in a deeply touching tribute:[15]

> The man Barili equaled the artist. Of quiet tastes, he devoted himself
> to his art, his family, and his intimate friends. His lightness and gayety
> [sic] of spirit were as real as his depth of soul. Ready with a good

story, free with his contagious laughter, an agile immaculate body, a youth which denied his eighty-one years, that is the indelible picture of Alfredo Barili which will remain with those who knew him.

And what more was there to say of his artistic achievements? Nothing really. As in the case of his celebrated aunt and friend Adelina Patti, it had all been said, countless times. Any respect paid to his artistic achievements would only be expected, such as those in *Musical America* (10 December, p.32), *Musical Courier* (14 December, p.20), and the *Peters Jahrbuch* (Leipzig, Germany, Vol. 55, 19, p.32). Perhaps one of the finest tributes had appeared while he was still alive, however. No eulogy would ever surpass the editorial that appeared in the *Journal* on 3 October 1932 when the Music Club honored him with their program. The writer obviously felt deeply about Barili, given the moving poetry he penned in the editorial. He (Mr. Jones again?) opens with a brief biographical summary of Barili's past. Then the second paragraph explains that these tales "end usually in the past tense. But Alfredo Barili belongs to an eternal present." That became even truer on 17 November 1935. "The young city to which he came years ago as a youthful artist with an Old World tradition was rich in courage and faith, for it had forged upward from the very ashes of war, and was rich in the enterprise that makes for prosperity. But in music it still awaited its prophet and leader. That vital want Mr. Barili supplied." Even better: "He not only instructed, he revealed, and inspired. His teaching and his rendering of the masters was the work of one who created in the footsteps of the creators. How many distinguished musicians today remember with gratitude the foundation he gave them, not merely in the technique but in the very soul of their art, and the loyalty with which he imbued them for its highest and purest standards."

Tirelessly, then, for his fifty-five years in Atlanta

". . . he poured out for us the riches of his knowledge and genius. By a thousand gracious touches, in a thousand fruitful ways, he led his chosen city in his chosen art—the most potent personal influence we have known for musical progress.

How quietly, yet how tellingly, he teaches and lives his gospel of beauty, as indifferent to the crowd and to the world's reward as that young knight who went questing for the Grail! Let us ever honor true captains of industry and commerce, true soldiers and statesmen. But let us never forget those rarer leaders—the poet, the painter, the sculptor, the musician—without whom the gleam would vanish from our earth, and the song from our hearts."

CODA

Emily outlived Alfredo less than five years, dying at the age of 82 in 1940, just one year older than he at his death. Alfredo left his entire estate to her in his will of 23 April 1921. The children received nothing, as he explained, "believing that it will be to their best interests and benefit that their mother should inherit my entire estate, and thereafter provide for them in such manner as she may deem appropriate." Emily and Louise moved from the Myrtle Street house to a small apartment at 794 Adair Street in 1937, where they both continued teaching.

By the time they moved their finances had tightened considerably. It appears that Emily and Alfredo had been living off the principal of Patti's bequest at about $1,000 a year since her death in 1919. This would have nearly depleted the money by 1937. Without the income from Alfredo's teaching, who likely was the strongest force financially, Emily and Louise probably found their income much reduced by the time they moved from the Myrtle Street house.

Emily lived until 3 May 1940. Mary Barili Goldsmith was with her at the end and recounts how she had lapsed into a coma, then rose suddenly, told Alfredo that she was coming, and finally expired. Again, Dr. Richard Orme Flinn led the funeral, after which Emily was buried near her beloved Alfredo in Westview Cemetery. The *Journal* (5 May 1940) once more recognized them for their contributions to Atlanta's cultural life, "These two admirably trained musicians brought to Atlanta musical standards which were of the highest, and their influence was immediate and lasting." Her death closed a remarkable era in music.

In 1944 Louise moved to 989 Amsterdam Avenue, where she taught music for years. Like her Aunt Adelina, she remained colorful, vibrant, and imperious. She continued writing poetry, corresponding with numerous friends and relatives, and keeping watch over the family archives. With her death on 1 September 1963 Atlanta lost a priceless witness to one of the most extraordinary musical families in American life.

It seems cruelly ironic that shortly after Emily's death, in 1944, the city *finally* became serious about its musical life. The next year it created the Atlanta Youth Symphony and hired a Chicago conductor and educator, Henry Sopkin, to conduct. Two years later the group began adding professional players and changed its name to the Atlanta Symphony Orchestra. The 1950's proved a labor of love as the low pay kept the players essentially on a part-time basis. The old Auditorium, once the pride of the city, was now, as one observer put it, "drafty, creaky, a hall better-suited for a Sousa band than a classical symphony orchestra" where a backstage telephone would ring maddeningly during the slow movement of a symphony. Things gradually improved, however. Sopkin, like Barili, labored on, and the orchestra grew in status until his retirement in 1966. The next year, Robert Shaw was selected as conductor and music director. For his first season in 1967, the orchestra was expanded to 87 musicians. For the 1968-69 season, it finally became staffed by players on full-time contracts. That same year, the orchestra and the Alliance Theater moved into the Atlanta Memorial Arts Center, which was renamed the Robert W. Woodruff Arts Center in 1983 in honor of the distinguished contributions he made to the arts. During Shaw's twenty-one year tenure he created the 200-member Atlanta Symphony Orchestra Chorus and the select 60-member Atlanta Symphony Orchestra Chamber Chorus. He retired in 1988 as music director emeritus and conductor laureate when Yoel Levi succeeded him. Under the direction of Levi, the orchestra traveled to Europe in 1991 for a highly acclaimed tour of fifteen cities. Since 1986 its recordings have garnered fourteen Grammy Awards, and it has moved into the top rank of symphonic organizations.

The Atlanta Opera followed suit. The Metropolitan Opera had returned to the city in 1940, resuming its annual tours until 1986, when expenses and scheduling problems finally forced it to discontinue touring. This development proved fortunate for the Atlanta opera, however. The energies and financial support which had gone to the Metropolitan for years were now redirected towards the Atlanta Opera, which was organized under William Fred Scott in 1985. Like Robert Shaw and the Atlanta Symphony, Scott proved to be exactly the right person for the opera; he has led the company to an artistic excellence scarcely imaginable a few years earlier. Though Atlanta still does not have an opera house, and may not for some time, it does have first-rate opera.

Other parts of the city have also moved forward musically. The Flora Glenn Candler Concert Series at Emory University has brought outstanding artists and ensembles for many years. The *Atlanta Constitution* confirmed Atlanta's cultural progress in 1985 by hiring Derrick Henry as the first full-time professional music critic. His impressive experience, insight, critical balance, and artisic vision have done much to enrich the city's musical life. With the opening of the Emily Spivey Concert Hall on the Clayton State College Campus, the city gained an outstanding performing space. Its season brings first-rate groups and performers regularly during the year, as well as local groups in their performances. In 1996 downtown Atlanta got its first major concert space since DeGive's Opera House was converted into the Paramount movie theater. The old Rialto Theater was remodeled as part of Georgia State University's School of Music into a world-class performing hall. Its 1,200 seats, excellent acoustics, and state-of-the art stage facilities will finally return active concert life to the heart of the city, and almost on the exact spot where it all started.

Alfredo Barili did more than any other musician to lay the groundwork for these achievements. He did not work alone, nor did he directly establish any of these institutions. But he did show Atlanta that it was possible, that the city only needed leadership, zeal, and talent. Performing space is critical, but it should not be a reason to shy away from supporting great music. Look at Atlanta Opera today.

By his own magnificent playing, by organizing the Atlanta Music Festival in 1883 and the Polymnia Club, and by producing a succession of outstanding students, Barili demonstrated that excellence was possible. All that was needed was commitment. Health reasons brought him to Atlanta, not the city's musical opportunities. Although he arrived before the city was ready artistically, which brought him no little frustration, he nevertheless quietly started with the talent in hand, carefully guided it along, and polished it until it shone. And that glow flickers strongly today.

For this reason Alfredo Barili will not be forgotten—"He belongs to an eternal present." He would radiate satisfaction upon seeing the musical activity in Atlanta today. One can fantasize about his returning via some imagined time warp to survey the city's musical life in the 1990's. He would be delighted with the sparkling musicality and engaging lyricism of the Lanier Trio at the Georgia State School of Music, or the sound of the magnificent Casavant organ at Glenn

Memorial United Methodist Church on the Emory campus. He would also thrill to hear Lucia go mad—once again—as she soared lyrically upward on the stage of the Atlanta Opera. The glorious sounds of the choir and organ at St. Philip's Cathedral would reassure him that church music too had come of age in the Gate City. He would then make his way to symphony hall in the newly remodelled Woodruff Arts Center, where the Atlanta Symphony Orchestra under Yoel Levi would amaze him with its superb balance, brilliant sheen, and vigorous playing. Finally, he would move up to the balcony to better hear the present day choral descendent of the outstanding chorus which he directed more than a century ago at the first Atlanta Music Festival. The ASO chorus, with its captivating choral tone, transcendent blend, and compelling power would undoubtedly astound him. One can just see him sitting there listening intently to the orchestra and chorus as Robert Shaw conducted the Finale to Beethoven's Ninth Symphony. As the last electrifying chords died away, he would not leap to his feat, yelling and clapping boisterously, for that was not his way. Rather, he would slowly break into that engaging smile, rise to his feet calmly, clap intensely, nod, and say to himself: "Excellent, Atlanta. I knew you could do it."

Appendix A

Grand Concert by the Brass Band of the Second Regiment Infantry
The New Concordia Hall - Marietta Street
May 9, 1877
J. A. Gibson, Director

Part I

Overture - Opera *La Dame blanche* .... Boieldieu
Cleopatra Waltzes .... Waltzes
Selections - Opera *Martha* .... Flotow
Traumerei (Reverie) .... Schumann
Selections - Opera *Norma* .... Bellini

Part II

Overture - Opera *L'italiana in Algeri* .... Rossini
Casandra Waltzes .... Gibson
Selections - Opera *Faust* .... Gounod
Golden Robin Polka .... Bousquet
Grand Potpourri - *Bohemian Girl* .... Balfe

The Rossini Club
May 18, 1877

Paradise and the Peri .... Schumann
Rossini Club and Orchestra, Soloists
"Ah, What Fate!" *Moses in Egypt* .... Rossini
Lima Waltz - Aria - "d'Abilita" .... Arditi
Loreley, an unfinished opera .... Mendelssohn
"Mi manco la voce" Quartet .... Rossini
"Dal l'uo stellaio soglio"-Prayer,
    Moses in Egypt .... Rossini
Aria Concertant, *Le pré aux clercs* .... Hérold
Grand March and Concert, *Tannhäuser* .... Wagner
Rossini Club and Orchestra

Theodore Thomas and His Unrivalled Symphony Orchestra

Sixty Distinguished Artists

Assisted by

The Musical Union's Fine Selected Chorus of Ninety Voices
under Alfredo Barili

at

DeGive's Opera House

Saturday, December 1, 1883

MATINEE

Wedding March. Overture   *Midsummer Nights's Dream* .... Mendelssohn

Larghetto, 2nd Symphony .... Beethoven

Ballet Music and Wedding Processional .... Rubinstein

    Torchlight Dance of the Bayaderes

    Torchlight March of the Brides of Cashmere

    Second Dance of the Bayaderes

    Wedding Procession

"Gypsy Life" .... Schumann

Hungarian Rhapsody, No. 2 .... Liszt

Intermission

Overture *Merry Wives of Windsor* .... Nicolai

Ave Maria   .... Bach-Gounod

Ballet Air *Paris and Helen* ....   _____

Symphonic Poem *Danse Macabre* .... Saint-Saëns

Lohengrin 3rd Act .... Wagner

    Introduction
    Nuptial Chorus
    March Movement
    "Hail Bright Adobe" - Chorus

Saturday Evening

Rakoczy March *Damnation of Faust* ....Berlioz

Overture *Tannhäuser* .... Wagner

Andante, 6th Symphony .... Beethoven

Gypsy Life - Chorus .... Schumann

Invitation to the Dance... Weber

Symphonic Poem *Les Préludes* .... Liszt

Intermission

Overture *William Tell*... Rossini

Träumerei .... Schumann

Spring Song .... Mendelssohn

Waltz *On The Beautiful Blue Danube*.. Strauss

"Heavens Are Telling" - Chorus ....Haydn

Bal Costume .... Rubinstein

* * *

Programme of the Five Entertainments
of
Atlanta Music Festival - November 15, 16, & 17 [1883]

Thursday Night
Part I

Jubel Overture - Grand Orchestra .... C. M. von Weber

"Inflammatus" *Stabat mater* .... Rossini
Mr. Jules Levy

Humoristique Fantasie on a popular German Air
(as it would have been written by Bach,
Haydn, Mozart, Verdi, Gounod, and Wagner) .... Schertz
Grand Orchestra

Bolero   *Sicilian Vespers* .... Verdi
Miss Letitia L. Fritch

Unfinished Symphony - Grand Orchestra .... Franz Schubert

Part II

Grand March and Chorus   *Tannhäuser* .... Richard Wagner
Music Festival Chorus and Grand Orchestra.
Under the direction of Alfredo Barili

Sweet Sixteen Waltz .... Rudolph Aronson
Mr. Jules Levy

Overture   *Maritana* .... Wm. Vincent Wallace
Grand Orchestra

Sweetheart .... Balfe
Miss Letitia L. Fritch

Overture   *William Tell* .... Rossini
Grand Orchestra

* * *

Friday Matinee
Part I

Overture   *Magic Flute* .... Mozart
Grand Orchestra

Levy - Athan Polka .... Levy
Mr. Jules Levy

Pastoral Symphony .... Beethoven
Grand Orchestra
Flor de Marghereta .... Arditi
Miss Bessie Pierce
Symphony in B Flat .... Haydn
Grand Orchestra

Part II
Grand March and Chorus *Tannhäuser*............................... Wagner
Music Festival Chorus and Grand Orchestra.
Under the direction of Alfredo Barili
Original Selections .... Levy
Mr. Jules Levy
Waking of the Lion .... Kontski
L'Albani Valse .... Arditi
Miss Bessie Pierce
Overture *Freischütz*... C. M. von Weber
Grand Orchestra

* * *

Friday Night
Part I
Overture *Midsummer Night's Dream* .... Mendelssohn
Grand Orchestra
The Lost Chord .... Sullivan
Mr. Jules Levy
Pastoral Symphony .... Beethoven
Polacca *I Puritani* .... Bellini
Miss Letitia L. Fritch
Duet - Flute and French Horn .... ──
Members of the Orchestra

Part II
Bridal Chorus, with Introduction, *Lohengrin* .... Wagner
Music Festival Chorus and Grand Orchestra.
Under the direction of Alfredo Barili

"O Luce di Quest Anima" .... Donizetti
Miss Bessie Pierce
Serenade for String Instruments Alone .... Haydn
Grand Orchestra
Grand Aria *Il Trovatore* .... Verdi
Mr. Jules Levy
Rhapsodie Hongroise .... Liszt
Grand Orchestra

* * *

Saturday Matinee
Part I
Overture *William Tell* .... Rossini
Grand Orchestra
Grand Arie *Il Trovatore* .... Verdi
Mr. Jules Levy
Forosseter Tarantelle .... Arditi
Miss Bessie Pierce
Fifth Symphony .... Beethoven
Grand Orchestra
Sweet Sixteen Waltz .... Rudolph Aronson
Mr. Jules Levy

Part II

Bridal Chorus, with Introduction, *Lohengrin* .... Wagner
Grand Orchestra
Ave Maria .... Gounod
Miss Letitia L. Fritch
Air Le Roi Louis XIII .... Ghys
Grand Orchestra
Love Me - Majourka .... Chopin
Miss Bessie Pierce
The Reformation Symphony .... Mendelssohn
Grand Orchestra

* * *

Saturday Night
Part I

Overture *Rienzi* .... Richard Wagner
Grand Orchestra
Whirlwind Polka .... Levy
Mr. Jules Levy
"Son Virgin vezzoza" Polacca *I Puritani* .... Bellini
Miss Letitia L. Fritch
Menuet (especially arranged for orchestra) .... Alfredo Barili
Grand Orchestra
"Inflammatus" *Stabat mater* .... Rossini
Mr. Jules Levy

Part II

Concerto in F Sharp Minor for Piano and Orchestra .... Ferdinand Hiller
Andante Expressione
Finale
Alfredo Barili
The Lotus Flower .... Schumann
Miss Letitia L. Fritch
Second Symphony .... Beethoven
Grand Orchestra
"The Heavens Are Telling" *Creation* .... Haydn
Music Festival Chorus and Orchestra

APPENDIX B

A partial listing of the books on music in the Young Men's Library given in the *Atlanta Constitution,* 9 February 1898:

Music and Morals, Dr. Hawels.

Philosophy of Music, Pole.

The Story of Music, Henderson.

Music Study in Germany, Amy Fay.

The Standard Operas, George P. Upton.

The History of Music, Matthews.

Life of Chopin, Franz Liszt.

Frederick Chopin, Willeby.

Wagner and His Works, Henry T. Finck.

Wagner as I Knew Him, Praeger.

Chopin and Other Musical Essays, Henry T. Finck.

My Musical Life, Dr. Hawels.

How to Listen to Music, Krehbiel.

From the Tone World, Ehlert.

Ruskin on Music.

Famous Comosers and Their Works, Paine.

Letters of Felix Mendelssohn, Bartholdy.

Wagner's Ring of the Nibelung, Gustav Cable.

Autobiography of Rubenstein, translated by Delano.

Life of Schubert, H. F. Frost.

Women in Music, George P. Upton.

The Great German, French, and Italian Composers.

The World of Music, Comtesse of Bremont.

Life of Mozart, Nohl.

Life of Beethoven, Nohl.

Cyclopedia of Music and Musicians, John D. Champlin, Jr., and William F. Apthorp.

Music of the Modern World, edited by Anton Seidl.

The Wagner Story Book, W. H. Frost.

APPENDIX C EXTANT WORKS

Barili only gave about half of his works opus numbers, which is reflected in the listing below. There are three sources for the list: (1) the Barili Collection at the Georgia Department of Archives and History; (2) listings of works on the back of published music; (3) one handwritten catalogue of works by Emily Barili, which is probably an early one, as it lacks some later works.

Works with Opus Numbers

"Pass'd Away," op. 4 [song]. Philadelphia: A. H. Rosewig, 1876. Dedicated to Mrs. Alfred Vezin. [Pub. copy].
Valse Gracieuse, op. 6 [piano]. Atlanta: Philips & Crew. [Emily Barili Cat.].
Cradle Song, op. 18 [piano]. Atlanta: Philips & Crew, 1881. Dedicated to Louise [Barili]. The work went through at least twenty-six editions. The copyright was renewed in 1909. [Pub. copy].
Fantasie Mazurka, op. 19 [piano]. Atlanta: Philips & Crew. [Emily Barili Cat.].
Menuet, op. 20 [piano]. Atlanta: Philips & Crew. Dedicated to Willie Howard. [Emily Barili Cat].
Tambourine (Danse Caprice), op. 21 [piano]. Atlanta: Pilips & Crew. [Emily Barili Cat].
Song of the Blacksmith, op. 22 [piano]. Atlanta: Philips & Crew. [Emily Barili Cat.].
Danse Caprice op. 23 [piano]. New York: Eduard Schuberth & Co., 1887. Dedicated to James B. Huneker. [Pub. copy].
Impromptu, op. 24 [piano]. Atlanta: Philips & Crew. [Emily Barili Cat.]
Miniature Gavotte, op. 25, no. 1 [piano]. Atlanta: Philips & Crew. Dedicated to Lucy Peel. [Pub. copy].
Minature Minuet, op. 25, no. 2 [piano]. Atlanta: Philips & Crew. Dedicated to Bertie Crew. [Pub. copy].
Moment Musical, op. 26, no. 1 [piano]. Atlanta: Philips & Crew, 1889. Dedicated to Madame Teresa Carreño. [Pub. copy].
Mazurka, op. 26, no. 2 [piano]. Atlanta: Philips & Crew, 1889. Dedicated to Madame Teresa Carreño. [Pub. copy].
Spanish Serenade, op. 27 [piano]. Atlanta: Philips & Crew. [Emily Barili Cat].

"Your Tender Love Is Best," pub. as op. 27 [song]. Atlanta: Philips & Crew, 1892. Words by Charles Hubner and Grace H. Duffield. Dedicated to William Frederickson. [Pub. copy].

Modern Minuet, op. 28 [piano]. Atlanta: Philips & Crew. Dedicated to Miss Neally Stevens of California, pianist. [Pub. copy].

"There Little Girl Don't Cry," op. 29 [song]. Atlanta: Philips & Crew, 1897. Words by James Whitcomb Riley. Dedicated to Miss Bessie Rathbon. [Pub. copy].

"Oh, Say Not Love's A Rover," op. 29 [song]. Atlanta: Philips & Crew, 1897. Words by Charles Hubner. Dedicated to Miss Bessie Rathbon. [Pub. copy].

Gavotte, op. 30, no. 1 [piano]. Atlanta: Philips & Crew, 1897. Dedicated to William Sherwood. [Pub. copy].

Butterfly (Valse Caprice), op. 30, no. 2 [piano]. Atlanta: Philips & Crew, 1897. Dedicated to William Sherwood. [Pub. copy].

Works without Opus Number

Album Leaf for Piano [Manuscript].

Gate City Guard-International Quickstep [piano]. By R. A. P. Sodie (pseudonymn for Alfredo Barili). Atlanta: Philips & Crew, 1887. [Pub. copy]. Republished as *The Atlanta March* by Philips & Crew in 1895 for the Cotton States Exposition.

Gavotte Number 1 [piano]. [Emily Barili Cat.].

Gavotte [piano]. Philadelphia [n. p.]. Dedicated to Charlotte M. Sharpless. [Emily Barili Cat.].

Gavotte in G [piano]. [Emily Barili Cat.].

"Good Night" [song]. Philadelphia: Boner. Dedicated to Mrs. G. Peacock. [Emily Barili Cat.].

"Love Is A Flower" [song]. Atlanta: Philips & Crew. Words by Myrta Avary. [Emily Barili Cat.].

"Maiden With Thy Mouth So Rosy" [song]. Manuscript.

Polonaise [piano]. [Emily Barili Cat.].

Romanza [piano]. [Emily Barili Cat.].

A Short Story [piano]. Atlanta: Philips & Crew. [Emily Barili Cat.].

"Thoughts of Thee" [song]. Manuscript.

APPENDIX D

Copy - Letter from Emily Barili to Hermine Augusta [?]

October 1927

Your Majesty

No doubt you will be surprised to receive a letter from Atlanta Ga U. S. A. and please pardon the liberty I am taking; but ever since I read "My Life" in the Sat. E. P. I have had the desire to write to your Majesty and tell you how very interesting your articles have been to all readers, but especially to me, who lived two years in Buckeburg at a select boarding school for young girls, that was kept by the Fraulein Meenkhoff, daughter of General Meenkhoff deceased. I saw your beautiful young mother often also her older sister, who was a wonderful horse-back rider, and the younger brother who was then about 8 years old. The young girls attending the school went to the weekly concerts given in your grandparents castle and the conductor was my music teacher. I was 15 years old but after all these years (I am 71 now) I remember everything vividly. We would take our daily walks in the beautiful beech forests and also in the castle part.

I want to tell you that I am glad that His Majesty the Kaiser has such a fine congenial companion for the evening of his tragic life and I am sure all those who know, that he only wished the best for his people, will feel the same.

I was born in Philadelphia of an American father and a German mother, daughter of Ober-Geheime Finanzrath Carl Kalisky and Emilie Lehman whose ancestor was General Lehman under Frederick the Great.

The Kaliskys emigrated from Poland during the religious persecutions and settled in Magdeburg; and my father's last french [sic] ancestor Pierre de Vezin left France for the same reason. The latter settled in Hanover where he married Marie Charlotte de Chateauneuf a Huguenot emigree. So you see I have many German ancestors. I have one brother C. V. a noted artist living in N. Y. and my brother Frederick Vezin who studied painting in Dusseldorf and married a german [sic], has lived there ever since and when the War broke out became a german [sic] subject. He had the honor of painting portraits of his Majesty, his father & grandfather; also the portrait of the late Empress for a public building in Elberfeld. His Majesty Emperor William II came to an Exposition in D[usseldorf] and my brother F. V. had a permit to follow His Majesty around for 3 1/2 hours and succeeded in getting a fine likeness.

My husband, whom I met at Cologne after I left Buckeburg, and was a fellow student under Dr. Ferdinand Hiller is a nephew of the late Adelina Patti Baroness Cederstrom. After completing his studies he returned to Philadelphia and after a 2 year engagement we were married and have lived in Atlanta nearly our whole married life.

I hope this long letter has not wearied you, but I wanted you to know that all the traditions of my family made me always love Germany, and that I have a warm feeling of interest for the family at Dooan. I hope you will receive this letter safely, for no matter what station in life one occupies, one always is glad to know that others like and admire you.

Yours respectfully,
    Emily Barili
        nee Vezin.
            October 1927

ENDNOTES

CHAPTER 1

1. Vera Brodsky Lawrence, *Strong on Music: The New York Music Scene in the Days of George Templeton Strong. Volume 2: Reverberations: 1850-1856* (Chicago: University of Chicago Press, 1995): 11; Herman Klein, *The Reign of Patti* (1920. Reprint, New York: Arno Press, 1977): 431.
2. Katherine K. Preston, *Opera on the Road* (Urbana and Chicago: University of Illinois Press, 1993): 101-22.
3. Richard Crawford, *The American Musical Landscape* (Berkeley: University of California Press, 1993): 73-74.
4. Lawrence Levine, *Highbrow/Lowbrow. The Emergence of Cultural Hierarchy in America* (Cambridge and London: Harvard University Press, 1988): 85-86; 97-99; Crawford, *American Musical Landscape,* p. 75.
5. *Atlanta Constitution* (hereafter AC), 9 June 1895.
6. Giovanni Schiavo, *Italian American History,* I (New York: The Vigo Press, 1947): 241; John Cone, *Adelina Patti* (Portland: Amadeus Press, 1993): 10.
7. Ibid.
8. Cone, *Adelina Patti,* p. 9; Schiavo, *Italian American History.* p. 405; *New Grove's Dictionary of Music and Musicians,* s. v. "Salvatore Patti;" Richard White, "Opera in New York," *The Century Magazine* 24, No. 2 (June 1882): 206.
9. Cone, *Adelina Patti,* pp. 11-12.
10. Cone, *Adelina Patti,* p. 13.

11.   Odell, George C. D. *Annals of the New York Stage,* 8 vols (1931; reprint, New York: AMS Press, 1970) V: 53; Preston, *Opera on the Road,* 129.

12.   Vera Brodsky Lawrence, *Strong on Music,* I (Oxford: Oxford University Press, 1988): 425-28; Preston, *Opera on the Road,* p. 130; Odell, *Annals* V: 300; Cone, *Adelina Patti,* p. 13.

13.   John Dizikes, *Opera in America* (New Haven: Yale University Press, 1993): 179

14.   Preston, *Opera on the Road,* p. 129-31; Lawrence, *Strong on Music* 1: 425-33; Odell, *Annals* V: 302.

15.   Preston, *Opera on the Road,* pp. 134; 398; Lawrence, *Strong on Music* 1: 454; 457.

16.   Preston, *Opera on the Road,* pp. 134-35; Lawrence, *Strong on Music* 1: 456-57.

17.   White, "Opera in New York," *The Century Magazine;* 23, No. 6 (April 1882): 880-81; quoted in Preston, *Opera on the Road,* p. 135.

18.   Lawrence, *Strong on Music* 1: 461; White, "Opera in New York," *The Century Magazine;* 23, No. 6 (April 1882): 877; 881.

19.   Cone, *Adelina Patti,* p. 17; Lawrence, *Strong on Music* 1: 466; Preston, *Opera on the Road,* pp. 135-36.

20.   Lawrence, *Strong on Music* 1: 497-501; Preston, *Opera on the Road,* p. 136.

21.   Lawrence, *Strong on Music* 1: 505; Preston, *Opera on the Road,* p. 138.

22.   Quoted in Lawrence, *Strong on Music* 1: 503, and Preston, *Opera on the Road,* p. 137.

23.   Odell, *Annals* V: 406; Preston, *Opera on the Road,* pp. 345-46; Cone, *Adelina Patti,* pp. 17-18; *Dwight's Journal of Music,* 8 September 1855, p. 181; 13 September 1856, p. 191; quoted in Lawrence, *Strong on Music* 2, 11, nl2. Richard Grant White, "Opera in New York," *The Century Magazine:* 23, No. 6 (April 1882): 877; 24, No. 1 (May 1882): 34.

24.   Laurence Lerner, "The Rise of the Impresario: Bernard Ullman and the Transformation of Musical Culture in Nineteenth-Century America" (Ph. D. diss., University of Wisconsin, 1970): 28-31.

25.   Preston, *Opera on the Road,* pp. 147; 49-75; Lerner, "The Rise of the Impresario," p. 33.

26.   L. Peltz, "Romance Years Ago," *Opera News,* 22 February 1964, pp. 12-13; Odell, *Annals* V: 406; VI: 92; Lawrence, *Strong on Music,* 1: 512; 592-93; Lerner, "Rise of the Impresario," pp. 38-39; Maurice Strakosch, *Souvenirs d'un Impresario,* 3rd ed. (Paris: Paul Ollendorf, 1887): 9.

27. All quotations in Preston, *Opera on the Road,* pp. 185-87.
28. Amalia Patti by this time had clearly established herself as a major singer. Most recently she had sung the role of Adalgisa for the brilliant debut of Teresa Parodi's *Norma* on 4 November 1850 at Astor Place.
29. Odell, *Annals* VI: 200-01; 64.
30. Quoted in Lawrence, *Strong on Music* 2: 290-91.
31. Quotations in Cone, *Adelina Patti*, pp. 26-31.
32. "Alfredo Barili," *Frank Leslie's Illustrated Newspaper,* 10 August 1872, p. 349.
33. Cone, *Adelina Patti*, pp. 31-32.
34. Ibid., p. 32.
35. The *New York Times* 19 & 20 February 1855; Lawrence, *Strong on Music* 2: 578-83.
36. Quoted from Lawrence, *Strong on Music* 2: 584.
37. Lawrence, *Strong on Music* 2: 584-85; Odell, *Annals* VI: 393-94.
38. Cone, *Adelina Patti,* pp. 21, 33.
39. Adelina Patti, "The Art of Song, Yesterday and To-Day." *The Independent,* 17 March 1904, pp. 606-07.
40. *Atlanta Journal,* 22 May 1927; Cone, *Adelina Patti,* p. 34.
41. Cone, *Adelina Patti,* p. 34.
42. Odell, *Annals* VI: 575-76.
43. Lerner, "Rise of the Impresario," pp. 126-28.
44. Ibid., pp. 130-31.
45. Ibid., pp. 133-34; 144-48.
46. Ibid., pp. 153-58.
47. Odell, *Annals* VII: 257-58.
48. Cone, *Adelina Patti,* p. 37; Klein, *The Reign of Patti,* p. 44; Odell, *Annals* VII: 258.
49. Quoted in Odell, *Annals* VII: 258-59; Cone, *Adelina Patti,* p. 39; Klein, *Reign of Patti,* p. 49.
50. Quoted in Odell, *Annals* VII: 259.
51. Quoted in Odell, *Annals* VI: 260; Cone, *Adelina Patti,* pp. 40-41.
52. Cone, *Adelina Patti,* pp. 42-48.
53. Odell, *Annals* VII: 511-12; *New Grove's Dictionary of Music,* s.v. "Carlotta Patti."
54. Klein, *Reign of Patti,* pp. 144-46.
55. James Gibbons Huneker, *Steeplejack* (New York: Charles Scribner's Sons, 1922): 40-41.

56. Quoted in Schiavo, *Italian American History,* p. 404.
57. Klein, *Reign of Patti,* p. 146.
58. Odell, *Annals* VII: 512-13; 560; 611; 693; 695.
59. All articles in the Barili Collection, Georgia Department of Archives and History.
60. The *Philadelphia Press,* 9 July 1868; The *Philadelphia Sunday Times,* 12 July 1868.
61. *Evening City Item,* 29 1871; The *Press; Philadelphia Inquirer,* n. d.; *Evening Bulletin* 22 March 1869; Barili Collection, GDAH.
62. *Philadelphia Evening City Item,* 13 April 1872.
63. *Watson's Art Journal,* 20 April 1872; *New York Sunday Times,* 21 April 1872.
64. *Evening Post,* 22 April 1872; "Alfredo Barili," *Watson's Art Journal,* 27 April 1872, p. 268.
65. 10 August 1872, p. 349.
66. Gilbert, Chase. *America's Music From the Pilgrims to the Present,* rev. 2nd. (New York and London: McGraw Hill Book Company, 1966): 325.
67. *New Grove's Dictionary of American Music,* s.v. "Ferdinand Hiller."
68. *New Grove's Dictionary of Music and Musicians,* s. v. "Friedrich Gernsheim"; *Baker's Biographical Dictionary of Musicians,* s. v. "James Kwast."
69. Barili Collection, GDAH.
70. Barili Collection, GDAH; *Dictionary of National Biography,* 2nd Supplement (London, 1912), III: 557-58
71. Huneker, *Steeplejack,* pp. 188; 42.
72. Huneker to Emily Barili, 23 March 1919, Josephine Huneker. *Letters of James Gibbons Huneker,* (New York: Charles Scribner's Sons, 1922): 274-75.

CHAPTER 2

1. *AC,* 2 March 1879.
2. Edward King, *The Great South: A Record of Journeys* (Hartford: American Publishing Company, 1875): 350.

3. *Daily New Era,* 10 May 1870. Cited in Grigsby H. Wotton, Jr. "New City of the South: Atlanta, 1843-1873" (Ph. D. diss., Johns Hopkins University, 1973): 208-10.

4. *Daily New Era,* 14 February 1867. Cited in Wotton, "New City of the South," p. 210.

5. Peggy Malott Gough, "Entertainment in Atlanta, Georgia: 1860-1870" (master's thesis, University of California, Santa Barbara, 1975): 4-14; also, "On Stage in Atlanta, 1860-1870",*The Atlanta Historical Bulletin* 21, no. 2 (summer 1977): 37-57; James M. Russell, "Atlanta, Gate City of the South, 1847 to 1885" (Ph. D. diss., Princeton University, 1971): 175-80.

6. Quoted in Gough, "Entertainment in Atlanta," p. 4.

7. Ibid., p. 17.

8. Ibid., pp. 4-6; Franklin M. Garrett, *Atlanta and Environs* I (Athens: University of Georgia Press, 1954): 375.

9. Preston, *Opera on the Road,* p. 246.

10. *AC,* 11 June 1888, cited in Gough, "Entertainment in Atlanta," pp. 5-6.

11. *Daily New Era,* cited in Wotton, "New City of the South," p. 64.

12. This discussion is largely based on Charles S. Watson, *Ante-bellum Charleston Dramatists* (University: University of Alabama Press, 1976): 2-26.

13. John Joseph Hindman, "Concert Life in Ante Bellum Charleston" (Ph. D. diss., University of North Carolina at Chapel Hill, 1971): 55; two other helpful sources on music in Charleston are Mary Julia Curtis, "The Early Charleston Stage 1703-1798" (Ph. D. diss., Indiana University, 1968); and Eola Wills, *The Charleston Stage in the XVIII Century* (New York: Benjamin Blom, 1933).

14. Hindman, "Concert Life in Ante Bellum Charleston," p. 67.

15. Preston, *Opera on the Road,* pp. 47-48; 78-88.

16. Ibid., pp. 147; 197-203.

17. Ibid., pp. 203-05.

18. Hindman, "Concert Life in Ante Bellum Charleston," pp. 127; 135; 184-96.

19. This discussion of music in Richmond is based on Albert Soutamire, *Music of the Old South: Colony to Confederacy* (Madison: Fairleigh Dickinson University Press, 1972).

20. *Richmond Dispatch,* 18 May 1852, quoted in Stoutamire, *Music of the Old South,* p. 205.

21.   Ibid., pp. 198-208.
22.   This discussion is based on Henry A. Kmen, *Music in New Orleans: The Formative Years, 1791-1841* (Baton Rouge, Louisiana State University Press, 1966).
23.   Ibid., pp. 111-14.
24.   19 March 1836, quoted in Kmen, *Music in New Orleans*, p. 198.
25.   Preston, *Opera on the Road*, p. 34.
26.   Ibid., pp. 278-79.
27.   Ibid., pp. 279-80.
28.   Ibid., pp. 128; 247-48.
29.   James Michael Russell, *Atlanta 1847-1890. City Building in the Old South and New* (Baton Rouge and London: Louisiana State University Press, 1988): 70.
30.   *Southern Confederacy,* 17 December 1861; cited in Peggy Gough, "On Stage Atlanta, 1860-1870," Atlanta Historical Bulletin 21, No. 2 (Summer 1977): 45-48.
31.   *AC* 6 December 1874; Carolyn Gaye Crannell, "In Pursuit of Culture:A History of Art Activity in Atlanta 1847-1926" (Ph.D. diss., Emory University, 1971): 9,4.
32.   *Atlanta Daily Intelligencer,* 31 January 1858, quoted in Crannell, "In Pursuit of Culture," p. 349; Hindman, "Concert Life in Ante Bellum Charleston," 2: 731-32
33.   *Daily Intelligencer*, 12 April 1866; 25 February 1860; cited in Gough, "Entertainment in Atlanta," pp. 83-85.
34.   Iline Fife, "The Confederate Theater in Georgia," *Georgia Review* 9 (Fall 1955; reprint in *Music in Georgia,* New York: Da Capo Press, 1984): 189-190.
35.   Gough, "On Stage Atlanta, 1860-1870," pp. 53-54.
36.   N. Lee Orr, "John Hill Hewitt: Bard of the Confederacy," *American Music Research Center Journal* 4 (1995): 31-75; *Daily Intelligencer,* 12, 16, & 18 July 1860; 9 & 12 October 1860.
37.   *Daily Intelligencer,* 31 December 1862.
38.   Gough, "Entertainment in Atlanta," pp. 26-29.
39.   Quoted in Russell, *Atlanta: 1847-1890,* pp. 114-15.
40.   Ibid., pp. 115-19.
41.   *Daily Intelligencer,* 24 August 1865; Arthur Reed Taylor, "From the Ashes: Atlanta During Reconstruction, 1865-1876" (Ph.D. diss., Emory University, 1973): 271.

42. Gough, "Entertainment in Atlanta," pp. 73-74.
43. *Daily New Era,* 7 October 1866, cited in Gough, "Entertainment in Atlanta," p. 74.
44. *Daily Intelligencer,* 17, 18, & 19 October 1866; *New Era,* 20 October 1866, cited in Gough, "Entertainment in Atlanta," pp. 74-75.
45. *Daily Intelligencer,* 21 October 1866, quoted in Gough, "Entertainment in Atlanta," p. 76.
46. Ibid., pp. 83-84.
47. Ibid., pp. 80-81; *AC,* 9 & 13 March 1870.
48. Ibid., p. 81.
49. Levine, *Highbrow/Lowbrow,* p. 102; *Daily New Era,* 24 May 1868.
50. Preston, *Opera on the Road,* pp. 316-17.
51. Taylor, "From the Ashes," pp. 275-71.
52. Quoted in Garrett, *Atlanta and Environs* I: 840; Taylor, "From the Ashes," p. 275.
53. Taylor, "From the Ashes," pp. 277-78; Meta Barker, "Some High Lights of the Old Atlanta Stage," The *Atlanta Historical Bulletin* 1, No. 2 (1928): 33-48; Garrett, *Atlanta and Its Environs* I: 840.
54. Taylor, "From the Ashes," p. 281.
55. Taylor, "From the Ashes," p. 273; *Daily New Era,* 26 November 1869, quoted in Russell, *Atlanta, 1847-1890; AC,* 15 November 1879.
56. Preston, *Opera on the Road,* pp. 256-57.
57. Levine, *Highbrow/Lowbrow,* p. 102.
58. *New Grove's Dictionary of American Music,* s.v. "Musical Theater"; *AC,* 20 November 1868.
59. *AC,* 4 August 1877; 8 March; 28 October 1879; *New Grove's Dictionary of American Music,* s.v. "Musical Theater."
60. Gough, "Entertainment in Atlanta," pp. 76-77.
61. *Atlanta Journal Magazine,* 31 March 1935.
62. *AC,* 28 April 1871.
63. Ibid.; *New Grove's Dictionary of Opera,* s.v. "Christine Nilsson."
64. Quoted in Russell, *Atlanta, 1847-1890,* p. 127.
65. *AC,* 8 May; 4 June, 16, 17 July; I September; 29 October 1872.
66. Writer's Program, *Atlanta. A City of the Modern South* (1942. Reprint, St. Clair Shores, Michigan, 1973): 128.
67. *AC,* 16 January; 4 March; 12 & 17 April 1873.
68. Taylor, "From the Ashes," pp. 284-85; *AC,* 3 & 18 February; 30 May; 23 October 1874.

69. *AC,* 13 & 21 February; 11 April 1875; *Daily Herald,* 26 March (in Russell, *Atlanta, 1847-1890); AC,* 11 & 16 December 1875.
70. *AC,* 10 January; 13 February 1877.
71. *AC,* 9 September 1923.
72. *AC,* 20 April; 5, 8, & 18 May; 6 June; 18 July; 24 August; 25 September 1877.
73. *AC,* 11, 15, & 23 February; 5 March; 16 April; 22 December 1879.

CHAPTER 3

1. Russell, *Atlanta, 1847-1890,* pp. 117; 233, 251-52.
2. Ibid.; Alexander K. McClure, *The South: Its Industrial, Financial, and Political Condition* (Philadelphia: J. B. Lippencott Company, 1886): 58-59.
3. Wallace P. Reed, *History of Atlanta, Georgia* (Syracuse: D. Mason & Co., 1889): 322-23.
4. *AC,* 7 May 1882; 27 August 1879; 13 & 27 June 1880.
5. *AC,* 8 April 1883.
6. Program; 30 April 1880. Barili Collection, GDAH.
7. *AC,* 30 April 1880.
8. Program, Barili Collection GDAH; *AC,* 5 November; 2 December 1880.
9. *AC,* 7 November 1880; *Evening Bulletin,* 15 November 1880; The *Item,* 21 November 1880.
10. *AC,* 20 September 1870; 29 August 1880; Leonora Raines, "Young Atlanta Knew Good Music," *The Atlanta Historical Bulletin* 7, No. 29 (October 1944): 186; Annie Miller, "Old Days at Ballard's School," *Atlanta Journal Magazine,* 13 December 1931, p. 4.
11. *AC,* 8 June 1882; *Evening Post* (Atlanta), 8 June 1882.
12. Ibid.
13. Programs in Barili Collection, GDAH.
14. *AC,* 18 March 1883.
15. *AC,* 2 April 1883.
16. *AC,* 3 April 1883; *Atlanta Post Appeal,* 3 April 1883; *Music and Drama,* 7 April 1883.
17. *AC,* 10 July; 19 September; 23 November; 12 December 1880.
18. *AC,* 1 & 9 January; 3 March; 25 August 1881.
19. *The New Grove's Dictionary of American Music,* s. v. "Patti."

20. *AC,* 19, 22 & 29 January 1882; Cone, *Adelina Patti,* pp. 137-43; 359-60.
21. *AC,* 23 October 1881; 2 February; 7 & 26 May; 7 & 26 November 1882; 14 January 1883.
22. AC, 5 & 31 January; 4 March; 7 August 1883.
23. AC, 9 August 1883.
24. Charles Hamm, *Music in the New World* (New York and London: W.W. Norton, 1983): 307-11.
25. *AC,* 19 August 1883.
26. *AC,* 21 October 1883.
27. *AC,* n. d. Barili Collection, GDAH; 11 November 1883; *Augusta Evening News,* n. d. GDAH
28. Programs for the entire festival are in the Barili Collection, GDAH.
29. *AC,* 16 & 17 November 1883; *The Musical World,* n. d. Barili Collection, GDAH.
30. *AC,* 2 January; 23 March; 28 September; 23 November 1884; 26 January; 3 February; 3 April; 23 October 1888.
31. *AC,* 4 February 1889.
32. Levine, *Highbrow/Lowbrow,* pp. 102-104.
33. *AC,* 5, 7 & 9 February 1889.
34. *AC,* 8 & 13 October 1885; 14 January 1886.
35. *AC,* 25 January; 14 February; 16 October 1886.
36. Hamm, *Music in the New World,* pp. 288-90.
37. *AC,* 18 & 19 April 1888.
38. *AC,* n. d.[about 1888]; 13 December 1885; 12 March; 7 May 1886; *Atlanta Journal,* 11 December 1885; *Evening Capitol,* 11 December 1885.
39. Articles in the Barili Collection, GDAH. Choral selections: Reinecke, "The Winter Hath Not a Blossom"; Hatton, "The Fisher Wife's Song"; Florio, "To the Spring"; Smart, "The Wood Nymphs"; Rubenstein, "Wanderer's Night Song"; Gilchrist, "The Sea Fairies."
40. *AC,* 21 & 23 May; 21 December 1886; other reviews without dates, Barili Collection, GDAH.
41. *AC,* 14 March 1886.
42. *Sunday Telegram,* 13 June 1886.
43. Folder for the school in Barili Collection, GDAH.
44. *AC,* 12 June 1887
45. *AC,* 7 June 1888.

46. *AC,* 5 June 1889.
47. *AC,* 13 December 1885; *Sunday Telegram,* 13 June 1886; Barili Collection, GDAH.
48. *Atlanta Journal,* n. d.; 5 June 1895; *AC,* n. d.; 9 June 1895; Barili Collection, GDAH.
49. *Atlanta Journal,* 5 June 1895; *AC,* 9 June 1895.
50. Interviews with the author: Evelyn Wall Robbins, 28 November 1979; Cherry Emerson, 28 September 1994.
51. *Musical Courier,* 21 March 1888, p. 158.
52. Elly Glover, "Alfred Barili," *Music. A Monthly Magazine* 12, no. 9 (September 1897): 575-78.
53. *AC,* 20 November 1885; *Atlanta Journal,* 20 November 1885; *Le Guide Musical* (Brussels): 31, No. 50 (10 December 1885): 364; *Le Menestrel* (Paris): 52, No. 6 (10 January 1886): 47.
54. Richard Crawford, ed., *The Civil War Songbook* (New York: Dover Publications, 1977): v; *The New Grove's Dictionary of American Music,* s. v. "Piano Music."
55. R. H. Ives Gammell, *The Boston Painters, 1900-1930* (Orleans, Mass.: Parnassus Imprints, 1986): 3.
56. Quoted in Nicolas E. Tawa, *The Coming of Age of American Art Music* (New York: Greenwood Press, 1991): 59; Gilbert Chase, *America's Music,* p. 166.
57. Quoted in Tawa, *The Coming of Age of American Art Music* p. 59.
58. n. d., Barili Collection, GDAH.
59. Charles W. Wilkinson, *Well-Known Piano Solos. How to Play Them* (Philadelphia: Theo. Presser Co., 1924): 26-28.
60. Duo-Art roll number 69007. I am indebted to Dr. Douglas Johnson of the University of Georgia for pointing this out.
61. n. d. about 1895.
62. Hamm, *Music in the New World,* pp. 454-56.
63. Nicholas E. Tawa, *Sweet Songs for Gentle Americans* (Bowling Green: Bowling Green Popular Press, 1980): 33-34.
64. Nicholas E. Tawa, A *Music for Millions* (New York: Prendragon Press, 1984): 41.
65. Boston: Ditson, 1857, quoted in Tawa, *A Music for the Millions,* p. 42.
66. *New Grove's Dictionary of American Music,* s. v. "James Huneker"; Josephine Huneker, ed., *Letters of James Gibbons Huneker,* pp. 34; 186.

67. Program in Barili Collection, GDAH; *Evening Capital,* 22 January 1887; AC, 22 January, 18 May 1887.
68. *AC,* 25 January 1889.
69. *Musical Courier,* n. d. 1888, Barili Collection, GDAH.
70. *AC,* 5 June 1888; *Evening Journal,* 5 June 1888.

CHAPTER 4

1. Russell, *Atlanta; 1847-1890,* pp. 240-65.
2. Ibid.
3. Robert C. McMath, Jr., *William Henry Emerson and the Scientific Discipline at Georgia Tech* (Atlanta: Emerson Publications, 1994): 50-59.
4. *AC,* 23 February 1890.
5. Ibid.
6. Cone, *Adelina Patti,* p. 184; Patti to Emily Barili, 12 July 1890, Barili Collection, GDAH.
7. *AC,* 7 January 1894.
8. *AC,* n. d., late April 1891, Barili Collection, GDAH.
9. *Atlanta Journal,* 6 June 1891; *AC,* 30 July 1891.
10. Mary Barili Goldsmith recounts a different version of this incident. In a letter dated 19 November 1995, she relates how she was told by her mother, Mary Hudgins Barili, that the uproar was caused by "a person who had become completely enamored with and pursued Alfredo....since her pursuit was relentless, Mother said it did cause a terrible dilemma-- and that he was not at fault."
11. *AC,* 11 February 1893.
12. *AC,* 11 September 1894.
13. *AC,* 17 April 1893; 1 April 1894.
14. *AC,* 2 February; 14 December 1890; 8 February 1892; 18 January 1893; 7 & 10 May 1893.
15. *AC,* 22 May 1891.
16. *AC,* 22 May 1891; 10 May; 11 & 23 October 1894.
17. *AC,* 25 January; 24 May 1891; 19 February; 11 December 1893.
18. *AC,* 5 October 1890; 4 June 1893; 19 March; 6 May 1894; 21 April; 6 May; 9 December 1895.
19. *AC,* ibid.

20. *AC,* 12 January 1893; 12 & 14 January 1894.
21. *AC,* 20 January 1895; *New Grove's Dictionary of American Music,* s.v. "Sissieretta Jones."
22. Garrett, *Atlanta and Environs,* II: 318-32; AC, 23 September; 13 October 1895.
23. Chase, *America's Music,* pp. 622-23.
24. Garrett, *Atlanta and Environs* II: 329.
25. *AC,* 6 January 1897.
26. Patti to Alfredo Barili, 7 January 1895; *Atlanta Journal,* 5 June 1895; *AC,* 9 June 1895.
27. Emily to friend, n. d., Barili Collection GDAH.
28. *AC,* 14 February; 19 November 1898; Patti to Louise Barili, 27 February 1898.
29. Patti to Alfredo Barili, 12 December 1898; Cone, *Adelina Patti,* pp. 221-22.
30. *AC,* 19 & 23 January 1896.
31. *AC,* 23 April 1896.
32. *AC,* 28 October 1897.
33. *AC,* 20 & 22 October 1898; Programs, The Atlanta Historical Society.
34. *AC,* 5 & 17 November; 4 & 17 December 1898.
35. *AC,* 9 & 24 February; 14 & 30 April 1898; program, Atlanta Historical Society.
36. *AC,* 9 December 1897; 25 January; 23 & 29 April 1898; N. Lee Orr, "Dudley Buck: Leader of a Forgotten Tradition," *The Tracker* 38, No. 3 (Fall 1994): 19.
37. *AC,* 24 May & 1 June 1891; 4 December 1892; 19 February 1893.
38. *AC,* 13 April 1895; 25 April 1896; 19 April & 6 October 1897.

CHAPTER 5

1. Garrett, *Atlanta and Its Environs* II: 387; 389; 397.
2. Edward MacDowell to Alfredo Barili, 8 July 1902. Barili Collection, GDAH. Patti to Alfredo Barili, 11 August 1902.
3. Patti to Alfredo Barili, 27 September; 31 October & 8 December 1902.
4. Cone, *Adelina Patti,* pp. 230-32.
5. *AC,* 8 & 9 February 1904.

6. Cone, *Adelina Patti,* pp. 233-37; Patti to Alfredo Barili, 4 March 1904.
7. Patti to Alfredo Barili, 27 November 1904; to Louise Barili, 6 December 1904.
8. Patti to Alfredo Barili, August 1905; 3 January 1906.
9. Patti to Louise Barili, 20 January; 26 October; 26 November 1905; 3 January & 8 March 1906.
10. Louise Barili to Barilis, 8 & 20 April 1906; *Atlanta Journal Magazine,* 2 May 1943, p. 4.
11. Louise Barili to Barilis, 20 April, 11 & 31 May 1906.
12. Louise Barili to Barilis, 11, 31, & 22 May 1906.
13. Cone, *Adelina Patti,* pp. 241-48.
14. *Atlanta Journal Magazine,* 2 May 1943, p. 4.
15. Quoted in Cone, *Adelina Patti,* p. 248.
16. Patti to Barilis, 8 April & 30 September 1908.
17. Patti to Barilis, 14 October & 22 November 1909.
18. Patti to Louise Barili, 27 June & 18 July 1908.
19. Patti to Barilis, 9 June & 7 July 1908.
20. Patti to Louise Barili, 8 April 1908. *Musical Courier,* 20 April 1904, p. 19.
21. Madeline Keipp to Louise Barili, 24 June; 26 July & 30 August 1908.
22. Patti to Barilis 27 July & 30 September 1908.
23. *AC,* 15-18 January 1900.
24. *AC,* 6 March 1900.
25. *AC,* 20 & 29 October 1901.
26. *AC,* 29 & 30 October 1901.
27. *AC,* 25 December 1904; 17 January 1905.
28. *AC,* 22 April 1900. Eddy's program included Guilmant: *Prelude, Theme, Variations, and Finale*; Wagner: Prelude to *Lohengrin;* Pilgrim's Chorus, *Tannhäuser;* Buck: "The Holy Night"; Bach: Fugue in G minor; Weber: Overture to *Euryanthe; AC,*18 November 1900; 15 December 1901.
29. *AC,* 24 January 1909.
30. *AC,* 13 January 1901; 11 April 1903.
31. *AC,* 28 January; 23 & 27 February; 10 & 11 March 1900.
32. *AC,* 3, 12 & 13 June 1900.
33. *AC,* 14 November; 2 December 1900; 17 December 1901.
34. *AC,* 10 November 1901; 3 & 18 January 1903; 5 April 1904.
35. *AC,* 9 January 1903.
36. *AC,* 27 January 1905.

37.   Garrett, *Atlanta and Environs* II: 493.

38.   *AC,* 26 May & 1 June 1907.

39.   T. Eldin Burton, "Music Festival of 1909," *Atlanta Historical Bulletin* 4, No. 18 (July 1939): 199-202.

40.   Ibid.

41.   Douglas Johnson, N. Lee Orr, and Melvin Potts, "The AGO in Atlanta," *The American Organist"* 14, No. 2 (February 1980): 38-39.

42.   Ibid.

43.   Ibid.

44.   Burton, "Music Festival of 1909," p. 202.

45.   Eldin Burton, "The Metropolitan Opera in Atlanta," *Atlanta Historical Bulletin* 5 No. 20 (April 1940): 37-61.

46.   Ibid.

47.   Barili Collection, GDAH.

48.   Patti to Emily Barili, 22 November 1910; Patti to Alfredo Barili, 9 June 1908.

49.   Quoted in Cone, *Adelina Patti,* p. 256.

50.   Louise to Emily Barili, 8 May 1911.

51.   Patti to Alfredo Barili, 14 March 1911; Cone, *Adelina Patti,* p. 259.

52.   *Musical America,* 14 September 1912, p. 4; Patti to Barilis, 12 August; 14 September; 10 & 29 December 1912.

53.   Patti to Barilis, 23 April & 3 June 1913.

54.   Cone, *Adelina Patti,* pp. 260-61.

55.   Cone, *Adelina Patti,* pp. 261-63.

56.   Ibid., p. 264.

57.   Letter from Guaranty Trust, London Branch to Barili, 28 April 1920.

58.   *AC,* 4 June 1913.

59.   Burton, "The Metropolitan Opera in Atlanta," 5 (April 1940): 40; 44-47; *AC,* 23 April 1950.

60.   Ibid., pp. 48-50.

61.   Ibid., pp. 54-57.

62.   Burton, "The Metropolitan Opera in Atlanta," 5, No. 20 (April 1940): 46-51.

63.   Ibid., pp. 54-57.

64.   Ibid., pp. 57-61.

65.   Burton, "The Metropolitan Opera in Atlanta," 5, No. 23 (October 1940): 285-88.

66. *AC,* 30 September; 22 October 1917; 3 February; 7 & 14 April; 30 June 1918.
67. Johnson, Orr, and Potts, "The AGO in Atlanta," pp. 41-42; The *Constitution of the American Guild of Organists,* Article 1, Sec. 2.
68. Ibid.
69. Ibid., *AC,* 2 September 1917.
70. Writer's Program. Georgia. *Atlanta. A City of the Modern South* (1942. Reprint, Clair Shores, Michigan: Somerset Publishers, 1973): 130.

CHAPTER 6

1. Raymond B. Jones, "What to See In Atlanta and Where to See It," *The City Builder* (October/November 1923): 26.
2. Helen Knox Spain, "Atlanta Symphony Orchestra," *The City Builder* (October/November 1923): p. 10.
3. *AC,* 19 December 1920.
4. Spain, "Atlanta Symphony Orchestra," p. 10; *AC,* 7 October 1923.
5. *AC,* 3 & 17 October 1920; 16 January 1921.
6. n. d. Late 1920s; *Atlanta Journal,* 18 May 1926.
7. *AC,* n. d. About 1932; 22 April 1933.
8. *Atlanta Journal,* 11 May 1926.
9. Barili Collection, GDAH.
10. Chase, *America's Music,* p. 384.
11. *AC,* 10 September 1922; Amy Beach to Louise Barili, 18 June 1922.
12. Barili Collection, GDAH.
13. Barili Collection, GDAH.
14. AC, 23 October, 1932; *Atlanta Journal,* 29 October 1932; Atlanta *Sunday American,* 30 October 1932; program in Barili Collection, GDAH; Works for piano: *Modern Minuet, Gavotte, Moment Musical, The Butterfly,* and *Cradle Song;* voice: "O, Say Not Love's a Rover," "There Little Girl Don't Cry", "Maiden With Thy Mouth So Rosy," and "Your Tender Love is Best."
15. *Atlanta Journal,* 19 December 1935.

BIBLIOGRAPHY

Research materials for this work came from five sources.

1. The *Atlanta Constitution*, 1870-1920.
2. The Barili Collection at the Georgia Department of Archives and History.
3. Materials still held by family members Mary Barili Goldsmith and Randy Barili Harris.
4. Conversations with surviving students and family of Alfredo Barili: Cherry Emerson, Edwin Hall Hanley, Evelyn Wall Robbins, Randy Barili Harris, and Mary Barili Goldsmith.
5. General Published materials.

Barker, Meta   "Some Highlights of the Old Atlanta Stage," *The Atlanta Historical Bulletin* 1, No. 2 (1928): 33-51.

Burton, T. Eldin   "Music Festival of 1909," *Atlanta Historical Bulletin* 4, No. 18 (July 1939): 199-202; "First Season of Metropolitan Opera Presentations," *AHB* 4, No. 19 (October 1939): 270-74; "The Metropolitan in Atlanta," *AHB* 5, No. 20 (April 1940): 37-61; "Metropolitan Opera in Atlanta, Part 3, 1917," *AHB* 5, No. 23 (October 1940): 285-95.

Chase, Gilbert   *America's Music From the Pilgrims to the Present,* rev. second ed. New York and London: McGraw Hill Book Company, 1966.

Charosh, Paul   "'Popular' and 'Classical' in the Mid-Nineteenth Century," *American Music* 10, No. 2 (Summer 1992): 118-35.

Cone, John Frederick   *Adelina Patti. Queen of Hearts.* Portland: Amadeus Press, 1993.

Crannell, Carolyn Gaye   "In Pursuit of Culture: A History of Art Activity in Atlanta, 1847-1926," Ph. D. diss., Emory University, 1971.

Crawford, Richard, ed.   *The Civil War Songbook.* New York: Dover Publications, 1977.

—————   *The American Musical Landscape.* Berkeley: University of California Press, 1993.

Dizikes, John   *Opera in America. A Cultural History.* New Haven and London: Yale University Press, 1993.

Dunglison, Robley   *A Dictionary of Medical Science.* Philadelphia: Blanchard and Lea, 1857.

Garrett, Franklin   *Atlanta and Environs.* 2 vols. Athens: University of Georgia Press, 1954.

Gerstmann, B. E. Hugo   *Das Geschlecht Hasenclever.* Remscheid und Leipzig: n. p., 1922.

Glover, Ellye   "Alfredo Barili," *Music. A Monthly Magazine* 12, No. 9 (September 1897): 575-79.

Gough, Peggy   "Entertainment in Atlanta, Georgia, 1860-1870," master's thesis, University of California, Santa Barbara, 1973.

—————   "On Stage Atlanta, 1860-1870," *The Atlanta Historical Bulletin* 21, No. 2 (summer 1977): 37-58.

Hamm, Charles   *Music in the New World.* New York and London: W. W. Norton, 1983.

—————   *Yesterdays.* New York and London: W. W. Norton, 1983.

Hindman, John Joseph   "Concert Life in Ante Bellum Charleston," Ph. D. diss., University of North Carolina at Chapel Hill, 1971.

Hoogerwerf, Frank, ed.   *Music in Georgia*. New York: Da Capo Press, 1984.

Huneker, James Gibbons   *Steeplejack*. New York: Charles Scribner's Sons, 1922.

Huneker, Josephine, ed.   *Letters of James Gibbons Huneker*. New York: Charles Scribner's Sons, 1922.

Ives Gammell, R. H.   *The Boston Painters, 1900-1930*. Orleans, Mass.: Parnassus Imprints, 1986.

Johnson, H. Douglas
Orr, N. Lee
Potts, J. Melvin   "The AGO in Atlanta," *The American Organist* 14, No. 3 (February 1980): 38-44.

King, Edward   *The Great South: A Record of Journeys*. Hartford: American Publishing Company, 1875.

Klein, Herman   *The Reign of Patti*. 1920. Reprint, New York: Arno Press, 1977.

Kmen, Henry A.   *Music in New Orleans*. Baton Rouge: Louisiana State University Press, 1966.

Lawrence, Vera Brodsky   *Strong on Music: The New York Scene in the Days of George Templeton Strong, 1836-1875. Volume 1: Resonances, 1836-1850*. New York: Oxford University Press, 1988.

—————   *Strong on Music: The New York Music Scene in the Days of George Templeton Strong. Volume 2: Reverberations: 1850-1856*. Chicago: University of Chicago Press, 1995.

Lerner, Laurence Marton   "The Rise of the Impresario: Bernard Ullman and the Transformation of Musical Culture in Nineteenth Century America." Ph. D. diss., University of Wisconsin, 1970.

Levine, Lawrence   *Highbrow/Lowbrow. The Emergence of Cultural Hierarchy in America*. Cambridge and London: Harvard University Press, 1988.

Mates, Julian   "The First Hundred Years of the American Lyric Theater," *American Music* 1, No. 2 (Summer 1983): 22-38.

—————— *Two Hundred Years of Musical Theater.* New York and London: Praeger, 1987.

McClure, Alexander K. *The South: Its Industrial, Financial, and Political Condition.* Philadelphia: J. B. Lippencott Company, 1886.

McMath, Jr., Robert C. *William Henry Emerson and the Scientific Discipline at Georgia Tech.* Atlanta: Emerson Publications, 1994.

New Grove's Dictionary of American Music.

Odell, George C. D. *Annals of the New York Stage.* 8 vols. 1931. Reprint, New York: AMS Press, 1970.

Orr, N. Lee "Alfredo Barili: Atlanta Musician, 1880-1935," *American Music* 2, No. 1 (Spring 1984): 43-60.

—————— "Dudley Buck: Leader of a Forgotten Tradition," *The Tracker* 38, No. 3 (1994): 10-22.

—————— "John Hill Hewitt: Bard of the Confederacy," *American Music Research Center Journal* 4 (1995): 31-75.

Ottenberg, June C. *Opera Odyssey. Toward a History of Opera in Nineteenth-Century America.* Westport: Greenwood Press, 1994.

Pelz, L. "Romance Years Ago," *Opera News* (22 February 1964): 12-15.

Preston, Katherine K. *Opera on the Road. Traveling Opera Troupes in the United States, 1825-60.* Urbana and Chicago, University of Illinois Press, 1993.

Raines, Leonora "Young Atlanta Knew Good Music," *The Atlanta Historical Bulletin* 7, No. 29 (October 1944): 184-95.

Reed, Wallace P. *History of Atlanta.* Syracuse: D. Mason & Co., 1889.

Russell, James Michael *Atlanta 1847-1890.* Baton Rouge and London: Louisiana State University Press, 1988.

Schiavo, Giovanni E. *Italian American History,* 2 vols. New York: The Vigo Press, 1947.

Stoutamire, Albert *Music of the Old South: Colony to Confederacy.* Madison: Fairleigh Dickinson University Press, 1972.

Strakosch, Maurice   *Souvenirs d'un Impresario.* 3rd ed. Paris: Paul
                         Ollendorf, 1887.

Taylor, Arthur Reed   "From the Ashes: Atlanta During Reconstruction,
                         1865-1876," Ph. D. diss., Emory University, 1973.

Tawa, Nicolas E   *The Coming of Age of American Art Music.* New
                         York: Greenwood Press, 1991.

———————   *A Music for the Millions.* New York: Prendragon
                         Press, 1984.

———————   *Sweet Songs for Gentle Americans.* Bowling
                         Green: Bowling Green Popular Press, 1980.

Watson, Charles S.   *Antebellum Charleston Dramatists.* University:
                         University of Alabama Press, 1976.

Wilkinson, Charles W.   *Well-Known Piano Solos. How to Play Them.*
                         Philadelphia: Theo. Presser Co., 1924.

Wotton, Grigsby Hart, Jr.   "New City of the South: Atlanta, 1843-1873,"
                         Ph. D. diss., Johns Hopkins University, 1973.

Writer's Program. Georgia   *Atlanta. A City of the Modern South.* 1942.
                         Reprint, Clair Shores, Michigan: Somerset
                         Publishers, 1973.

INDEX

Caliph of Baghdad, Boieldieu, Adrien (1775-1834),
    French composer, 75
Calvé, Julie, French actress/singer, 175
Camille, 70
Campanari, Giuseppe, 193
Campania (ship), 174
Campbell Minstrel's & Brass Band, 53, 62
Campobello, Enrico, 157
Campobello Company, 158
Canada, French Steamer, 49
Canada, 183
Capitol Theater, Atlanta, 209
Carlisle, Professor, 155
Carlsbad, 173, 200
Carnegie Hall, 160, 172
Carraway, W.L., 161
Carreño, Teresa (1853-1917), Venezuelan pianist/
    composer, 80, 112
Caruso, Enrico (1873-1921), Italian tenor, 175, 196,
    194, 202-05
Casavant organ, Glenn United Methodist Church,
    Emory University, 223
Caselli, Luisa, 8
Castle Garden, New York, 8, 23
Catani, Italy, 9
Cathedral of St. Philip, Atlanta, 167
Cederström, Rolf Baron, 162, 172, 174, 175,
    198, 200, 201
Centennial Exhibition, Philadelphia, 115
Central Presbyterian Church, Atlanta, 122
Central Congregational Church, Atlanta, 167
Century Magazine, 14
Chadwick, George Whitefield (1854-1931), Composer/
    teacher/conductor, 44, 134, 137, 167, 180,
    "The Miller's Daughter," 164
Charles Ford's English Opera Company, 114
Charles Towne Courtroom, 56
Charleston, South Carolina, 19, 52, 55-58, 61, 63, 64, 68,
    74, 105, 115
Charlotte, North Carolina, 76
Chase, Gilbert (b. 1906), Music historian/critic, 42, 135
Chestnut Street Theater, Philadelphia, 15, 60
Chicago, ix, 22, 114, 120, 130, 152, 206, 222
Chicago Symphony Orchestra, 186
Chicago World's Fair, 1892, 160
Chickering, Jonas (1797-1853), piano manufacturer, 134
Chickering Hall, New York, 40

Maretzek, Max (1821-97), conductor/
impresario, 11, 19, 20, 23-25,29, 57, 58
Crotchets & Quavers, 20
Maretzek Opera Company, 19
Sharps & Flats, 20
Marie Tavary Grand Opera Company, 164
Marino, Concepcion, 9
Mario, Giovanni Matteo (1810-83), Italian tenor, 23
Mariotti Italian Opera Troupe, 72
Marseniella, 67
Marshbank, J. W., 185
Marston, "The Lord is King", 185
Martin, Riccard, 194, 196, 203
Mascagni, Pietro (1863-1945), Italian composer
Cavaleria Rusticana, 157, 183
Massenet, Jules (1842-1921), French composer
Manon, 204
Matthews, Carrie, 109, 125-27, 129, 140, 153
Matthews, W. S. B. (1837-1912), editor/writer,
131, 170
Matzenaur, Margaret, 210
McCaully Opera Company, 157
McClain, Professor, 165
McClure, A. K., 104
McCormack, John (1884-1945), tenor, 206
McCulloch, Miss, 68, 69
McCulloch Opera Troupe, 67
McPherson Army Post Regimental Band, 157
Meefie, Tom (Blind), 62
Meek, Mrs., 202
Méhul, Etienne-Nicolas (1763-1817), French composer, 59
Melba, Dame Nellie (1861-1931), Australian soprano, 175
Memphis, Tennessee, 183
Men and Women, 154
Mendelssohn, Felix (1809-47), German composer,
xii, 44, 59, 129, 134, 135, 147, 165, 216, 217
Hear My Prayer, 126
Hymn of Praise, 193
Piano Concerto, xi, 39, 40
Quintette in B flat, Op. 87, 139
Rondo Capriccioso, 110, 127, 157
Sonata No. 6 for Organ, 195
Songs Without Words, 110, 157
St. Paul, 185
Symphony No 5 in D Minor, "Reformation," 117
Variations sérieuses, 110, 197
Violin Concerto in E Minor, 193
Wedding March, 78

New York Sunday Dispatch, 42
New York Sunday Times, 34
New York Symphony and Oratorio Societies, 156
New York Times, 24, 31, 42, 120, 139
New York Tribune, 30
New York World, 139
Niblo, William (1789-1878), Irish restaurateur/
    entrepreneur, 16, 28
Niblo's Concert Saloon, 28, 34
Nicolai, Otto (1810-49), German composer
    The Merry Wives of Windsor, 67
Nicolini, Ernest (1834-98), French tenor, 112, 113, 162
"Nightingales Echo song," 22
Nilsson, Christina (1843-1921), Swedish soprano, 75, 114
Nordica, Lillian (1857-1914), American soprano, 163, 189
Norfolk, Virginia, 105
North Avenue Presbyterian Church, Atlanta, 170, 206

O'Donnelly, J. P., Atlanta organist, 144, 145, 157, 166, 185
Odell, George C. D. (1866-1949), American theater
    historian, 29
Offenbach, Jacques (1819-80), French composer, 121
Oglethorpe University, Atlanta, 196
Old Charleston Theater (Dock Street), 55, 56
Old Joe Sweeney's Great Burlesque Opera Troupe, 53
Oliver Doud Byron Troupe, 70
Olk, Hugo, violinist, 193
Opera di Santa Maria del Fiore, 23
The Orange Girl, 119
The Orleans Theater, New Orleans, 59, 60
Orpheus Glee Club, 155
Orr, N. Lee, xii, 2, 4

Pacini, Giovanni (1796-1867), Italian composer
    Valerie ossia La Cieca, 9
Paderewski, Ignace Jan (1860-1941), Polish pianist/
    composer, xi, 157, 163, 169, 186, 188
    Minuet in A, 186
Paine, John Knowles (1839-1906), composer/teacher,
    44, 134, 135, 137, 166
Palermo, Sicily, 9
Palmetto Band, 64
Palmo's Opera House, New York, 10-13, 15
Pappenheimer, Oscar, 187
Paramount movie theater, Atlanta, 223
Paravelli, Eliza Valentini, 25